Workshop on Multimodal Augmented Generation via Multimodal Retrieval (MAGMaR 2025)

Vienna, Austria
1 August 2025

ISBN: 979-8-3313-2413-1

Printed from e-media with permission by:

Curran Associates, Inc.
57 Morehouse Lane
Red Hook, NY 12571

Some format issues inherent in the e-media version may also appear in this print version.

Printed with permission by Curran Associates, Inc. (2025)

For permission requests, please contact the Association for Computational Linguistics at the address below.

Association for Computational Linguistics
209 N. Eighth Street
Stroudsburg, Pennsylvania 18360

Phone: 1-570-476-8006
Fax: 1-570-476-0860

acl@aclweb.org

Additional copies of this publication are available from:

Curran Associates, Inc.
57 Morehouse Lane
Red Hook, NY 12571 USA
Phone: 845-758-0400
Fax: 845-758-2633
Email: curran@proceedings.com
Web: www.proceedings.com

MAGMaR 2025

Workshop on Multimodal Augmented Generation via Multimodal Retrieval

Proceedings of the Workshop

August 1, 2025

Introduction

We are excited to welcome you to MAGMaR 2025, the first workshop on Multimodal Augmented Generation via Multimodal Retrieval. MAGMaR is being held in Vienna, Austria on August 1, 2025, and is co-located with ACL 2025, which takes place from July 28th-August 1st.

While information retrieval systems for text documents have been extensively studied for decades, the landscape has shifted; vast amounts of information today are stored as videos with minimal text metadata. For instance, online commercial platforms host billions videos. Despite the explosion of multimodal data, there remains a dearth of research around the efficient retrieval, processing, and synthesis of these massive multimodal collections. Existing systems largely still rely on text metadata (e.g., human written descriptions), overlooking the rich semantic content embedded within the multimodal data itself.

Individual research groups have independently begun addressing this challenge, leading to parallel yet disconnected efforts to define the research space. MAGMaR was conceived as a collaborative venue to unify these efforts and foster dialogue, which we believe is crucial for advancing the field. The MAGMaR workshop focuses on two primary areas: (1) the retrieval of multimodal content, which spans text, images, audio, video, and multimodal data (e.g., image-language, video-language); and (2) retrieval-augmented generation, with an emphasis on multimodal retrieval and generation.

To further this goal, we hosted a shared task on event-based video retrieval and understanding, designed to spark interest and facilitate research development in both retrieval and generation. This task's primary retrieval metric, nDCG@10, compared the final ranked lists of videos produced by participant systems.

The shared task was built around MultiVENT 2.0 (Kriz et al., 2024). While prior datasets like MSR-VTT (10,000 videos) and MultiVENT (2,400 videos; Sanders et al., 2023) made progress toward multilingual and event-centric video retrieval, they remain small compared to typical text retrieval corpora—e.g., HC4 from the 2022 NeuCLIR shared task, which contains 6 million documents. To address this gap, we introduced MultiVENT 2.0, a large-scale benchmark with over 217,000 videos and 2,549 event-centric queries for a test collection of 109,800 videos. The dataset covers a diverse range of real-world current events and is designed to facilitate both retrieval and generation research.

MultiVENT 2.0 has been made publicly available on HuggingFace[1] and includes extracted features such as visual frames, transcribed speech, embedded text, and frame-level captions. Relevance judgments for the training set were released publicly, while those for the test set were hosted on an Eval.ai leaderboard[2]. The primary task setting restricts participants to use only the raw video content; using additional metadata or text descriptions is permitted only in an oracle setting.

Several teams submitted strong systems to the leaderboard. The best-performing submission, OmniEmbed, was developed by the Tevatron group from the University of Waterloo: Jiaqi Samantha Zhan, Crystina Zhang, Shengyao Zhuang, Xueguang Ma, and Jimmy Lin. Their best non-oracle system achieved an nDCG@10 of 0.709, a significant improvement over the strongest original baseline (0.324).

This year, the program of MAGMaR includes two keynote talks, one presentation session, and one poster session. In our inaugural year, we received 21 submissions and accepted 14, for an overall acceptance rate of 67%. Of these, five were accepted as oral presentations. The members of our Program Committee and Organizing Comittee did an excellent job in reviewing the submitted papers, and we thank them for their essential role in selecting the accepted papers and helping produce a high quality program for the conference.

[1]https://huggingface.co/datasets/hltcoe/MultiVENT2.0

[2]https://eval.ai/web/challenges/challenge-page/2507

A workshop requires the hard work of numerous people, both behind the scenes and those that you will see more prominently. First off, we want to say thank you to our two keynote speakers, Desmond Elliott (University of Copenhagen) and Joel Brogan (Oak Ridge National Laboratory) whose interdisciplinary talks are a nice resource for the broader NLP and ACL communities. Both Dr. Elliott's talk "Recent Experiments in Retrieval-Augmented Image Captionin" and Dr. Brogan's talk "When you Don't Quite Know What You Want: Bridging the Multimodal Search Intention Gap" cover challenging, state-of-the-art problems at the unique intersection of the focus of MAGMaR and we appreciate the insights that they are sharing. Additonally, we would be remiss to not mention the people who helped organize (and participated) in our shared task on retrieving events in videos. Our online leaderboard received numerous submissions and we continue to have people engaging with it even though the official evaluation is closed.

Finally, we thank all contributors, reviewers, and attendees who helped make MAGMaR 2025 possible. We hope you enjoy a day full of engaging talks, thought-provoking posters, and stimulating discussion.

Reno Kriz and Kenton Murray, Editors

Organizing Committee

Organizers

Reno Kriz, Human Language Technology Center of Excellence, Johns Hopkins University
Kenton Murray, Human Language Technology Center of Excellence, Johns Hopkins University
Eugene Yang, Human Language Technology Center of Excellence, Johns Hopkins University
Francis Ferraro, University of Maryland, Baltimore County
Kate Sanders, Johns Hopkins University
Cameron Carpenter, Johns Hopkins University
Benjamin Van Durme, Johns Hopkins University and Microsoft

Program Committee

Program Committee

Reno Kriz, Human Language Technology Center of Excellence, Johns Hopkins University
Kenton Murray, Human Language Technology Center of Excellence, Johns Hopkins University
Eugene Yang, Human Language Technology Center of Excellence, Johns Hopkins University
Francis Ferraro, University of Maryland, Baltimore County
Jeremy Gwinnup, Air Force Research Laboratory
Kate Sanders, Johns Hopkins University
Cameron Carpenter, Johns Hopkins University
Will Walden, Human Language Technology Center of Excellence, Johns Hopkins University
David Etter, Human Language Technology Center of Excellence
Andrew Yates, Human Language Technology Center of Excellence, Johns Hopkins University
Alex Martin, Johns Hopkins University
Gaurav Kumar, University of California San Diego

Invited Speakers

Joel Brogan, Oak Ridge National Laboratory
Desmond Elliot, University of Copenhagen

Keynote Talk

Recent Experiments in Retrieval-Augmented Image Captioning

Dr. Desmond Elliott
Associate Professor
Department of Computer Science
University of Copenhagen
2025-08-01 09:45:00 – Room: **2.44**

Abstract: Retrieval-augmentation has proven useful in a wide-range of classification and generation tasks, and it is now powering the next generation of Large Language Models. In this talk, I will present recent research on applying retrieval-augmentation to image caption generation. I will start by outlining how retrieval-augmentation can work in this task, and present a parameter-efficient image captioning model that can describe images from a variety of domains by hot-swapping the contents in the retrieval data store without retraining the model. Then I will describe two approaches to multilingual image captioning: one based on prompting an LLM without any training, the other based on supervised training with either multilingual or monolingual data. Finally, I will speak about our efforts to understand and explain the success and failure modes of retrieval-augmented image captioning

Bio: Dr. Desmond Elliot is an Associate Professor and a Villum Young Investigator at the University of Copenhagen. His main research interests are tokenization-free language modelling, and multilingual and multimodal processing. Dr. Elliot's work received a Best Paper Honorable Mention at the CVPR 2025 Workshop on Visual Concepts, the Best Long Paper Award at EMNLP 2021, and an Area Chair Favourite paper at COLING 2018. His research is funded by the Velux Foundations, the Innovation Foundation Denmark, the Novo Nordisk Foundation, the Poul de Jensen Foundation, Meta, and Google.

Keynote Talk

When you Don't Quite Know What You Want: Bridging the Multimodal Search Intention Gap

Dr. Joel Brogan
Research Group Lead – Multimodal Sensor Analytics
Center for AI Security Research
Energy Systems and Technology Directorate
Oak Ridge National Laboratory, Department of Energy
2025-08-01 16:00:00 – Room: **2.44**

Abstract: In research and analysis, the most valuable insights often lie beyond what we think to look for. Yet building systems that can surface these unknown unknowns remains a fundamental challenge. How do you design retrieval methods for discoveries you can't define upfront, and how do you measure success when you didn't know what you wanted in the first place? In this talk, I will share some of the practical ways our team at the Multimodal Sensor Analytics Group has approached this problem. We will explore how multimodal retrieval, combining vector stores and graph-based approaches, can bridge the gap between what you are searching for and what you truly need to find. I will discuss examples where these systems have surfaced unexpected but meaningful patterns, and reflect on the limitations, opportunities, and design choices when aiming to build retrieval systems that broaden rather than narrow human attention.

Bio: Dr. Joel Brogan is a Research Professional and Group Lead of the Multimodal Sensing Analytics Group at Oak Ridge National Laboratory, a US DOE national lab. There, he leads a team of 13 researchers who perform work in inverse imaging, graph analytics, biometrics, and adversarial AI vulnerability mitigation. Dr. Brogan received his PhD in computer vision at the University of Notre Dame, where he worked under the DARPA MediFor program to design image and video retrieval and analysis algorithms to help detect and understand the dynamics of misinformation spread. He joined Oak Ridge National Laboratory in 2019, where he is currently the Evaluation Lead for the IARPA BRIAR Program, Biometric Recognition and Identification at Altitude and Range, which aims to perform large-scale biometric characterization human action from video at long distances and altitudes. Additionally, Dr. Brogan is a founding member of the Center for AI Security Research, or CAISER, through which he and his design content retrieval tools that aim to discover previously unknown patterns in large pools of multimodal data. His work has been nominated for the 2023 R&D100 awards and the AFCEA 2023 FedID Best Operational Success Award. In 2024, Dr. Brogan was Honored as a Finalist in the FedScoop 50 "Most Inspiring Up & Comer" category.

Table of Contents

Program

Friday, August 1, 2025

09:30 - 09:45 *Opening Remarks*

09:45 - 10:30 *Keynote 1 (Desmond Elliott, PhD)*

10:30 - 11:00 *Break*

11:00 - 12:30 *Oral Presentations*

MT2ST: Adaptive Multi-Task to Single-Task Learning
Siyuan Yuan

One Pic is All it Takes: Poisoning Visual Document Retrieval Augmented Generation with a Single Image (Short Paper)
Ezzeldin Shereen, Dan Ristea, Burak Hasircioglu, Shae McFadden, Vasilios Mavroudis and Chris Hicks

M2IV: Towards Efficient and Fine-grained Multimodal In-Context Learning in Large Vision-Language Models
Yanshu Li, Yi Cao, Xi Xiao and Tianyang Wang

Q2E: Query-to-Event Decomposition for Zero-Shot Multilingual Text-to-Video Retrieval
Shubhashis Roy Dipta and Francis Ferraro

OmniEmbed-MultiVent: Unified End-to-end All-modality Retrieval
Jiaqi Samantha Zhan, Crystina Zhang, Shengyao Zhuang, Xueguang Ma and Jimmy Lin

12:30 - 14:00 *Lunch*

14:00 - 15:30 *Poster Session*

15:30 - 16:00 *Break*

16:00 - 16:45 *Keynote 2 (Joel Brogan, PhD)*

16:45 - 17:30 *Best Paper Award and Closing*

MultiReflect: Multimodal Self-Reflective RAG-based Automated Fact-Checking

Uku Kangur[1] **Krish Agrawal**[2] **Yashashvi Singh**[3] **Ahmed Sabir**[1] **Rajesh Sharma**[1,4]
[1]University of Tartu, Institute of Computer Science, Estonia, [2]Indian Institute of Technology Indore [3]Indian Institute of Information Technology Dharwad, [4]Plaksha University, India

Abstract

In this work, we introduce MultiReflect, a novel multimodal self-reflective Retrieval Augmented Generation (RAG)-based automated fact-checking pipeline. MultiReflect is designed to address the challenges of rapidly outdated information, limitations in human query capabilities, and expert knowledge barriers in fact-checking. Our proposed pipeline leverages the latest advancements in Large Language Models (LLMs) and Retrieval Augmented Generation (RAG) to enhance fact verification across text and images. Specifically, by integrating multimodal data processing with RAG-based evidence reflection, our system improves the accuracy of fact-checking by utilizing internet-sourced verification. We evaluate our results on the VERITE benchmarks and using several multimodal LLMs, outperforming baselines in binary classification.[1]

1 Introduction

Information plurality, particularly on the internet, presents both opportunities and challenges in identifying accurate and up-to-date information. Given the increasing reliance on online platforms for news consumption, learning, and interaction (Eurostat, 2022), developing effective mechanisms to distinguish between truthful and false information has become more critical. However, the increase of coordinated misinformation movements by spam bots, and other forms of informational chaos have significantly complicated this process. Therefore, more advanced and systematic approaches are required to evaluate and verify (*fact-check*) the credibility of information sources.

With the emergence of Large Language Models (LLMs), which can understand and learn from billions of texts, automated fact-checking has grown in popularity as an alternative to traditional manual methods (Guo et al., 2022). While LLMs are state-of-the-art tools for various language understanding and reasoning tasks, they still face several limitations, such as hallucinations, overconfidence, and bias (Xu et al., 2024b; Li et al., 2024). To address these issues, several studies have employed Retrieval Augmented Generation (RAG) techniques, which allow the model to check based on externally verified information (Lewis et al., 2021; Gao et al., 2024).

Language, however, is only part of the challenge when it comes to fact-checking information on the internet. Online information is presented in various forms, including text, images, video, and sound. As a result, fact-checking also requires the retrieval and reasoning of information across multiple modalities (Akhtar et al., 2023b; Martin et al., 2025). More recently, several state-of-the-art models, such as GPT-4V (OpenAI, 2023), GPT-4o (OpenAI, 2024), DeepSeek-VL2 (Wu et al., 2024) and Claude 3 (Anthropic, 2024), have made reason across multimodal data possible. These rapid advancements highlight the need for multimodal fact-checking, which has grown with the increased prevalence of complex information that spans various data types: text, image, video, and audio. Systems like COSMOS (Aneja et al., 2021), Twitter-COMMs (Biamby et al., 2022), EXMULF (Amri et al., 2022), ChartBERT (Akhtar et al., 2023a), RED-DOT and (Papadopoulos et al., 2024a) have made significant progress in tackling the challenges posed by multimodal data.

However, despite their successes, these systems have not fully taken advantage of RAG, a crucial component for dynamic and context-aware evidence retrieval in the multimodal setting. To address this gap, we introduce **MultiReflect**, illustrated in Figure 1, which integrates multimodal fact-checking (image + text) with a self-reflective RAG framework. Our system is designed to dynamically retrieve, evaluate, and rank supporting

[1]https://github.com/ukangur/MultiReflect

Proceedings of the 1st Workshop on Multimodal Augmented Generation via Multimodal Retrieval (MAGMaR 2025), pages 1–17
August 1, 2025 ©2025 Association for Computational Linguistics

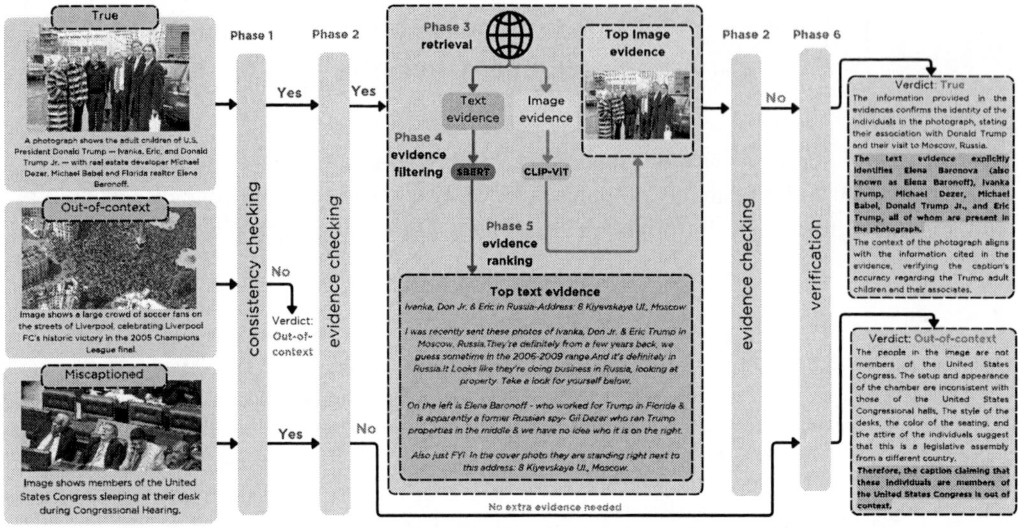

Figure 1: **MultiReflect** system overview. The proposed pipeline contains six phases: (1) consistency checking, (2) evidence checking, (3) retrieval, (4) evidence filtering, (5) evidence ranking and (6) verification. The colors indicate using both modalities in gray/**black**, or only image data in yellow, or only text data in blue.

evidence, improving reasoning capabilities and accuracy of multimodal fact verification.

We summarize our contributions as follows:

- We propose a novel pipeline **MultiReflect**, a multimodal self-reflective RAG-based automated fact-checking pipline.
- The novelty of the approach is in combining RAG-based evidence reflection with multimodal fact-checking.
- Our MultiReflect system achieves state-of-the-art results in binary classification in the Multimodal fact-checking VERITE benchmark.

2 Data

For our experiments, we utilize the VERITE dataset, a multimodal *fack-checking* benchmark dataset (Papadopoulos et al., 2024b). The dataset contains 892 different image-text pairs with the labels "True" (302), "Miscaptioned" (302), and "Out-of-context" (288). The dataset incorporates a wide range of real-world data while specifically excluding "asymmetric multimodal misinformation" (Asymmetric-MM), which refers to scenarios where one form of modality significantly amplifies misinformation while others have minimal impact. Also, the data implements "modality balancing," ensuring that each image and caption are represented twice in the dataset: once within truthful contexts and once within misleading pairs.

3 Proposed Method: MultiReflect

In this section, we introduce our proposed six-phase pipeline: (1) consistency checking, (2) evidence checking, (3) retrieval, (4) evidence filtering, (5) evidence ranking, and (6) verification.

3.1 Phase 1: Consistency checking

In this phase, we filter inputs by checking the alignment between the image and the caption. If inconsistent, the post is marked as OUT-OF-CONTEXT (as shown in Figure 1 with the second example). Three strategies are evaluated to determine the best method for consistency checking. The best strategy is used in the pipeline for the consistency checking phase.

Image-to-Text consistency: Using CLIP Large-336 (Radford et al., 2021), cosine similarity between image-caption embeddings determines consistency based on the best threshold of 0.28 estimated via grid search within the range [0.10 - 0.39].

Text-to-Text consistency: BLIP-2 (Li et al., 2023) generates descriptions for images, compared to captions using cosine similarity via SBERT (Reimers and Gurevych, 2019), with best threshold 0.10 for all model (BLIP-$2_{2.7\text{B}}$, BLIP-$2_{6.7\text{B}}$ and BLIP-2 FLAN) estimated similar to Image-to-Text method.

Multimodal consistency: Since multimodal LLMs can comprehend and perform reasoning on both text and images, we use the image-caption pairs to evaluate their consistency. We adopt

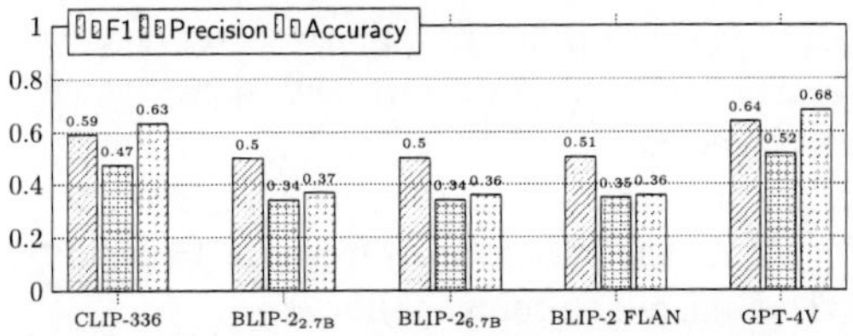

Figure 2: Performance Metrics of Different Consistency Checking Strategies (Phase 1). We rely on three validation methods: Image-to-Text consistency using CLIP, Text-to-Text consistency using BLIP (via SBERT), and Multimodal consistency using GPT-4V model.

a prompt-based approach wherein each image-caption pair is evaluated to ascertain the alignment between the provided text and the associated image. Specifically, the prompt instructs the model to assign a binary score [0,1] whether the caption accurately describes the depicted image. We evaluate multimodal consistency using GPT-4V (OpenAI, 2023). Figure 2 shows that the LLM multimodal consistency strategy has the highest F1-score, therefore, we adopt this strategy in our pipeline.

3.2 Phase 2: Evidence checking

The aim of this phase is for the model to evaluate if extra evidence is needed, inspired by the work of (Asai et al., 2023). We do this to differentiate between information that contains changing or unchanging events. For example, political events may require external evidence for up-to-date information, while physics or nature-related statements, like the world being round, generally remain consistent over time. Additionally, this phase allows the model to be more dynamic when evaluating how much information is needed to fact-check something. We can see this phase in Figure 1, where the first example requires evidence and the third example does not.

We employ the use of multimodal LLM (*e.g.* GPT-4o-mini) for this task as it allows the model to evaluate the post and the evidence text and image data at the same time. This phase can occur several times during fact-checking one post, as the model can ask for additional evidence several times. To keep this process more efficient, in the evidence retrieval phase, we collect more evidence the first time around and then only provide additional evidence if it is asked in the next iterations of phase 2.

3.3 Phase 3: Evidence retrieval

In this phase, we retrieve both textual and visual evidence required to fact-check the original input post. We collect the evidence for both modalities using at least 3 sources to lower the chances of bias brought by single-source dependency. In addition, we collect all evidence straight from the internet without using any static databases. We do this to ensure the most up-to-date information. We explain the full procedure of evidence collection in the following subsections, as shown in Figure 1 with the top (True) example.

Textual evidence: We retrieve textual evidence from three sources - Wikipedia, Google search, and Bing search. For Wikipedia (Wikimedia, 2024), we search for the top 10 articles. For Google, we use the Google Custom Search API (Google, 2024) to get the top 10 Google search results and collect their textual data. We also use the Google Cloud Vision API (Cloud, 2024) to collect textual information from pages that include a fully or partially matching reverse image search result with our original multimodal post. For Bing search, we use the Bing Web Search API (Microsoft, 2024b) to get the top 10 Bing search results and collect the textual data from each of them. We additionally use the Bing Visual Search API v7 (Microsoft, 2024a) to collect textual information from pages that include a matching image search result with our multimodal post.

Visual evidence: We retrieve visual evidence from three sources - Wikimedia Commons, Google Image Search, and Bing Image Search. For Wikimedia Commons, we use the Wikimedia Commons API (Wikimedia, 2024) to retrieve the top 10 images by querying for each entity from the textual caption of the original post. For Google Image Search, we use Google Custom Search (Google, 2024) to get the top 10 regular image search results by querying all the entities from the textual caption. With Bing Image Search, we use the Bing Image Search API v7 (Microsoft, 2024a) to get the top 10 regular image search results by querying all the entities from the textual caption.

3.4 Phase 4: Evidence filtering

In this phase, we filter the retrieved evidence based on consistency with the original post data to ensure we do not rank unrelated evidence (as shown in Figure 1). The differences in filtering for textual and visual evidence are introduced as follows:

Textual evidence: With textual evidence, we first split each piece of evidence into paragraphs or if paragraphs are not given, then into sentence chunks of 250 words maximum. We use SBERT (Reimers and Gurevych, 2019) to find the top 3 most semantically similar paragraphs to the original post caption from each online source (*i.e.* Wikipedia, Google Search, Google Inverse Search, Bing Search, Bing Visual Search). Then, we extract the top matching paragraph from each textual evidence and dismiss all other paragraphs. By filtering irrelevant details, we retain only text relevant to domain-specific fact-checking. For example, focusing on Biden's political decisions while excluding information about his private life events.

Visual evidence: With visual evidence, we embed the images with CLIP Large-336 (Radford et al., 2021) and then use cosine similarity to filter out irrelevant images to the original post and find the top 3 images from each source (*i.e.* Wikimedia Commons, Google Image Search and Bing Image Search).

3.5 Phase 5: Evidence ranking

We use this phase to evaluate the quality of the given evidence based on five attributes: (1) **Authority**, (2) **Timeliness**, (3) **Relevancy**, (4) **Support** and (5) **Usefulness**. We compute a unified score to rank the evidence based on these attributes. After this we extract the top ranking text evidence and top ranking image evidence (as shown in Figure 1 with the first example). We keep the other ranking scores in case the pipeline requires additional evidence.

Authority This attribute captures how authoritative is the source of the evidence. We check the authority on how factual, biased, and reliable the sources are. For example, if a source contains factual content, which is neutral and is also reliable, then it is considered authoritative. To label the sources with these attributes in mind, we use the source bias dataset as introduced by Kangur et al. (2024). This dataset provides aggregated factuality, bias and reliability annotations of the top 500 sources used in X Community Notes (Community Notes, 2024) using pre-defined labels from three trusted media monitoring institutions: Media bias fact-check[2], Allsides[3], and Adfontes[4]. As these labels are ordinal (*i.e.* they can be ordered), we transform the labels into predefined scores ranging from 0 to 1, except for the factuality score, which is calculated on a scale from -1 to 1, to additionally penalize unfactual sources. The authority score for evidence is calculated as the sum of the factuality, bias and reliability scores as shown:

$$S_{\text{Authority}} = A_{\text{Factuality}} + A_{\text{Bias}} + A_{\text{Reliablity}}$$

$$A_{\text{Factuality}} = \begin{cases} 1.0 & \text{if rated } \textit{Very High Factuality} \\ 0.66 & \text{if rated } \textit{High Factuality} \\ 0.33 & \text{if rated } \textit{Mostly Factual} \\ 0.0 & \text{if rated } \textit{Mixed Factuality} \\ -0.33 & \text{if rated } \textit{Low Factuality} \\ -0.66 & \text{if rated } \textit{Very Low Factuality} \\ -1.0 & \text{if rated } \textit{Satire} \\ 0.0 & \text{otherwise.} \end{cases}$$

$$A_{\text{Bias}} = \begin{cases} 0.0 & \text{if rated as } \textit{Left} \text{ or } \textit{Right} \\ 0.5 & \text{if rated as } \textit{Left-Center} \text{ or } \textit{Right-Center} \\ 1.0 & \text{if rated as } \textit{Center} \\ 0.0 & \text{otherwise} \end{cases}$$

$$A_{\text{Reliablity}} = \begin{cases} 1.0 & \text{if rated as } \textit{Reliable} \\ 0.5 & \text{if rated as } \textit{Generally Reliable} \\ 0.0 & \text{if rated as } \textit{Mixed Reliability} \\ 0.0 & \text{otherwise} \end{cases}$$

Relevancy evaluates how well the evidence pertains to the multimodal post. The goal is to assess if the evidence is relevant to the factual accuracy of the image or caption. We use a multimodal LLM (*e.g.* GPT-4o-mini) to label evidence as relevant ($S_{\text{Relevancy}} = 1$) or irrelevant ($S_{\text{Relevancy}} = 0$).

Support evaluates how well the evidence backs the claims in the post. We use a multimodal LLM (*e.g.* GPT-4o-mini) to assess the factual accuracy of the input text and image, by examining their alignment with the evidence based solely on the provided information. An entailment scale is used to assign scores based on the degree of support:

$$S_{\text{Support}} = \begin{cases} 1 & \text{if Fully Supported} \\ 0.5 & \text{if Partially Supported} \\ 0 & \text{if No Support/Contradictory} \end{cases}$$

Usefulness measures how informative and relevant the evidence is for accepting or rejecting the claim in the post. We use a multimodal LLM (*e.g.* GPT-4o-mini) to assess how well the evidence helps determine the factuality of the input image and caption. A 5-point scale is used to score the evidence, with utility scores mapped to numeric values as follows:

$$S_{\text{Usefulness}} = \begin{cases} +1 & \text{if score = 5 (Highly informative)} \\ +0.5 & \text{if score = 4 (Mostly sufficient)} \\ 0 & \text{if score = 3 (Adequate)} \\ -0.5 & \text{if score = 2 (Limited)} \\ -1 & \text{if score = 1 (Irrelevant)} \end{cases}$$

[2]mediabiasfactcheck.com

[3]allsides.com

[4]adfontes.com

Timeliness evaluates how recently the information in the evidence is provided. Evidence E is considered timely if its date $t(E) < 2$ years, and it has a positive score in at least one of **Relevancy**, **Support**, or **Usefulness**. This ensures that only relevant and meaningful recent evidence is prioritized, avoiding the ranking of irrelevant but recent content. The score is assigned as follows:

$$S_{\text{Timeliness}} = \begin{cases} 1 & \text{if } t(E) < 2 \text{ years and} \\ & S_{\text{Relevancy}} + S_{\text{Support}} + \\ & S_{\text{Usefulness}} > 0 \\ 0 & \text{otherwise} \end{cases}$$

Combined Evidence Score: The overall evidence score is calculated as the sum of all of the five attributes. Based on this score, we extract the top ranking (highest scored) image and textual evidence. These are passed into the evidence checking (phase 2) and verification (phase 6) phases.

However, our human evaluation showed that **Timeliness** and **Authority** are hard to discern from visual evidence alone due to potential reuploads that may not reflect the original context. Therefore, we use all five attributes to rank textual evidence, but only **Relevancy**, **Support**, and **Usefulness** for visual evidence.

3.6 Phase 6: Verification

This phase verifies whether the original post is FALSE, OUT-OF-CONTEXT, or TRUE. For verification, we prompt a multimodal LLM model (*e.g.* GPT-4o-mini) to assess the factual accuracy of the input image and caption using the provided evidence, labeling the output as OUT-OF-CONTEXT, MISCAPTIONED, or TRUE. If the pipeline fails at any stage (*e.g.* due to LLM policy filters), we mark the original post as TRUE during verification, adhering to the principle of innocent until proven guilty. As baselines, we used the available benchmarks of the VERITE dataset. In Figure 1, we can also see the verdicts and explanations for the first and third examples. These explanations also allow the user to understand the reasoning process of the model.

4 Experimental Results

In the following section, we introduce our (1) baselines and experimental results (2).

4.1 Baselines

VERITE (Papadopoulos et al., 2024b). The VERITE dataset paper introduces a transformer-based model for detecting misinformation by combining image and text information. It uses CLIP ViT-L/14 to extract visual and textual features, which are merged into a single vector representing the image-caption pair. The vector is then processed by a transformer encoder that omits positional encodings and applies average pooling with multi-head self-attention. A final classification layer predicts the label of the image-caption pair. The model is trained on datasets like CLIP-NESt and CHASMA-D, which include synthetic multimodal misinformation. To handle class imbalance, random down-sampling was used, and the model was trained using categorical cross-entropy loss for multiclass classification.

RED-DOT (Papadopoulos et al., 2024a). The Relevant Evidence Detection Directed Transformer (RED-DOT) is a model for multimodal fact-checking that focuses on identifying and leveraging relevant evidence. It uses CLIP-ViT-L/14 to extract visual features from images and textual features from captions. An evidence re-ranking module emphasizes relevant content via intra-modal similarity, while irrelevant items are filtered using hard negative sampling. Features from both modalities are fused using element-wise operations and concatenation, then processed by a transformer to predict evidence relevance and the overall class. RED-DOT is trained on the NewsCLIPings+ dataset with multi-task learning and evaluated using Out-of-Distribution Cross-Validation (OOD-CV).

MultiReflect models. We compare the efficiency of our pipeline using five different vision LLM models: GPT-4V (OpenAI, 2023), GPT-4o-mini (OpenAI, 2024), Gemma 3 (Team et al., 2025), LLaVA-CoT (Xu et al., 2024a) and DeepSeek-VL2 (Wu et al., 2024). GPT-4V is a large vision-language model that integrates advanced visual and textual reasoning across different domains. GPT-4o-mini builds on this by offering a lighter, faster variant optimized for real-time, low-latency interaction. Gemma 3 (12B) is a general-purpose multimodal foundation model using a modified SigLIP vision encoder. LLaVA-CoT (11B) brings visual inputs together with step-by-step reasoning, improving performance on tasks that require both understanding and explanation. We select LLaVA-CoT and Gemma 3 as they perform on par with GPT-4o-mini on reasoning benchmarks. DeepSeek-VL2 (4.2B) similarly focuses on multimodal reasoning, using techniques like mixture-of-experts, dynamic image tiling and multi-head latent attention to ex-

Type	Class	GPT-4V				GPT-4o-mini				LLaVA-CoT (11B)				DeepSeek-VL2 (4.2B)				Gemma 3 (12B)			
		Acc.	Prec.	Rec.	F1	Acc.	Prec.	Rec.	F1	Acc.	Prec.	Rec.	F1	Acc.	Prec.	Rec.	F1	Acc.	Prec.	Rec.	F1
M	ALL	0.49	0.53	0.49	0.46	**0.50**	0.53	0.50	**0.50**	0.38	0.59	0.38	0.30	0.36	0.38	0.36	0.31	0.44	0.52	0.44	0.37
	TRUE		0.69	0.62	**0.65**	-	0.60	0.48	0.53	-	0.41	0.69	0.51	-	0.38	0.53	0.44	-	0.47	0.71	0.56
	MC		0.54	0.16	0.25	-	0.56	0.34	0.42	-	1.00	0.00	0.01	-	0.34	0.49	0.40	-	0.41	0.59	**0.49**
	OOC		0.37	0.69	0.48	-	0.43	0.70	**0.53**	-	0.34	0.45	0.38	-	0.42	0.04	0.07	-	0.71	0.02	0.03
B	ALL	**0.78**	0.75	0.74	**0.74**	0.72	0.70	0.72	0.71	0.56	0.64	0.56	0.57	0.54	0.59	0.54	0.56	0.63	0.68	0.63	0.64
	TRUE		0.69	0.62	**0.65**	-	0.60	0.48	0.53	-	0.41	0.69	0.51	-	0.38	0.53	0.44	-	0.47	0.71	0.56
	FALSE		0.81	0.86	**0.83**	-	0.76	0.84	0.80	-	0.75	0.49	0.59	-	0.70	0.55	0.62	-	0.80	0.59	0.68

Table 1: Performance results of the proposed pipeline MultiReflect on the VERITE dataset. The results are shown for both the binary case (denoted as B, with labels TRUE and FALSE) and the multi-class case (denoted as M, with labels TRUE, MISCAPTIONED [MC], and OUT-OF-CONTEXT [OOC]). The drop in performance in the multi-class classification indicates that the model struggles to distinguish between MISCAPTIONED and OUT-OF-CONTEXT datapoints. The best overall accuracy and F1-scores for both binary and multi-class settings are **highlighted**. We observe that GPT-4o-mini performs best in the multi-class setting, while GPT-4V performs best in the binary classification setting.

Model	Accuracy	
	Multi-class	Binary
VERITE (Papadopoulos et al., 2024b)	**0.52**	0.73
RED-DOT (Papadopoulos et al., 2024a)		0.77
GPT-4V (OpenAI, 2023)	0.49	**0.78**
GPT-4o-mini (OpenAI, 2024)	0.50	0.72
LLaVA-CoT (11B) (Xu et al., 2024a)	0.38	0.56
DeepSeek-VL2 (4B) (Wu et al., 2024)	0.36	0.54
Gemma 3 (12B) (Team et al., 2025)	0.44	0.63

Table 2: The results show that MultiReflect with GPT-4V outperforms all baselines in binary classification. However, all MultiReflect versions underperform against the original VERITE baseline in multi-class classification.

tract and align the most relevant visual and textual features. We select DeepSeek-VL2 as a comparison due to its reliance on mixture-of-experts and good performance on reasoning benchmarks given its relatively small size.

4.2 Results

The VERITE dataset provides three classes: TRUE, MISCAPTIONED, and OUT-OF-CONTEXT. For binary classification, however, MISCAPTIONED and OUT-OF-CONTEXT are combined into a single FALSE class. We evaluate both binary and multi-class (taking into account all three classes).

Multi-class results: In the multiclass setting, our pipeline achieved the best result with GPT-4o-mini with a macro F1-score of 0.50 and accuracy of 0.50, slightly lower than the VERITE benchmark accuracy of 0.52 (see Table 2). Surprisingly, the score for the larger GPT-4V is lower, suggesting that the pipeline struggles to differentiate false subclasses. This is also shown when we look at the TRUE class, as the GPT-4V model performs the best with a F1-score of 0.65, the highest among all classes. However, for the MISCAPTIONED class GPT-4V showed a low F1-score of 0.25, driven by a recall of 0.16, indicating difficulty in identifying MISCAPTIONED posts. The same difficulty arised for LLaVA-CoT, which only identified a single MISCAPTIONED post due to being overconfident in the verification stage. Surprisingly, Gemma 3 performs the best win identifying MISCAPTIONED posts with an F1-score of 0.49 showing its capability of using evidence critically. For OUT-OF-CONTEXT, GPT-4o-mini achieved an F1-score of 0.53, primarily due to low precision (0.43) of OUT-OF-CONTEXT class. DeepSeek-VL2, performs the worst out of the four with an F1-score of 0.36 due to misclassifying OUT-OF-CONTEXT posts. We note that these results highlight the pipelines poor capability to differentiate which modality includes the false information.

Binary results: In the binary setting, we see that GPT-4V performs the best out of the three models in all metrics achieving a F1-score of 0.74 and an accuracy of 0.78, exceeding the VERITE benchmark of 0.72 and RED DOT baseline of 0.77 (see Table 2). The TRUE class retained its F1-score of 0.65, while the combined false class achieved 0.83 as shown in Table 1. The overall result against other baselines is shown in Table 2, our model achieves the best binary results in the VERITE benchmark dataset. The open-source models (Gemma 3, LLaVA-CoT and DeepSeek-VL2) all perform worse in both classes compared to the OpenAI models. This performance gap may be attributed to less effective use of evidence in the verification process.

Type	Class	No Evidence				All Evidence			
		Acc.	Prec.	Rec.	F1	Acc.	Prec.	Rec.	F1
Multi-Class	ALL	0.49	0.53	0.49	**0.46**	0.50	0.53	0.50	**0.50**
	TRUE	-	0.69	0.62	0.65	-	0.60	0.48	0.53
	MISCAPTIONED	-	0.54	0.16	0.25	-	0.56	0.34	0.42
	OUT-OF-CONTEXT	-	0.37	0.69	0.48	-	0.43	0.70	0.53
Binary	ALL	0.78	0.75	0.74	**0.74**	0.72	0.70	0.72	**0.71**
	TRUE	-	0.69	0.62	0.65	-	0.60	0.48	0.53
	FALSE	-	0.81	0.86	0.83	-	0.76	0.84	0.80

Table 3: Performance results on the VERITE dataset under **No Evidence** and **All Evidence** conditions using GPT-4V. The results are shown for both the multi-class (TRUE, MISCAPTIONED, and OUT-OF-CONTEXT) and binary (TRUE, FALSE) settings. The "ALL" row gives the overall accuracy (Acc.), while per-class rows show only precision (Prec.), recall (Rec.), and F1.

5 Ablation Study

We conduct an ablation study of our best-performing model, GPT-4V, on the benchmark to evaluate the role of evidence within the **MultiReflect** pipeline. This analysis focuses on two key questions: (1) Is any evidence necessary for effective verification? (2) Does the ranking of evidence contribute meaningfully to performance? To address the first question, we evaluate the system's performance when no evidence is provided during the verification stage. For the second, we provide all available evidence without applying any ranking. The results demonstrate that RAG-enhanced retrieval and ranking both play a critical role in strengthening multimodal reasoning.

5.1 No evidence

This subsection analyzes the pipeline without using evidence, excluding phases 2 to 5, for both multi-class and binary settings. This means that this variation of the pipeline only checks for consistency and then goes directly into verification if the post is found to be consistent.

Multi-class results: Without evidence, the model achieves an F1-score of 0.41, which is lower than the pipeline's 0.46, as shown in Table 3. This indicates that evidence improves multi-class verification. Specifically, for the TRUE class, the F1-score drops to 0.46 from 0.65. Interestingly, MISCAPTIONED posts perform better without evidence, achieving an F1-score of 0.29 compared to 0.25, suggesting that evidence may mislead in this category. In both evaluation scenarios, the F1-score for MISCAPTIONED posts remains consistently low, highlighting the model's persistent difficulty in accurately distinguishing them from the other classes.

Binary results: As detailed in Table 3, without evidence, the model's overall F1-score is 0.63, underperforming compared to 0.74 in the full pipeline. The classwise F1-scores for TRUE and FALSE drop to 0.46 and 0.79 from 0.65 and 0.83, respectively, highlighting the importance of evidence in binary settings. The larger drop in the TRUE class score highlights that evidence is crucial for reducing false negatives and confirming truthful posts, as its absence increases uncertainty.

5.2 All evidence

This subsection analyzes the pipeline without phase 2 (evidence checking), providing all retrieved evidence in the verification phase for both multi-class and binary settings.

Multi-class results: Providing all evidence does not improve the F1-score beyond 0.46, matching the regular pipeline's performance as reflected in Table 3. This suggests that adding more evidence does not necessarily enhance the model's accuracy. However, giving all of the evidence adds additional computational costs to the pipeline, making the regular pipeline more preferable. The classwise F1-scores for all classes are lower than in the full pipeline, except for MISCAPTIONED, which increases to 0.30 from 0.25.

Binary results: With all evidence included, the F1-score decreases to 0.72 compared to 0.74 in the full pipeline, confirming that an overload of evidence can hinder effective reasoning, as shown in Table 3. The F1-scores for TRUE and FALSE are slightly lower at 0.63 and 0.81, respectively, than those in the regular pipeline. This highlights the need for careful evidence selection methods as providing all of the retrieved evidence can make the reasoning noisy in the verification phase.

Fact-Checking System	Evidence Retrieval	Multimodal	Verification	Evidence Ranking	RAG
COSMOS (Aneja et al., 2021)	×	✓	✓	×	×
EXMULF (Amri et al., 2022)	×	✓	✓	×	×
Twitter-COMMs (Biamby et al., 2022)	×	✓	✓	×	×
MuRAG* (Chen et al., 2022)	✓ (static knowledge base)	✓	×	✓	✓
CCN (Abdelnabi et al., 2022)	✓ (internet)	✓	✓	×	×
BERT + LSTM (Hammouchi and Ghogho, 2022)	✓ (internet)	✓	✓	✓ (source credibility)	×
Self-RAG* (Asai et al., 2023)	✓ (internet + static knowledge base)	×	×	✓ (relevancy, supportedness, usefulness)	✓
ChartBERT (Akhtar et al., 2023a)	×	✓	✓	×	×
FakeNewsGPT4 (Liu et al., 2024)	×	✓	✓	×	×
RED-DOT (Papadopoulos et al., 2024a)	✓ (internet)	✓	✓	✓ (similarity)	×
MultiReflect (Ours)	✓ (internet)	✓	✓	✓	✓

Table 4: Overview of related works and associated features. We highlight that our work **MultiReflect** is the only one to utilize RAG for the multimodal verification task. The (*) refers to work in the domain of Question-Answering.

6 Related Works

In this section, we introduce several related methods and papers to our work. We additionally highlight the main feature differences between the methods in Table 4.

Automated Fact-Checking. Fact-checking methods have significantly evolved with advancements in artificial intelligence, particularly through the development of LLMs and automated systems. Early systems such as those introduced by Thorne et al. (2018) and Thorne and Vlachos (2021) relied on static knowledge bases for evidence retrieval for fact-checking and correction. However, these systems lacked the ability to update their knowledge bases dynamically, which is critical in the fast-paced information era.

Recent efforts have seen the integration of Retrieval Augmented Generation (RAG) techniques to enhance the reliability and accuracy of fact-checking systems. For instance, models such as MuRAG (Chen et al., 2022) and Self-RAG (Asai et al., 2023) have utilized not only static knowledge bases but also the internet to retrieve current and relevant information. These models enhance the fact-checking process by employing RAG for dynamic evidence retrieval, allowing for a more accurate verification of facts by evaluating various aspects of information quality. This approach significantly surpasses earlier models that relied only on static databases or lacked evidence ranking mechanisms (Gao et al., 2024).

Multimodal Fact-Checking. The need for multimodal fact-checking has grown with the increased prevalence of complex information that spans various data types: text, image, video, and audio. Systems like COSMOS (Aneja et al., 2021), Twitter-COMMs (Biamby et al., 2022), EXMULF (Amri et al., 2022), ChartBERT (Akhtar et al., 2023a), RED-DOT and (Papadopoulos et al., 2024a) have made significant progress in tackling the challenges posed by multimodal data. However, prior works rely heavily on training, limiting usability in low-resource settings, and often focus only on intra-modal relationships, overlooking nuanced cross-modal relationships.

To the best of our knowledge, our MultiReflect approach is the first to integrate evidence retrieval, multimodality, verification, evidence ranking, and RAG into a single fact-checking pipeline.

7 Conclusions

We introduce **MultiReflect**, a novel multi-modal RAG-based fact-checking pipeline. The novelty of the pipeline lies in its new evidence ranking and reflection scheme over multimodal posts. We validate the efficiency of the pipeline using a specialized multimodal fact-checking benchmark dataset VERITE. Our results show that MultiRelflect underperforms in the multiclass setting but outperforms other baselines in the binary class scenario. Future works could improve this pipeline by focusing on how to better identify in which modality the error exists. Additionally, incorporating modality-specific retrieval strategies could help disentangle complex cross-modal contradictions.

8 Ethics Statement

The VERITE dataset used in this study is publicly available and specifically designed for benchmarking multimodal fact-checking systems. All annotation work was done by the study authors without crowd-sourcing. VERITE consists of fact-checked articles from Snopes and Reuters, curated by experts. Our pipeline retrieves only publicly available evidence using official APIs of search engines that comply with the Robots Exclusion Protocol.

Acknowledgment

This work has received funding from the EU H2020 program under the SoBigData++ project (grant agreement No. 871042), by the CHIST-ERA grant No. CHIST-ERA-19-XAI-010, (ETAg grant No. SLTAT21096), and partially funded by HAMISON project.

References

Sahar Abdelnabi, Rakibul Hasan, and Mario Fritz. 2022. Open-domain, content-based, multi-modal fact-checking of out-of-context images via online resources. Preprint, arXiv:2112.00061.

Mubashara Akhtar, Oana Cocarascu, and Elena Simperl. 2023a. Reading and reasoning over chart images for evidence-based automated fact-checking. In Findings of the Association for Computational Linguistics: EACL 2023, pages 399–414, Dubrovnik, Croatia. Association for Computational Linguistics.

Mubashara Akhtar, Michael Schlichtkrull, Zhijiang Guo, Oana Cocarascu, Elena Simperl, and Andreas Vlachos. 2023b. Multimodal automated fact-checking: A survey. In Findings of the Association for Computational Linguistics: EMNLP 2023, pages 5430–5448, Singapore. Association for Computational Linguistics.

Sabrine Amri, Dorsaf Sallami, and Esma Aïmeur. 2022. Exmulf: An explainable multimodal content-based fake news detection system. In Foundations and Practice of Security, pages 177–187, Cham. Springer International Publishing.

Shivangi Aneja, Chris Bregler, and Matthias Nießner. 2021. Cosmos: Catching out-of-context misinformation with self-supervised learning. Preprint, arXiv:2101.06278.

Anthropic. 2024. The claude 3 model family: Opus, sonnet, haiku.

Akari Asai, Zeqiu Wu, Yizhong Wang, Avirup Sil, and Hannaneh Hajishirzi. 2023. Self-rag: Learning to retrieve, generate, and critique through self-reflection. Preprint, arXiv:2310.11511.

Giscard Biamby, Grace Luo, Trevor Darrell, and Anna Rohrbach. 2022. Twitter-COMMs: Detecting climate, COVID, and military multimodal misinformation. In Proceedings of the 2022 Conference of the North American Chapter of the Association for Computational Linguistics: Human Language Technologies, pages 1530–1549, Seattle, United States. Association for Computational Linguistics.

Wenhu Chen, Hexiang Hu, Xi Chen, Pat Verga, and William W. Cohen. 2022. Murag: Multimodal retrieval-augmented generator for open question answering over images and text. Preprint, arXiv:2210.02928.

Google Cloud. 2024. Detect web entities and pages - cloud vision api.

Community Notes. 2024. Introduction.

Eurostat. 2022. Consumption of online news rises in popularity. Accessed: 2024-04-13.

Yunfan Gao, Yun Xiong, Xinyu Gao, Kangxiang Jia, Jinliu Pan, Yuxi Bi, Yi Dai, Jiawei Sun, Meng Wang, and Haofen Wang. 2024. Retrieval-augmented generation for large language models: A survey. Preprint, arXiv:2312.10997.

Google. 2024. Programmable search engine - google for developers.

Zhijiang Guo, Michael Schlichtkrull, and Andreas Vlachos. 2022. A survey on automated fact-checking. Transactions of the Association for Computational Linguistics, 10:178–206.

Hicham Hammouchi and Mounir Ghogho. 2022. Evidence-aware multilingual fake news detection. IEEE Access, 10:116808–116818.

Uku Kangur, Roshni Chakraborty, and Rajesh Sharma. 2024. Who checks the checkers? exploring source credibility in twitter's community notes. Preprint, arXiv:2406.12444.

Patrick Lewis, Ethan Perez, Aleksandra Piktus, Fabio Petroni, Vladimir Karpukhin, Naman Goyal, Heinrich Küttler, Mike Lewis, Wen tau Yih, Tim Rocktäschel, Sebastian Riedel, and Douwe Kiela. 2021. Retrieval-augmented generation for knowledge-intensive nlp tasks. Preprint, arXiv:2005.11401.

Junnan Li, Dongxu Li, Silvio Savarese, and Steven Hoi. 2023. Blip-2: Bootstrapping language-image pre-training with frozen image encoders and large language models. Preprint, arXiv:2301.12597.

Yingji Li, Mengnan Du, Rui Song, Xin Wang, and Ying Wang. 2024. A survey on fairness in large language models. Preprint, arXiv:2308.10149.

Xuannan Liu, Peipei Li, Huaibo Huang, Zekun Li, Xing Cui, Jiahao Liang, Lixiong Qin, Weihong Deng, and Zhaofeng He. 2024. Fakenewsgpt4: Advancing multimodal fake news detection through knowledge-augmented lvlms. Preprint, arXiv:2403.01988.

Alexander Martin, Reno Kriz, William Gantt Walden, Kate Sanders, Hannah Recknor, Eugene Yang, Francis Ferraro, and Benjamin Van Durme. 2025. Wikivideo: Article generation from multiple videos. Preprint, arXiv:2504.00939.

Microsoft. 2024a. Bing visual search v7 - microsoft learn.

Microsoft. 2024b. Bing web search v7 - microsoft learn.

OpenAI. 2023. Gpt-4 technical report. arXiv, abs/2303.08774.

OpenAI. 2024. Gpt-4o system card. Preprint, arXiv:2410.21276.

Stefanos-Iordanis Papadopoulos, Christos Koutlis, Symeon Papadopoulos, and Panagiotis C. Petrantonakis. 2024a. Red-dot: Multimodal fact-checking via relevant evidence detection. Preprint, arXiv:2311.09939.

Stefanos-Iordanis Papadopoulos, Christos Koutlis, Symeon Papadopoulos, and Panagiotis C Petrantonakis. 2024b. Verite: a robust benchmark for multimodal misinformation detection accounting for unimodal bias. International Journal of Multimedia Information Retrieval, 13(1):4.

Alec Radford, Jong Wook Kim, Chris Hallacy, Aditya Ramesh, Gabriel Goh, Sandhini Agarwal, Girish Sastry, Amanda Askell, Pamela Mishkin, Jack Clark, Gretchen Krueger, and Ilya Sutskever. 2021. Learning transferable visual models from natural language supervision. Preprint, arXiv:2103.00020.

Nils Reimers and Iryna Gurevych. 2019. Sentence-bert: Sentence embeddings using siamese bert-networks. In Proceedings of the 2019 Conference on Empirical Methods in Natural Language Processing. Association for Computational Linguistics.

Gemma Team, Aishwarya Kamath, Johan Ferret, Shreya Pathak, Nino Vieillard, Ramona Merhej, Sarah Perrin, Tatiana Matejovicova, Alexandre Ramé, Morgane Rivière, et al. 2025. Gemma 3 technical report. arXiv preprint arXiv:2503.19786.

James Thorne and Andreas Vlachos. 2021. Evidence-based factual error correction. In Proceedings of the 59th Annual Meeting of the Association for Computational Linguistics and the 11th International Joint Conference on Natural Language Processing (Volume 1: Long Papers), pages 3298–3309, Online. Association for Computational Linguistics.

James Thorne, Andreas Vlachos, Christos Christodoulopoulos, and Arpit Mittal. 2018. FEVER: a large-scale dataset for fact extraction and VERification. In Proceedings of the 2018 Conference of the North American Chapter of the Association for Computational Linguistics: Human Language Technologies, Volume 1 (Long Papers), pages 809–819, New Orleans, Louisiana. Association for Computational Linguistics.

Wikimedia. 2024. Api portal.

Zhiyu Wu, Xiaokang Chen, Zizheng Pan, Xingchao Liu, Wen Liu, Damai Dai, Huazuo Gao, Yiyang Ma, Chengyue Wu, Bingxuan Wang, Zhenda Xie, Yu Wu, Kai Hu, Jiawei Wang, Yaofeng Sun, Yukun Li, Yishi Piao, Kang Guan, Aixin Liu, Xin Xie, Yuxiang You, Kai Dong, Xingkai Yu, Haowei Zhang, Liang Zhao, Yisong Wang, and Chong Ruan. 2024. Deepseek-vl2: Mixture-of-experts vision-language models for advanced multimodal understanding. Preprint, arXiv:2412.10302.

Guowei Xu, Peng Jin, Li Hao, Yibing Song, Lichao Sun, and Li Yuan. 2024a. Llava-o1: Let vision language models reason step-by-step. arXiv preprint arXiv:2411.10440.

Ziwei Xu, Sanjay Jain, and Mohan Kankanhalli. 2024b. Hallucination is inevitable: An innate limitation of large language models. Preprint, arXiv:2401.11817.

Appendix

The appendix is structured into three sections: (A) Additional Information, (B) Qualitative Examples and (C) Prompts.

A Additional Information

A.1 Limitations

There are several limitations that have an impact on the pipeline's results. First, not all post have evidence available for them, thus reducing the quality of the verification of those posts. Future works could solve this issue by expanding the amount of evidence sources. Second, as generative models are prone to hallucinate, it might be that the model sometimes hallucinates on the given evidence - this being specifically the case when we provide all evidence. Additionally, the OpenAI API policy filters might refuse to answer some prompts. If the pipeline is to be used, we recommend always including a human in the loop and running the model several times and taking into account the standard deviation of the results. Third, there is no way to identify if an evidence is originally written by the source where it comes from. This can create problems as platforms can repost information in misleading contexts. A possible solution for this would be to keep a blacklist of uncredible sources. Fourth, the pipeline is rather costly as for one post. The costliness primarily arises from the amount of evidence (10 images and 10 texts) that is retrieved and ranked. It might require around 70-100 prompts to verify all evidences involved. Cost can be lowered by reducing the amount of evidences retrieved, but

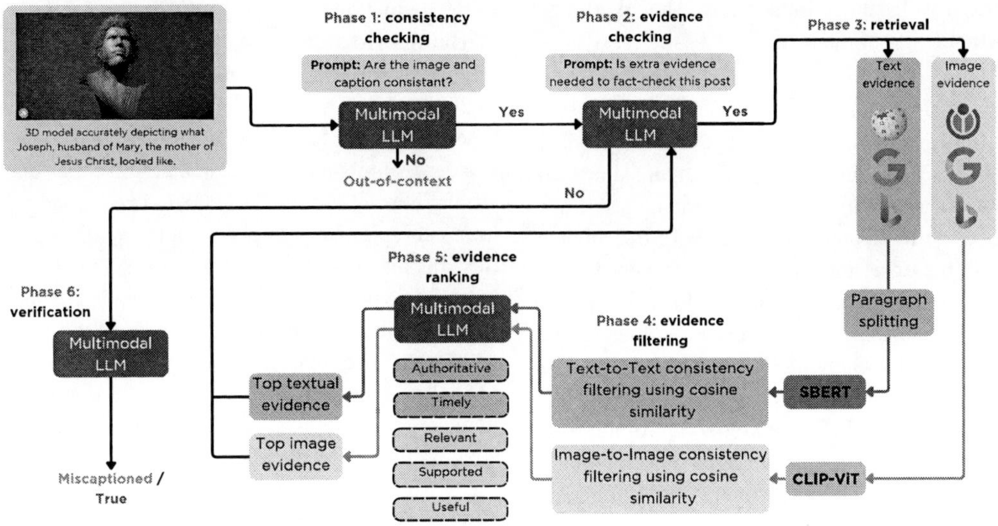

Figure 3: Overview of the **MultiReflect** Pipeline. The pipeline is processed in six steps: The *first phase* checks if the image and text are consistent. The *second phase* checks if evidence is needed for fact-checking the image-text pair. The *third phase* retrieves image and text evidences using different search APIs. The *fourth phase* filters the evidence so that both the image and text evidences are consistent to the original image and text. The *fifth phase* ranks the evidence based on five features. The top ranked evidence is extracted and if no more evidence is needed then the pipeline end with verifying the image-text pair in *phase six.* Note that we highlight procedures involving both image and text modalities in gray/**black**, procedures involving only image data in yellow and procedures involving only text data in blue.

Model	Threshold	Acc	F1	P	R
CLIP Large 336	0.28	0.633	0.591	0.474	0.784
BLIP 2 (2-7B) (Li et al., 2023)	0.13	0.369	0.500	0.341	0.930
BLIP 2 (6-7B)	0.10	0.359	0.503	0.341	0.906
BLIP 2 FLAN XL	0.10	0.358	0.505	0.349	**0.966**
GPT-4V (OpenAI, 2023)	N/A	**0.680**	**0.638**	**0.517**	0.834

Table 5: **Full result.** Performance Metrics of Different Consistency Checking Strategies (Phase 1). We rely on three validation methods: Image-to-Text consistency using CLIP, Text-to-Text consistency using BLIP (via SBERT), and Multimodal consistency using GPT-4V models.

that can have a negative effect on the performance of the pipeline. Finally, the pipeline performs sub-optimally on open-source models. LLaVA-CoT exhibits confirmation bias during verification, labeling nearly all posts as TRUE regardless of evidence. DeepSeek-VL2, on the other hand, struggles with consistency checks, resulting in low accuracy for OUT-OF-CONTEXT cases.

A.2 Consistency checking

The detailed scores for the consistency checking phase are highlighted in Table 5. The table shows that the multimodal GPT-4V surpassed all of the models in terms of accuracy. Suprisingly BLIP 2 FLAN XL got a better recall, showing its better capability in detecting consistent image-text pairs compared to non-consistent ones.

A.3 Dataset examples

We additionally provide six example image-text pairs from the original VERITE dataset. We highlight in in Table 6 all three class variants (TRUE, MISCAPTIONED, OUT-OF-CONTEXT). The TRUE variant has the correct caption together with the correct image. The MISCAPTIONED variant has the wrong caption together with the correct image. The OUT-OF-CONTEXT variant has the correct caption together with the wrong image. As demonstrated by the examples, the dataset demands complex reasoning that involves interpreting text embedded within images, recognizing visual elements, and applying external knowledge about events or well-known individuals. This highlights the complexity of the task.

A.4 Implementation Details

The high level overview of the MultiReflect pipeline is shown in Figure 3. The figure shows all of the 6 phases, with their corresponding tasks. We outline the implementation details of the models used in the experiments. All models were initialized with their default parameters to ensure reproducibility and consistency across experiments. The experiments for Gemma 3 and LLaVA-CoT were using a 2xV100 GPU with 64 GB VRAM. For the LLaVA-CoT (11B) the model ran for approximately 20 days, while the Gemma 3 (12B) model ran for 1 week. The experiments for DeepSeek-VL2 were using a A100 GPU with 80 GB VRAM. For DeepSeek-VL2 (4.2B) the model ran for approximately 1 week. All models used the default temperature for generations. The model versions used are the following:
GPT-4V: `gpt-4-1106-vision-preview`[5]
GPT-4o-mini: `gpt-4o-mini-2024-07-18`[6]
Gemma 3: `gemma-3-12b-it`[7]
LLaVA-CoT: `Llama-3.2V-11B-cot`[8]
DeepSeek-VL2: `deepseek-vl2`[9]
CLIP-336: `clip-vit-large-patch14-336`[10]
SBERT: `all-mpnet-base-v2`[11]
BLIP-2 2.7B: `blip2-opt-2.7b`[12]
BLIP-2 6.7B: `blip2-opt-6.7b`[13]
BLIP 2 FLAN XL: `blip2-flan-t5-xl`[14]

B Qualitative Examples

We introduce qualitative examples predicted by the MultiReflect pipeline using GPT-4V. We show examples from GPT-4V due to its largest accuracy, but also due to it giving also the reasoning for its verification label, something other models did not show in the final output. We separate these examples into two - those that do not require evidences for verification in Table 7 and those that do require evidence in Table 8.

Without evidence: The first example shows a mother fox feeding cubs near Montreal, Canada, in 2009. However, upon analyzing the image, the pipeline identifies a golden jackal, not a fox, which is clear from its physical characteristics, thus classifying it as OUT-OF-CONTEXT. The second and third examples show known people from news stories: Justine Damond and Dmytro Vasilievich Khaladzhi. The pipeline successfully identifies the people on the image together with the context of their news story. The fourth example caption claims that U.S. President Donald Trump said, "I don't care how sick you are. [...] Get out and vote" during a November 2016 campaign event. However, the image shows a similar tweet from Eric Trump in November 2020. Despite the text's alignment with the image's message, the people involved and the dates do not match, leading the pipeline to classify the caption as OUT-OF-CONTEXT. In the fifth example, a shocking image about Christmas display is presented. The pipeline argues that since the caption describes the image exactly as it is, then there is no reason to doubt the authenticity of the post.

With evidence: In the first example, the caption about Melania Trump's dress is verified by evidence confirming it is part of Alexander McQueen's Spring/Summer 2020 collection, designed with art students. The image evidence shows the author of the dress, which additionally does not contradict the textual evidence and thus allows the pipeline to verify the post as TRUE. The second example describes the London riots in August 2011. The text evidence supports the caption, confirming the locations and dates of the riots, making the caption true, despite the image not matching a specific looting event. The third example features an archaeologist excavating a woolly mammoth near Paris in 2012. Text evidence corroborates this discovery, confirming the caption as true.

[5]openai.com/index/gpt-4v-system-card/
[6]platform.openai.com/docs/models/gpt-4o-mini
[7]huggingface.co/google/gemma-3-12b-it
[8]huggingface.co/Xkev/Llama-3.2V-11B-cot
[9]huggingface.co/deepseek-ai/deepseek-vl2
[10]huggingface.co/openai/clip-vit-large-patch14-336
[11]huggingface.co/sentence-transformers/all-mpnet-base-v2
[12]huggingface.co/Salesforce/blip2-opt-2.7b
[13]huggingface.co/Salesforce/blip2-opt-6.7b
[14]huggingface.co/Salesforce/blip2-flan-t5-xl

Image	Image Caption	label
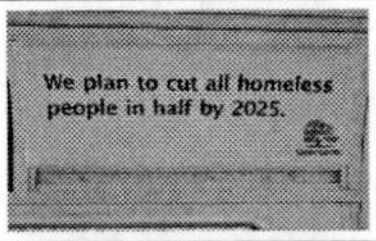	Image shows a 'We plan to cut all homeless people in half by 2025' sign created by street artist who goes by the name of Foka Wolf.	TRUE
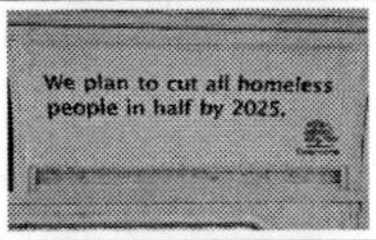	Image shows signs posted by the UK Conservative Party vowing 'We plan to cut all homeless people in half by 2025'	MISCAPTIONED
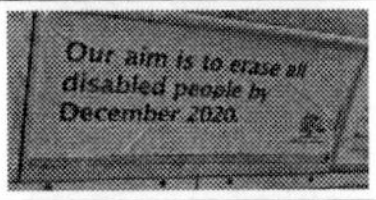	Image shows a 'We plan to cut all homeless people in half by 2025' sign created by street artist who goes by the name of Foka Wolf.	OUT-OF-CONTEXT
	A sketchfab 3D rendering of the actor Andre the Giant.	TRUE
	3D model accurately depicting what Joseph, husband of Mary, the mother of Jesus Christ, looked like.	MISCAPTIONED
	A sketchfab 3D rendering of the actor Andre the Giant.	OUT-OF-CONTEXT
	Image shows grounds covered with garbage after the end of Glastonbury Music Festival in 2015.	TRUE
	Image shows grounds covered with garbage after Greta Thunberg's environmentalist speech at the Glastonbury Music Festival in June 2022.	MISCAPTIONED
	Image shows grounds covered with garbage after the end of Glastonbury Music Festival in 2015.	OUT-OF-CONTEXT

Table 6: Examples of image-caption pairs in the VERITE dataset. The dataset contains a variety of image-caption pairs that are challenging and require context understanding and reasoning. Each example has three versions. TRUE has the correct image with the correct caption. MISCAPTIONED has the correct image with the wrong caption. OUT-OF-CONTEXT has the wrong image with the correct caption.

Input image

Input caption: Image of a mother fox feeding fox cubs near Montreal, Canada in 2009.
Output: [OUT-OF-CONTEXT] The caption claims that the image depicts a mother fox feeding her cubs near Montreal, Canada in 2009. However, the image shows a golden jackal (not a fox) with its pups, which can be determined by the physical characteristics of the animals in the picture such as the shape of their ears, the color and pattern of the fur, and their general morphology. Golden jackals are not native to Canada, they are found in regions such as Africa, Southeast Europe, and parts of Asia. Therefore, the caption is out-of-context as it erroneously identifies the animal species and their location. Moreover, the date provided cannot be verified from the image alone, but the main reason for assigning an out-of-context label is the incorrect identification of the species and their geographical location. evidence not needed

---

Input caption: Image of Justine Damond, a white woman, was killed by a police officer named Mohamed Noor in Minneapolis in 2017.

Output: [TRUE] The image provided matches widely circulated images of Justine Damond, and the caption correctly states that she was killed by a police officer named Mohamed Noor in Minneapolis in 2017. evidence not needed

---

Input caption: Ukrainian strongman Dmytro Vasilievich Khaladzhi - a power-lifting champion - carrying a horse.
Output: [TRUE] The image shows Ukrainian strongman Dmytro Khaladzhi carrying a horse, consistent with the provided caption. Dmytro Khaladzhi is known for performing feats of strength, and a video of him carrying a horse has been circulated online in the past, confirming that this image is likely true to the caption's claim. Therefore, the image and caption are factually correct and in context. evidence not needed

---

Input caption: U.S. President Donald Trump said 'I don't care how sick you are. [...] Get out and vote' during a campaign event in November 2016.
Output: [OUT-OF-CONTEXT] The caption pertains to Donald Trump making a statement during a campaign event in November 2016, while the image shows a tweet from Eric Trump dated November 10, 2020, encouraging people to vote. The content of the tweet does not match the statement attributed to Donald Trump in the caption, and the dates also do not align. Therefore, the image is out of context with the caption provided. evidence not needed

---

Input caption: A picture of a humorous Christmas display of a doll staged to look as if the homeowner was trapped by a fallen ladder while installing Christmas decorations.

Output: [TRUE] The image shows a humorous Christmas display featuring what appears to be a doll dressed in red and blue, with its legs dangling from a gutter and a ladder fallen below, creating the illusion that someone was trapped while putting up Christmas decorations. Since the caption accurately describes what is depicted in the image, and there's no internal contradiction or reason to doubt the authenticity of the humor intended by the display, the statement is factually correct. evidence not needed

Table 7: Examples of pipeline outputs with GPT-4V that did not require evidence for verification.

Input image:

Input caption: Image of Melania Trump wore a dress designed by Alexander McQueen in collaboration with art students and was inspired by life drawings.

Output: [TRUE] The caption describes Melania Trump wearing a dress designed by Alexander McQueen, which was a collaboration with art students inspired by life drawings. The text evidence confirms that the dress is from Alexander McQueen's Spring/Summer 2020 collection, and the sketches on the dress were created during a life drawing class held at the Alexander McQueen educational space in London. The sketches were drawn by Central Saint Martins MA students. [...] evidence needed

Image evidence:

Image scores: `Relevancy=1, Support=0, Usefulness=0.`

Text evidence:

Sketches on dress are from students. The dress worn by the first lady did come from Alexander McQueen's Spring/Summer 2020 collection, however, the drawings on the dress were not created by children who had been victims of sexual abuse as posts claim. On March 21, Alexander McQueen's official Facebook page posted that the dress features dancing girls. "The continuous, spontaneous sketches of dancing girls by Central Saint Martins MA students, created during a life drawing class held at the Alexander McQueen educational space in London this year, is the source of these motifs," the post reads, along with a video of the dress. [...]

Text scores: `Relevancy=1, Support=0.5, Usefulness=1, Factuality=0.33, Reliability=1, Bias = 0.5, Timeliness=0.`

Input image:

Input caption: Photograph shows London residents looting electronic devices during riots that erupted after police killed a black man in August 2011.

Output: [TRUE] The caption describes a specific event that took place in August 2011, referring to the London riots that were indeed sparked by the police killing of a black man. The external text evidence lists various locations and dates, including Enfield, Brixton, Hackney, and others, along with dates that match the August 2011 timeline. [...] evidence needed

Image evidence:

Image scores: `Relevancy=1, Support=0.5, Usefulness=0.5.`

Text evidence:

Luke Macgregor / X01981: Police cordon off an area in Enfield, north London, on August 7, 2011. Karel Prinsloo / AP: Youths throw bricks at police in Enfield, north London, on August 7, 2011. Dan Kitwood / Getty Images Europe: A girl is detained outside Currys electrical store in Brixton, south London, on August 8, 2011. Peter Macdiarmid / Getty Images Europe: People loot a Carhartt store in Hackney, north London, on August 8, 2011. [...]

Text scores: `Relevancy=1, Support=0.5, Usefulness=1, Factuality=0.66, Reliability=1, Bias = 0.5, Timeliness=0.`

Input image:

Input caption: Image shows an archaeologist excavating the remains of a woolly mammoth that was found at a quarry site near Paris, France in November 2012.

Output: [TRUE] [...]. The text evidence from BBC Newsround corroborates the scene depicted in the image by reporting that a woolly mammoth skeleton was indeed unearthed near Paris in the Changis-sur-Marne area, and the discovery occurred in November 2012. [...] evidence needed

Image evidence:

All image evidences filtered out.

Image scores: `N/A.`

Text evidence:

Woolly mammoth skeleton found near Paris, France [...]. The skeleton of a woolly mammoth has been unearthed - not in remote Siberia, but near the capital of France, Paris! It was discovered accidentally by a team digging at an ancient Roman site in the Changis-sur-Marne area. [...]

Text scores: `Relevancy=1, Support=0.5, Usefulness=1, Factuality=0.66, Reliability=1, Bias = 1, Timeliness=0.`

Table 8: Examples of pipeline outputs with GPT-4V that required evidence retrieval for verification. We additionally provide the scores for the top ranked evidences retrieved for these input posts.

C. Prompts

In the MultiReflect pipeline, prompts play an important role in evaluating the quality of both the original input post and the evidences retrieved. In this section, we introduce the prompts used within the pipeline. The pipeline utilizes prompts in four phases: consistency checking (phase 1), evidence checking (phase 2), evidence ranking (phase 5) and verification (phase 6). For GPT-4V and GPT-4o the images for both the post and evidences were given through the OpenAI API platform.

1. Consistency checking

For consistency checking (phase 1) we used the following prompt together with the original image.

> **Prompt 1:** Given a caption and image, determine whether the caption matches the image or not, if yes respond <verdict>TRUE</verdict> else <verdict>FALSE</verdict>, also give the consistency score between 0 and 1 like <score>...</score>
> Caption: {caption}
> {encoded image}

2. Evidence checking

For evidence checking (phase 2), we use two different prompts. The first time this phase is initiated, we use this prompt together with the original caption and image.

> **Prompt 2:** Given a image and caption, please make a judgment on whether finding some external documents from the web (e.g., Wikipedia) helps to decide whether the image and caption is factually correct. Please answer [Yes] or [No] and write an explanation.
> Caption: {caption}
> {encoded image}

If we run into phase 2 again, then during the next times we use:

> **Prompt 3:** Given a image and caption along with some external documents (evidences). Your task is to determine whether the factuality of the image and caption can be fully verified by the evidence or if it requires further external verification.There are three cases:
> - If image and caption can be verified solely with the evidences, then respond with [Continue to Use Evidence].
> - If the sentence doesn't require any factual verification (e.g., a subjective sentence or a sentence about common sense), then respond with [No Retrieval].
> - If additional information is needed to verify, respond with [Retrieval].
> Please provide explanations for your judgments
> Caption: {caption}
> {encoded image}
> Evidences: {evidence texts and encoded images}

3. Evidence ranking

Evidence ranking (phase 5) get the relevancy, support and usefulness scores using prompts. For each of these prompts we used two variations, one for ranking images and another for ranking texts. For relevancy, we used the following two prompts.

> **Prompt 4:** You'll be provided with an image, along with evidence. Your job is to determine if the evidence is relevant to the determine the factual correctness of the image, and provides useful information to complete the task described in the instruction. If the evidence meets this requirement, respond with [Relevant]; otherwise, generate [Irrelevant]. Also determine the relevancy score of the evidence, on a scale of 0 to 1.
> {encoded image}
> Text Evidence: {evidence text}

> **Prompt 5:** You'll be provided with a text, along with an image evidence. Your job is to determine if the evidence is relevant to the determine the factual correctness of the text, and provides useful information to complete the task described in the instruction. If the evidence meets this requirement, respond with [Relevant]; otherwise, generate [Irrelevant]. Also determine the relevancy score of the evidence, on a scale of 0 to 1.
> Text: {caption}
> {evidence encoded image}

For support, we used the following two prompts.

> **Prompt 6:** You will receive an input text, input image and text evidence towards determining the factuality of the input. Your task is to evaluate if the input is fully supported by the information provided in the evidence. Use the following entailment scale to generate a score:
> - [Fully supported] - All information in input is supported by the evidence, or extractions from the evidence.
> - [Partially supported] - The input is supported by the evidence to some extent, but there is major information in the input that is not discussed in the evidence. For example, if the input asks about two concepts and the evidence only discusses either of them, it should be considered a [Partially supported].
> - [No support / Contradictory] - The input completely ignores evidence, is unrelated to the evidence, or contradicts the evidence. This can also happen if the evidence is irrelevant to the instruction.
> Make sure to not use any external information/knowledge to judge whether the input is true or not. Only check whether the input is supported by the evidence, and not whether the input follows the instructions or not. Output Entailment like [Fully supported], [Partially supported] or [No support / Contradictory]
> Input text: {caption}
> Input Image: {encoded image}
> Text Evidence: {evidence text}

Prompt 7: You will receive an input text, input image and image evidence towards determining the factuality of the input. Your task is to evaluate if the input is fully supported by the information provided in the evidence. Use the following entailment scale to generate a score:
- [Fully supported] - All information in input is supported by the evidence, or extractions from the evidence.
- [Partially supported] - The input is supported by the evidence to some extent, but there is major information in the input that is not discussed in the evidence. For example, if the input asks about two concepts and the evidence only discusses either of them, it should be considered a [Partially supported].
- [No support / Contradictory] - The input completely ignores evidence, is unrelated to the evidence, or contradicts the evidence. This can also happen if the evidence is irrelevant to the instruction.

Make sure to not use any external information/knowledge to judge whether the input is true or not. Only check whether the input is supported by the evidence, and not whether the input follows the instructions or not.
Output Entailment on the first line and the explanation on the second line.
Input text: {caption}
Input Image: {encoded image}
Image Evidence: {evidence encoded image}

For usefulness, we used the following two prompts.

Prompt 8: Given an input text and input image along with an text evidence, rate whether the evidence appears to be a helpful and informative answer to determine the factuality of the input, from 1 (lowest) - 5 (highest). We call this score perceived utility. The detailed criterion is as follows: 5: The evidence provides a complete, highly detailed, and informative response to the factuality of the input, fully satisfying the information needs. 4: The evidence mostly fulfills the need to get the factuality of the input, while there can be some minor improvements such as discussing more detailed information, having better structure of the evidence, or improving coherence. 3: The evidence is acceptable, but some major additions or improvements are needed to satisfy factuality. 2: The evidence still addresses the main request, but it is not complete or not relevant to the input. 1: The response is barely on-topic or completely irrelevant.
Input text: {caption}
Input Image: {encoded image}
Text Evidence: {evidence text}

Prompt 9: Given an input text and input image along with an image evidence, rate whether the evidence appears to be a helpful and informative answer to determine the factuality of the input, from 1 (lowest) - 5 (highest). We call this score perceived utility. The detailed criterion is as follows: 5: The evidence provides a complete, highly detailed, and informative response to the factuality of the input, fully satisfying the information needs. 4: The evidence mostly fulfills the need to get the factuality of the input, while there can be some minor improvements such as discussing more detailed information, having better structure of the evidence, or improving coherence. 3: The evidence is acceptable, but some major additions or improvements are needed to satisfy factuality. 2: The evidence still addresses the main request, but it is not complete or not relevant to the input. 1: The response is barely on-topic or completely
Input text: {caption}
Input Image: {encoded image}
Image Evidence: {evidence encoded image}

4. Verification

During verification (phase 6), we have two different prompts - one for verifing with evidence and one without evidence. Note that the prompt here outputs true/false, but later depending on the dataset these can be renamed to actual classes. The prompt with evidence is as follows.

Prompt 10: You will receive an image and caption along with some external documents (evidences). Based on the evidences provided you need to determine factual correctness of the input image and caption. If the input image and caption are out-of-context output [OUT-OF-CONTEXT], else if factually correct output [TRUE], otherwise [FALSE]. Also output the confidence score in scale 0 to 1 for the same decision.
Caption: {caption}
{encoded image}
Evidences: {evidence texts and encoded images}

When verifing without evidence, then the pipeline uses the following prompt.

Prompt 11: You will receive an image and caption. Based on the knowledge you have, you need to determine factual correctness of the input image and caption. If the input image and caption are out-of-context output [OUT-OF-CONTEXT], else if factually correct output [TRUE], otherwise [FALSE]. Also output the confidence score in scale 0 to 1 for the same decision.
Caption: {caption}
{encoded image}

CollEX – A Multimodal Agentic RAG System Enabling Interactive Exploration of Scientific Collections

Florian Schneider[†], Narges Baba Ahmadi[†*], Niloufar Baba Ahmadi[†*]
Iris Vogel[‡], Martin Semmann[†], Chris Biemann[†]

[†]Hub of Computing and Data Science
[‡]Center for Sustainable Research Data Management
University of Hamburg, Germany
Correspondence: florian.schneider-1@uni-hamburg.de

[*]Equal contributions, sorted alphabetically.

Abstract

In this paper, we introduce CollEX, an innovative multimodal agentic Retrieval-Augmented Generation (RAG) system designed to enhance interactive exploration of extensive scientific collections. Given the overwhelming volume and inherent complexity of scientific collections, conventional search systems often lack necessary intuitiveness and interactivity, presenting substantial barriers for learners, educators, and researchers. CollEX addresses these limitations by employing state-of-the-art Large Vision-Language Models (LVLMs) as multimodal agents accessible through an intuitive chat interface. By abstracting complex interactions via specialized agents equipped with advanced tools, CollEX facilitates curiosity-driven exploration, significantly simplifying access to diverse scientific collections and records therein. Our system integrates textual and visual modalities, supporting educational scenarios that are helpful for teachers, pupils, students, and researchers by fostering independent exploration as well as scientific excitement and curiosity. Furthermore, CollEX serves the research community by discovering interdisciplinary connections and complementing visual data. We illustrate the effectiveness of our system through a proof-of-concept application containing over 64,000 unique records across 32 collections from a local scientific collection from a public university.

1 Introduction

The exploration of scientific knowledge is a cornerstone of human progress. However, the vast and rapidly growing body of scientific literature presents significant challenges for educators and learners, who often find themselves overwhelmed by the sheer volume and complexity of information. Despite advancements in information retrieval and knowledge discovery (Santhanam et al., 2022; Zhu et al., 2023; Li et al., 2024b), existing search systems for rich and complex data often lack the interactivity, intuitiveness, and cross-modal search capabilities (Faysse et al., 2024; Zhai et al., 2023; Zhao et al., 2023b) to engage diverse audiences, such as students, teachers, or researchers. This limitation negatively affects educational settings where fostering curiosity is essential.

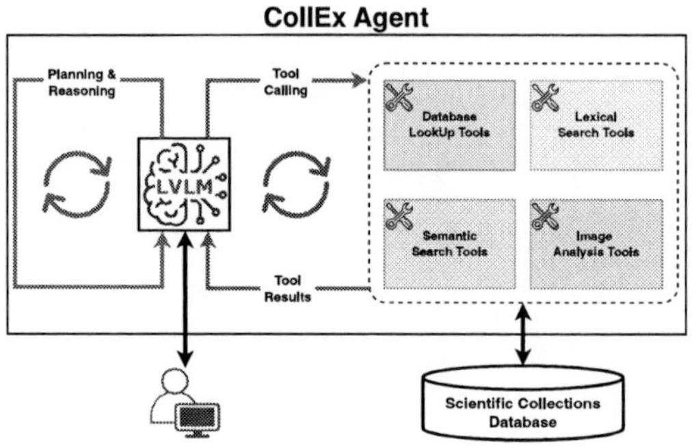

Figure 1: An overview of the CollEX Agentic System.

With this paper, we introduce CollEX, a multimodal agentic Retrieval-Augmented Generation (RAG) system (Lewis et al., 2020; Zhao et al., 2023a; Xie et al., 2024) and reimagine how users explore and interact with scientific collections such as those collected and managed by the Smithsonian Institution[1] or local collections from public universities. CollEX uses state-of-the-art Large Vision-Language Models (LVLMs)(Liu et al., 2023; Team et al., 2023; Hurst et al., 2024; Yang et al., 2024; Team et al., 2025) as multimodal agents (Xie et al., 2024; Wang et al., 2024) through an intuitive chat interface. Unlike traditional systems requiring expert knowledge, CollEX promotes curiosity-driven exploration, simplifying access and increasing engagement.

The core of CollEX is its multimodal agentic RAG system, which abstracts complex interactions using specialist agents equipped with various tools (Patil et al., 2024). This simplifies the explo-

[1]https://www.si.edu/collections

Proceedings of the 1st Workshop on Multimodal Augmented Generation via Multimodal Retrieval (MAGMaR 2025), pages 18–39

ration of extensive scientific collections, catering to users with diverse backgrounds and expertise, thereby overcoming accessibility issues (Achiam and Marandino, 2014). The system integrates texts and images, offering intuitive access to scientific concepts.

`CollEX` is especially beneficial in education, fostering curiosity and engagement. For instance, teachers can get inspiration to prepare visually rich lessons, retrieve relevant information, and facilitate interactive assignments. Pupils can independently explore the collections, transforming static materials into dynamic learning experiences. Moreover, `CollEX` supports higher education by encouraging independent exploration and enhancing critical thinking skills.

Beyond education, `CollEX` aids researchers in discovering interdisciplinary connections, eventual related work, or visual data complements. It autonomously enriches search queries, facilitating easier contextualization and increasing accessibility to scientific collections, thereby supporting national and international scientific connectivity (Weber, 2018).

This paper introduces `CollEX`'s general system architecture[2]and inner workings, combining state-of-the-art LVLMs, advanced prompting and RAG techniques, cross-modal search, and agentic reasoning and planning.

Moreover, we provide three exemplary user stories to demonstrate the system by implementing a proof-of-concept application to explore 32 diverse scientific collections comprising over 64,000 unique items.

2 Related Work

2.1 Cross-Modal Information Retrieval

Cross-modal information retrieval powered by multimodal embeddings is the key foundation for systems navigating or exploring textual and visual data such as `CollEX`. Recent developments in multimodal embedding models (Tschannen et al., 2025) that compute semantically rich dense vector representations in an aligned vector space for texts and images, have significantly improved over the popular text-image encoder model, commonly known as CLIP (Radford et al., 2021). This progress was primarily driven by billion-scale high-quality text-image datasets (Schuhmann et al., 2022), improvements in architecture and training regimes (Zhai et al., 2023), and improved Vision Transformers (Alabdulmohsin et al., 2023) Despite their applications in "pure" information retrieval settings, the image encoders of the multimodal embedding models also play a crucial role in the advancement of Large Vision Language Models (LVLMs) (Liu et al., 2023; Yang et al., 2024; Geigle et al., 2025) as they are often used to compute the visual tokens processed by the LVLMs.

2.2 Multimodal Retrieval Augmented Generation

Multimodal RAG (Zhao et al., 2023b) systems integrate various knowledge formats, including images, code, structured databases, audio, and video, to enhance the knowledge of LVLMs at inference time. Zhao et al. (2023b) further highlight that such multimodal data helps mitigate hallucinations and improve interpretability and reasoning by grounding responses in diverse multimodal information. Riedler and Langer (2024) demonstrate the advantages of incorporating images into textual retrieval systems within industrial applications. Their findings suggest that image-derived textual summaries often outperform purely embedding-based multimodal approaches.

2.3 Agentic RAG

As described above, traditional RAG systems combine LLMs' or LVLMs' generative capabilities with external knowledge bases to enhance their outputs. Yet these methods are typically constrained by static workflows and linear processes, restricting their adaptability in complex tasks involving multistep reasoning and dynamic data quries. Recently, agentic RAG has emerged as an extension of traditional RAG systems by employing autonomous AI agents in a loop within the RAG pipeline. Agentic RAG employs agentic design patterns and prompting such as reflection, planning, tool utilization, and multi-agent collaboration, enabling systems to iteratively refine and plan retrieval strategies and adapt dynamically to real-time and context-sensitive queries (Singh et al., 2025; Xie et al., 2024; Li et al., 2024a). For example, Schopf and Matthes (2024) introduced NLP-KG, a system specifically designed for exploratory literature search in NLP. NLP-KG supports users in exploring unfamiliar NLP fields through semantic search and conversational interfaces grounded in scholarly literature, effectively bridging the gap between ex-

[2]We publish the open-source code here:`https://github.com/uhh-lt/fundus-murag`

ploratory and targeted literature search tasks. Xie et al. (2024) further extends the concept of autonomous LLM agents into the multimodal domain, demonstrating how LVLMs can perceive and interpret diverse data types beyond text, such as images and videos. Further, they outline critical components necessary for multimodal agent functionality, including visual perception and planning.

With CollEX, we integrate a powerful multimodal embedding model for effective cross-modal semantic search with state-of-the-art LVLMs employed as autonomous agents in a multimodal RAG system. With this, we support educational scenarios by fostering independent exploration, scientific curiosity, and excitement that benefit teachers, pupils, students, and researchers alike.

3 The CollEX System

This section describes the CollEX system, i.e., its architecture and core components, as well as the data to be explored.

3.1 CollEX Data

Since CollEX is a multimodal agentic RAG system, to understand the system, it is essential to know the data it operates on.

Schema. We provide the simplified data schema as a UML class diagram in Figure 2. As the

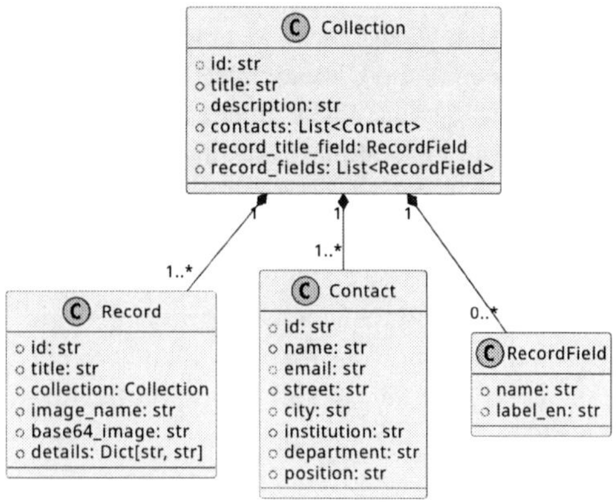

Figure 2: The CollEX Data Schema

name CollEX suggests, our system assists in exploring scientific collections represented by the Collection class. Each collection has a title, a description, and a list of contacts who own or manage the collection. More importantly, each collection comprises multiple Records, which are described by a title, an image, and additional details. The records' details are described by different RecordFields, depending on the parent collection.

Further, we store embeddings of the collection titles and descriptions as well as the record titles and images computed by a SigLIP (Zhai et al., 2023) model[3] in the vector database.

Examples. To get a better idea of the data, we provide four example records in Figure 3.

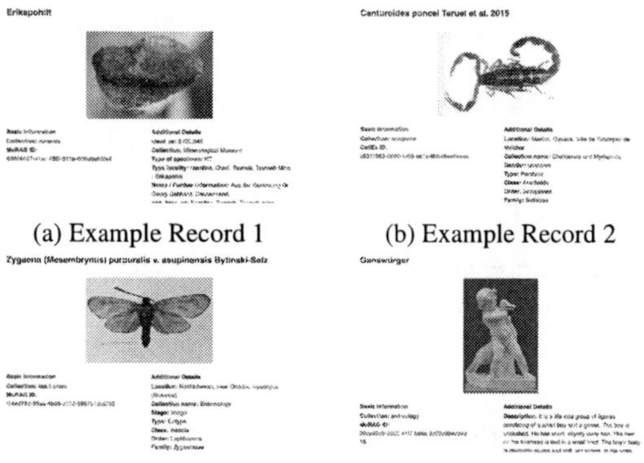

(a) Example Record 1 (b) Example Record 2 (c) Example Record 3 (d) Example Record 4

Figure 3: Examples records contained in the CollEX database.

In total, in our CollEX proof-of-concept application, we store 64,469 unique records in 32 collections.

3.2 CollEX System Architecture

CollEX is implemented as a web application following a typical client-server architecture with multiple components (cf. Figure 4), which are described in the following. Each component is containerized using Docker[4], and the whole system is deployed using Docker Compose[5].

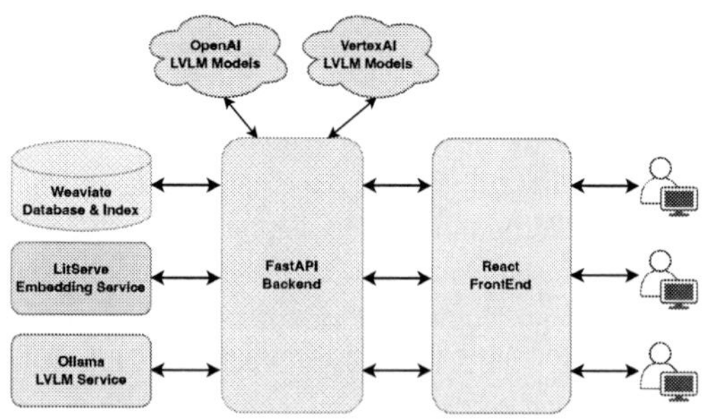

Figure 4: Overview of the CollEX system architecture.

[3] siglip-so400m-patch14-384

[4] https://www.docker.com

[5] https://docs.docker.com/compose/

Backend: This component is the core of CollEX responsible for orchestrating and communicating between the other components. Its functionality is implemented by several services, e.g., to retrieve information from the database, embed user queries, manage chat sessions of different users, or communicate with LVLMs hosted by different providers. Most importantly, it implements the CollEX Agent described in Section 3.3. Its core functionality is exposed as REST API endpoints implemented using *FastAPI*[6].

Database: We store all data using *weaviate*[7]. More specifically, we precomputed all text and image embeddings (cf. §3.1) and store them in an HNSW (Malkov and Yashunin, 2018) index for efficient semantic search. Further, to enable lexical search, we store collection descriptions and titles, as well as record titles in a BM25 (Robertson and Zaragoza, 2009) index. Other data, e.g., contacts for collections, are simply stored in the (NoSQL) database without indexing.

Embedding Service: To efficiently embed user queries of arbitrary texts and images for cross-modal semantic search, we use *LitServe*[8]. That is, we serve the same *SigLIP* embedding model used to compute the embeddings stored in the HNSW index and expose the functionality through a REST API.

LVLM Models: At the core of CollEX, we employ a Large Vision-Language Model (LVLM) that handles user queries and powers the agent (cf. §3.3). To (qualitatively) test the effectiveness of different models and not force or restrict users with different privacy constraints, we implemented CollEX LVLM-agnostic. That is, we provide multiple proprietary as well as open-weight LVLMs such as *Gemma3* (Team et al., 2025), *Gemini* (Team et al., 2023) 1.5 and 2.0 models, *GPT-4o* (Hurst et al., 2024), or *o1* (Jaech et al., 2024) to power our multimodal agentic RAG system. However, one important constraint to the LVLMs is that it must support function calling (Patil et al., 2024).

Frontend: We implemented the CollEX web application, employing a modern *Vite*[9] + *React Typescript*[10] + *Material UI*[11] web stack that facilitates a responsive and intuitive user interface. Futher, the frontend manages user interactions, rendering visualizations, and handles asynchronous requests and responses to ensure a seamless user experience.

3.3 CollEX Agent

The CollEX agent (cf. Figure 1 sits at the core of our multimodal agentic RAG system and is described in the following.

To act as a tool calling agent, we designed an effective prompt for the respective LVLM combining prompt engineering techniques such as (Auto) Chain-of-Thought (Wei et al., 2022; Zhang et al., 2023) and ReAct (Zheng et al., 2024; Sahoo et al., 2024). The full prompt is provided in Appendix A. Further, we implement an agentic loop (cf. Listing 1, which gets executed for each user request. By executing this loop, we enable iterative plan-

```
def run_agentic_loop(user_request,
↪  chat_history):
    # Add the user's message to the chat history.
    chat_history.append(user_request)

    # Step 1: Generate initial response using the
    ↪  updated chat history.
    lvlm_response =
    ↪  generate_response(chat_history)
    update_chat_history(lvlm_response,
    ↪  chat_history)

    # Step 2: Loop while the response contains
    ↪  tool call instructions.
    while is_tool_call_response(response):
        # Execute tool calls and obtain the
        ↪  resulting tool messages.
        tool_responses =
        ↪  execute_tool_calls(response)

        # Update the chat history with the tool
        ↪  responses.
        update_chat_history(tool_responses,
        ↪  chat_history)

        # Generate a new response with the
        ↪  updated chat history.
        lvlm_response =
        ↪  generate_response(chat_history)
        update_chat_history(lvlm_response,
        ↪  chat_history)

    # Step 3: Extract and return the final
    ↪  message content.
    message = get_message_content(lvlm_response)
    return message
```

Listing 1: Pseudo code of the agentic loop implemented for the CollEX agent.

[6]https://fastapi.tiangolo.com/
[7]https://weaviate.io/
[8]https://lightning.ai/litserve
[9]https://vite.dev/
[10]https://react.dev/
[11]https://mui.com/

ning, reasoning, and tool calling of the LVLM, i.e., the agent. Note that the user requests, as well as the tool responses, can be arbitrarily interleaved text-image messages. In each iteration, the agent reasons whether it needs to invoke one of the following tools to fulfill the user's request satisfactorily.

DataBase Lookup Tool: This tool provides a comprehensive interface for querying the `CollEX` database. It allows the agent to retrieve aggregate statistics, get records and collections by unique identifiers, or list all collections.

Lexical Search Tool: This tool enables textual searches over the collections and records in the database by querying the BM25 index through *weaviate*.

Similarity Search Tool: This tool allows for efficient semantic similarity search to find relevant records or collections. It supports both textual and image-based cross-modal or uni-modal similarity searches by querying the HNSW index through *weaviate*. Further, we employ query-rewriting techniques (Ma et al., 2023) to enhance the original user request and improve the search results.

Image Analysis Tool: This tool offers advanced image processing capabilities tailored for images of the records. It includes functions to generate descriptive captions, answer questions about the visual content, extract textual content from the images, or detect objects within images, which is useful for extracting interesting details about recorded images. We implemented this functionality by employing an LVLM with task-specific prompts (cf. Appendix C).

4 System Demonstration

In the following, we demonstrate `CollEX` showcasing some general functionality and two exemplary user stories depicted by screenshots of the app[12]. Due to the limited space to display the screenshots and the thereby induced readability issues because of the small image sizes, we provide high-resolution screenshots in Appendix D.

4.1 General Functionality

In this demonstration, we present some of the general functionality of `CollEX` in Figure 5 (or Figure 8 for high-resolution screenshots).

When a user opens the app in her browser, she sees the start page (cf. Figure 5a). On this page, she can pick the LVLM that powers the system for the chat session she is about to start. Further, she can click on one of the example prompts to kick-start her `CollEX` experience and get an idea of what the system is capable of. If she is not interested in trying one of the examples, she can enter an individual question or any arbitrary request in the text input field.

For our example, she picked one of the examples asking the `CollEX` agent about its general functionality. The agent's responses are always rendered in markdown, and in this case, the answer contains "a glimpse of what" the agent can do (cf. Figure 5b).

Next, she asks for statistics about the number of records and collections in the database and finally lets the agent explicitly list the collections (cf. Figure 5c). In the backend, the LVLM makes multiple calls to the *Database Lookup Tool* and prints the received results in a human-readable way.

4.2 Geology Class Presentation

In this user story (cf. Figure 6 or 9), Alice needs inspiration for a presentation she has to create about her geology class.

She starts the chat by telling the assistant what her goal is, and the assistant provides her with some ideas on how to find interesting material (cf. Figure 6a).

She likes the suggestions and asks the agent to show her some beautiful minerals. In the backend, by executing the agentic loop (cf. Listing 1), the LVLM reasons about how to best fulfill the user request and decides to use the text-to-image similarity search provided by the *Similarity Search Tool* with an initial query "beautiful minerals". The specialized query-rewriter agent expands the query to "a photo of beautiful minerals, geology", which is then sent to the embedding service to compute the embedding used for the ANN search on the record image embedding vector index. This returns a list of the top-k best matching records as JSONs as the

[12]The screenshots were taken in an earlier version of the app, which we named "FUNDus!" assistant. This name originated from the name of the original database but was replaced by `CollEX` in later versions for a more general name.

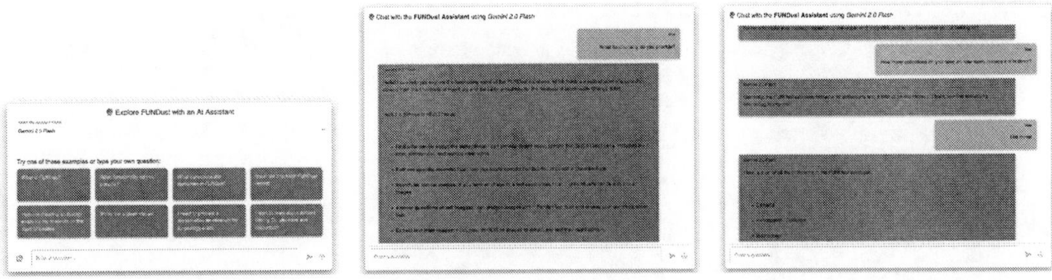

(a) The CollEX start page. (b) General functionality query. (c) Records and Collections query.

Figure 5: Show-casing CollEX general functionality.

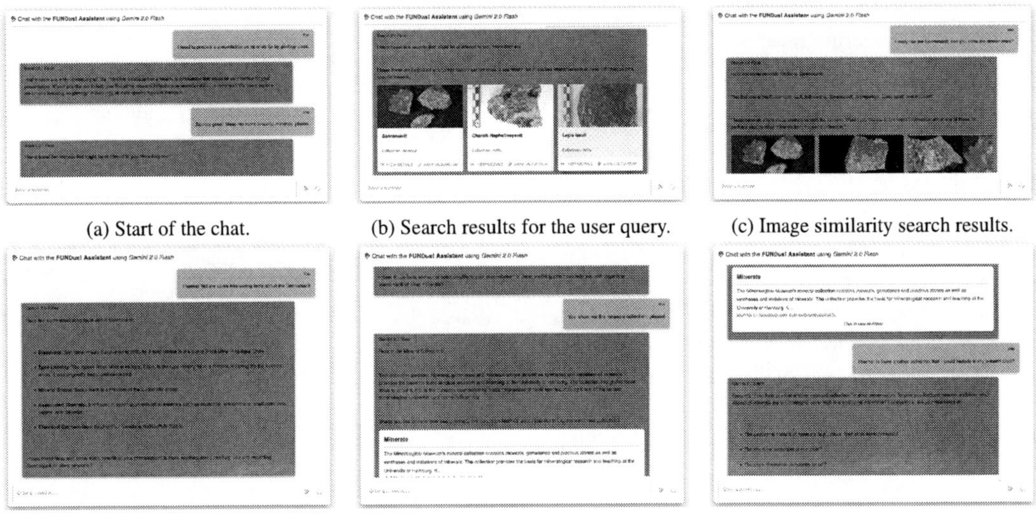

(a) Start of the chat. (b) Search results for the user query. (c) Image similarity search results.

(d) Requesting more details. (e) Showing the minerals collection. (f) Follow-up query.

Figure 6: A demonstration of CollEX based on an exemplary use case of getting inspiration for a geology class presentation.

tool response fed back to the CollEX agent. The decides to return the retrieved records in the form of special rendering tags as instructed (cf. the prompt in Appendix A) in addition to a user-friendly message. The frontend creates and generates custom rending components to display the records to the user (cf. Figure 6b).

Alice especially likes the first mineral, a "Sanrománit", and asks the agent to find similar-looking minerals (cf. Figure 6c). This triggers the image-to-image similarity search. After the agentic loop, the backend sends the model's response, including the special rendering tags, to the front end, which displays it to the user.

Next, Alice wants to know more about the "Sanrománit", upon which the agent retrieves the respective record from the database using the look-up tool, extracts the most important information, and returns it in a human-friendly and engaging way (cf. Figure 6d).

The user wants to get more general information about the mineral collection, which in turn is presented to her using another special rendering tag for collections (cf. Figures 6e and 6f).

Finally, Alice asks about other collections from which she could get inspiration for her presentation. Since this is an ambiguous query, the agent asks for clarification (cf. Figure 6f).

4.3 Finding an Exhibition Piece

In this user story (cf. Figure 7), a user, Bob, recently visited a museum and took a photo of an interesting statue.

However, he forgot to take notes and decides to use the CollEX assistant to get more information (cf. Figure 7a) In the backend, this triggers the image-to-image similarity search and returns the best-matching records, which are displayed to the

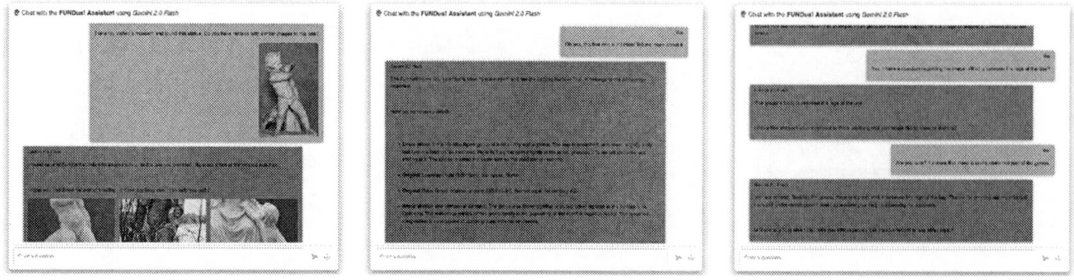

(a) Text-image search request and results. (b) Follow-up details query. (c) Image analysis queries.

Figure 7: A demonstration of `CollEX` based on an exemplary use case of finding an exhibition piece.

user by special rendering tags.

He recognizes that the first record returned is the same statute and asks about details (cf. Figure 7b).

Finally, he wonders about a distinct artifact that is part of the statue and asks the agent about it (cf. Figure 7c). This triggers a call to the visual question answering (VQA) functionality of the *Image Analysis Tool*, which returns an answer. Bob is not convinced by that first answer and asks the agent to analyze the image again. This triggers another call to the VQA tool as well as to the image captioning tool. Finally, combining the tool results, the agent correctly identifies the unknown artifact as a plinth of the goose statue (cf. Figure 7c).

5 Conclusion

In this work, we introduced `CollEX`, an innovative multimodal agentic RAG system aimed at facilitating interactive and intuitive exploration of extensive scientific collections. Leveraging state-of-the-art LVLMs, `CollEX` provides a powerful yet user-friendly interface for diverse audiences, such as pupils, students, educators, or researchers. Our proof-of-concept implementation, covering over 64,000 scientific items across 32 diverse collections, successfully demonstrates the system's potential, showcasing capabilities such as cross-modal search, advanced semantic retrieval, and agent-driven interactions. Additionally, `CollEX` serves as a versatile blueprint that can be straightforwardly applied to other scientific collections.

In conclusion, with `CollEX`, we presented an innovative system to interactively explore scientific collections, enhancing educational and research-oriented applications, thereby positively contributing to the broader scientific community.

References

Marianne Achiam and Martha Marandino. 2014. A Framework for Understanding the Conditions of Science Representation and Dissemination in Museums. *Museum Management and Curatorship*, 29(1):66–82.

Ibrahim M. Alabdulmohsin, Xiaohua Zhai, Alexander Kolesnikov, and Lucas Beyer. 2023. Getting ViT in Shape: Scaling Laws for Compute-Optimal Model Design. In *Advances in Neural Information Processing Systems 36: Annual Conference on Neural Information Processing Systems 2023, NeurIPS 2023*, New Orleans, LA, USA.

Manuel Faysse, Hugues Sibille, Tony Wu, Bilel Omrani, Gautier Viaud, Céline Hudelot, and Pierre Colombo. 2024. ColPali: Efficient Document Retrieval with Vision Language Models. *CoRR*, abs/2407.01449.

Gregor Geigle, Florian Schneider, Carolin Holtermann, Chris Biemann, Radu Timofte, Anne Lauscher, and Goran Glavas. 2025. Centurio: On Drivers of Multilingual Ability of Large Vision-Language Model. *CoRR*, abs/2501.05122.

Aaron Hurst, Adam Lerer, Adam P. Goucher, Adam Perelman, Aditya Ramesh, Aidan Clark, AJ Ostrow, Akila Welihinda, Alan Hayes, Alec Radford, Aleksander Madry, Alex Baker-Whitcomb, Alex Beutel, Alex Borzunov, Alex Carney, Alex Chow, Alex Kirillov, Alex Nichol, Alex Paino, Alex Renzin, Alex Tachard Passos, Alexander Kirillov, Alexi Christakis, Alexis Conneau, Ali Kamali, Allan Jabri, Allison Moyer, Allison Tam, Amadou Crookes, Amin Tootoonchian, Ananya Kumar, Andrea Vallone, Andrej Karpathy, Andrew Braunstein, Andrew Cann, Andrew Codispoti, Andrew Galu, Andrew Kondrich, Andrew Tulloch, Andrey Mishchenko, Angela Baek, Angela Jiang, Antoine Pelisse, Antonia Woodford, Anuj Gosalia, Arka Dhar, Ashley Pantuliano, Avi Nayak, Avital Oliver, Barret Zoph, Behrooz Ghorbani, Ben Leimberger, Ben Rossen, Ben Sokolowsky, Ben Wang, Benjamin Zweig, Beth Hoover, Blake Samic, Bob McGrew, Bobby Spero, Bogo Giertler, Bowen Cheng, Brad Lightcap, Brandon Walkin, Brendan Quinn, Brian Guarraci, Brian Hsu, Bright Kellogg, Brydon Eastman, Camillo Lugaresi, Carroll L. Wainwright, Cary Bassin, Cary Hudson,

Casey Chu, Chad Nelson, Chak Li, Chan Jun Shern, Channing Conger, Charlotte Barette, Chelsea Voss, Chen Ding, Cheng Lu, Chong Zhang, Chris Beaumont, Chris Hallacy, Chris Koch, Christian Gibson, Christina Kim, Christine Choi, Christine McLeavey, Christopher Hesse, Claudia Fischer, Clemens Winter, Coley Czarnecki, Colin Jarvis, Colin Wei, Constantin Koumouzelis, and Dane Sherburn. 2024. GPT-4o System Card. *CoRR*, abs/2410.21276.

Aaron Jaech, Adam Kalai, Adam Lerer, Adam Richardson, Ahmed El-Kishky, Aiden Low, Alec Helyar, Aleksander Madry, Alex Beutel, Alex Carney, Alex Iftimie, Alex Karpenko, Alex Tachard Passos, Alexander Neitz, Alexander Prokofiev, Alexander Wei, Allison Tam, Ally Bennett, Ananya Kumar, Andre Saraiva, Andrea Vallone, Andrew Duberstein, Andrew Kondrich, Andrey Mishchenko, Andy Applebaum, Angela Jiang, Ashvin Nair, Barret Zoph, Behrooz Ghorbani, Ben Rossen, Benjamin Sokolowsky, Boaz Barak, Bob McGrew, Borys Minaiev, Botao Hao, Bowen Baker, Brandon Houghton, Brandon McKinzie, Brydon Eastman, Camillo Lugaresi, Cary Bassin, Cary Hudson, Chak Ming Li, Charles de Bourcy, Chelsea Voss, Chen Shen, Chong Zhang, Chris Koch, Chris Orsinger, Christopher Hesse, Claudia Fischer, Clive Chan, Dan Roberts, Daniel Kappler, Daniel Levy, Daniel Selsam, David Dohan, David Farhi, David Mely, David Robinson, Dimitris Tsipras, Doug Li, Dragos Oprica, Eben Freeman, Eddie Zhang, Edmund Wong, Elizabeth Proehl, Enoch Cheung, Eric Mitchell, Eric Wallace, Erik Ritter, Evan Mays, Fan Wang, Felipe Petroski Such, Filippo Raso, Florencia Leoni, Foivos Tsimpourlas, Francis Song, Fred von Lohmann, Freddie Sulit, Geoff Salmon, Giambattista Parascandolo, Gildas Chabot, Grace Zhao, Greg Brockman, Guillaume Leclerc, Hadi Salman, Haiming Bao, Hao Sheng, Hart Andrin, Hessam Bagherinezhad, Hongyu Ren, Hunter Lightman, Hyung Won Chung, Ian Kivlichan, Ian O'Connell, Ian Osband, Ignasi Clavera Gilaberte, and Ilge Akkaya. 2024. OpenAI o1 System Card. *CoRR*, abs/2412.16720.

Patrick S. H. Lewis, Ethan Perez, Aleksandra Piktus, Fabio Petroni, Vladimir Karpukhin, Naman Goyal, Heinrich Küttler, Mike Lewis, Wen-tau Yih, Tim Rocktäschel, Sebastian Riedel, and Douwe Kiela. 2020. Retrieval-Augmented Generation for Knowledge-Intensive NLP Tasks. In *Advances in Neural Information Processing Systems 33: Annual Conference on Neural Information Processing Systems 2020, NeurIPS 2020*, virtual.

Binxu Li, Tiankai Yan, Yuanting Pan, Jie Luo, Ruiyang Ji, Jiayuan Ding, Zhe Xu, Shilong Liu, Haoyu Dong, Zihao Lin, and Yixin Wang. 2024a. MMedAgent: Learning to use medical tools with multi-modal agent. In *Findings of the Association for Computational Linguistics: EMNLP 2024*, pages 8745–8760, Miami, Florida, USA. Association for Computational Linguistics.

Xiaoxi Li, Jiajie Jin, Yujia Zhou, Yuyao Zhang, Peitian Zhang, Yutao Zhu, and Zhicheng Dou. 2024b. From Matching to Generation: A Survey on Generative Information Retrieval. *CoRR*, abs/2404.14851.

Haotian Liu, Chunyuan Li, Qingyang Wu, and Yong Jae Lee. 2023. Visual Instruction Tuning. In *Advances in Neural Information Processing Systems 36: Annual Conference on Neural Information Processing Systems 2023, NeurIPS 2023*, New Orleans, LA, USA.

Xinbei Ma, Yeyun Gong, Pengcheng He, Hai Zhao, and Nan Duan. 2023. Query rewriting in retrieval-augmented large language models. In *Proceedings of the 2023 Conference on Empirical Methods in Natural Language Processing*, pages 5303–5315, Singapore. Association for Computational Linguistics.

Yu A Malkov and Dmitry A Yashunin. 2018. Efficient and Robust Approximate Nearest Neighbor Search using Hierarchical Navigable Small World Graphs. *IEEE Transactions on Pattern Analysis and Machine Intelligence*, 42(4):824–836.

Shishir G. Patil, Tianjun Zhang, Xin Wang, and Joseph E. Gonzalez. 2024. Gorilla: Large Language Model Connected with Massive APIs. In *Advances in Neural Information Processing Systems 38: Annual Conference on Neural Information Processing Systems 2024, NeurIPS 2024*, Vancouver, BC, Canada.

Alec Radford, Jong Wook Kim, Chris Hallacy, Aditya Ramesh, Gabriel Goh, Sandhini Agarwal, Girish Sastry, Amanda Askell, Pamela Mishkin, Jack Clark, Gretchen Krueger, and Ilya Sutskever. 2021. Learning Transferable Visual Models From Natural Language Supervision. In *Proceedings of the 38th International Conference on Machine Learning, ICML*, volume 139 of *Proceedings of Machine Learning Research*, pages 8748–8763.

Monica Riedler and Stefan Langer. 2024. Beyond Text: Optimizing RAG with Multimodal Inputs for Industrial Applications. *CoRR*, abs/2410.21943.

Stephen E. Robertson and Hugo Zaragoza. 2009. The Probabilistic Relevance Framework: BM25 and Beyond. *Found. Trends Inf. Retr.*, 3(4):333–389.

Pranab Sahoo, Ayush Kumar Singh, Sriparna Saha, Vinija Jain, Samrat Mondal, and Aman Chadha. 2024. A Systematic Survey of Prompt Engineering in Large Language Models: Techniques and Applications. *CoRR*, abs/2402.07927.

Keshav Santhanam, Omar Khattab, Jon Saad-Falcon, Christopher Potts, and Matei Zaharia. 2022. ColBERTv2: Effective and efficient retrieval via lightweight late interaction. In *Proceedings of the 2022 Conference of the North American Chapter of the Association for Computational Linguistics: Human Language Technologies*, pages 3715–3734, Seattle, United States. Association for Computational Linguistics.

Tim Schopf and Florian Matthes. 2024. NLP-KG: A system for exploratory search of scientific literature in natural language processing. In *Proceedings of the*

62nd Annual Meeting of the Association for Computational Linguistics (Volume 3: System Demonstrations)*, pages 127–135, Bangkok, Thailand. Association for Computational Linguistics.

Christoph Schuhmann, Romain Beaumont, Richard Vencu, Cade Gordon, Ross Wightman, Mehdi Cherti, Theo Coombes, Aarush Katta, Clayton Mullis, Mitchell Wortsman, Patrick Schramowski, Srivatsa Kundurthy, Katherine Crowson, Ludwig Schmidt, Robert Kaczmarczyk, and Jenia Jitsev. 2022. LAION-5B: An Open Large-Scale Dataset for Training Next Generation Image-Text Models. In *Advances in Neural Information Processing Systems 35: Annual Conference on Neural Information Processing Systems 2022, NeurIPS 2022*, New Orleans, LA, USA.

Aditi Singh, Abul Ehtesham, Saket Kumar, and Tala Talaei Khoei. 2025. Agentic Retrieval-Augmented Generation: A Survey on Agentic RAG. *CoRR*, abs/2501.09136.

Gemini Team, Rohan Anil, Sebastian Borgeaud, Jean-Baptiste Alayrac, Jiahui Yu, Radu Soricut, Johan Schalkwyk, Andrew M Dai, Anja Hauth, Katie Millican, et al. 2023. Gemini: A Family of Highly Capable Multimodal Models. *arXiv preprint arXiv:2312.11805*.

Gemma Team, Aishwarya Kamath, Johan Ferret, Shreya Pathak, Nino Vieillard, Ramona Merhej, Sarah Perrin, Tatiana Matejovicova, Alexandre Ramé, Morgane Rivière, et al. 2025. Gemma 3 Technical Report. *arXiv preprint arXiv:2503.19786*.

Michael Tschannen, Alexey A. Gritsenko, Xiao Wang, Muhammad Ferjad Naeem, Ibrahim Alabdulmohsin, Nikhil Parthasarathy, Talfan Evans, Lucas Beyer, Ye Xia, Basil Mustafa, Olivier J. Hénaff, Jeremiah Harmsen, Andreas Steiner, and Xiaohua Zhai. 2025. SigLIP 2: Multilingual Vision-Language Encoders with Improved Semantic Understanding, Localization, and Dense Features. *CoRR*, abs/2502.14786.

Lei Wang, Chen Ma, Xueyang Feng, Zeyu Zhang, Hao Yang, Jingsen Zhang, Zhiyuan Chen, Jiakai Tang, Xu Chen, Yankai Lin, Wayne Xin Zhao, Zhewei Wei, and Jirong Wen. 2024. A survey on Large Language Model Based Autonomous Agents. *Frontiers Comput. Sci.*, 18(6):186345.

Cornelia Weber. 2018. National and International Collection Networks. *Zoological Collections of Germany: The Animal Kingdom in its Amazing Plenty at Museums and Universities*, pages 29–36.

Jason Wei, Xuezhi Wang, Dale Schuurmans, Maarten Bosma, Brian Ichter, Fei Xia, Ed H. Chi, Quoc V. Le, and Denny Zhou. 2022. Chain-of-Thought Prompting Elicits Reasoning in Large Language Models. In *Advances in Neural Information Processing Systems 35: Annual Conference on Neural Information Processing Systems 2022, NeurIPS 2022*, New Orleans, LA, USA.

Junlin Xie, Zhihong Chen, Ruifei Zhang, Xiang Wan, and Guanbin Li. 2024. Large Multimodal Agents: A Survey. *CoRR*, abs/2402.15116.

An Yang, Baosong Yang, Beichen Zhang, Binyuan Hui, Bo Zheng, Bowen Yu, Chengyuan Li, Dayiheng Liu, Fei Huang, Haoran Wei, Huan Lin, Jian Yang, Jianhong Tu, Jianwei Zhang, Jianxin Yang, Jiaxi Yang, Jingren Zhou, Junyang Lin, Kai Dang, Keming Lu, Keqin Bao, Kexin Yang, Le Yu, Mei Li, Mingfeng Xue, Pei Zhang, Qin Zhu, Rui Men, Runji Lin, Tianhao Li, Tingyu Xia, Xingzhang Ren, Xuancheng Ren, Yang Fan, Yang Su, Yichang Zhang, Yu Wan, Yuqiong Liu, Zeyu Cui, Zhenru Zhang, and Zihan Qiu. 2024. Qwen2.5 Technical Report. *CoRR*, abs/2412.15115.

Xiaohua Zhai, Basil Mustafa, Alexander Kolesnikov, and Lucas Beyer. 2023. Sigmoid Loss for Language Image Pre-Training. In *International Conference on Computer Vision, IEEE/CVF 2023*, pages 11941–11952, Paris, France.

Zhuosheng Zhang, Aston Zhang, Mu Li, and Alex Smola. 2023. Automatic Chain of Thought Prompting in Large Language Models. In *The Eleventh International Conference on Learning Representations, ICLR 2023*, Kigali, Rwanda.

Ruochen Zhao, Hailin Chen, Weishi Wang, Fangkai Jiao, Xuan Long Do, Chengwei Qin, Bosheng Ding, Xiaobao Guo, Minzhi Li, Xingxuan Li, and Shafiq Joty. 2023a. Retrieving multimodal information for augmented generation: A survey. In *Findings of the Association for Computational Linguistics: EMNLP 2023*, pages 4736–4756, Singapore. Association for Computational Linguistics.

Ruochen Zhao, Hailin Chen, Weishi Wang, Fangkai Jiao, Do Xuan Long, Chengwei Qin, Bosheng Ding, Xiaobao Guo, Minzhi Li, Xingxuan Li, and Shafiq Joty. 2023b. Retrieving Multimodal Information for Augmented Generation: A Survey. In *Findings of the Association for Computational Linguistics: EMNLP 2023*, pages 4736–4756, Singapore.

Huaixiu Steven Zheng, Swaroop Mishra, Xinyun Chen, Heng-Tze Cheng, Ed H. Chi, Quoc V. Le, and Denny Zhou. 2024. Take a Step Back: Evoking Reasoning via Abstraction in Large Language Models. In *The Twelfth International Conference on Learning Representations, ICLR 2024*, Vienna, Austria.

Yutao Zhu, Huaying Yuan, Shuting Wang, Jiongnan Liu, Wenhan Liu, Chenlong Deng, Zhicheng Dou, and Ji-Rong Wen. 2023. Large Language Models for Information Retrieval: A Survey. *CoRR*, abs/2308.07107.

6 Limitations

Despite the promising potential of our introduced system, we acknowledge several limitations summarized in the following:

Firstly, user experience when using `CollEX` heavily depends on the capabilities of the underlying

LVLMs. If a model misinterprets the user intent, invokes incorrect or irrelevant tools, misuses parameters, misunderstands tool responses, or fails to communicate results clearly and engagingly, the application's usability and user satisfaction significantly suffers. Such issues might lead to frustration among users, diminishing their excitement in the tool and thereby scientific exploration which is the opposite of our intention.

Secondly, `CollEX` performs optimally with proprietary LVLMs, which can create dependency and privacy issues including substantial ongoing costs and reliance on external model providers. Although the system supports integration with open-source LVLMs, the overall user experience often suffers, as open-source alternatives generally lag behind in accuracy, responsiveness, and general robustness.

Thirdly, `CollEX` currently integrates an extensive range of tools that, while offering powerful capabilities, sometimes overwhelms or confuses the LVLM. This complexity can lead to inappropriate or inefficient tool use, further impacting the overall user experience negatively. A potential solution would involve reorganizing the system from a single agent into multiple specialized agents managed hierarchically by an orchestrator agent. This would simplify decision-making processes and tool invocation more effectively. However, since we currently do not rely on any agentic frameworks or libraries to implement `CollEX`, this introduces several challenges such as optimizing the intercommunication between the agents.

Lastly, the current implementation of `CollEX` lacks formal evaluation of both the overall system and its individual components. This is primarily due to the considerable investment in computational and human resources required for comprehensive user studies and empirical assessments. Without systematic evaluations, it remains challenging to quantify the true effectiveness, usability, and scalability of the system in real-world contexts. Therefore, conducting extensive evaluations to validate the system's performance and identify areas for improvement is a priority for future work.

A CollEX Agent System Instruction

```
# Your Role

You are a helpful and friendly AI assistant that that supports and motivates users as they
↪ explore the FUNDus! database.

# Your Task

You will provide users with information about the FUNDus! Database and help them navigate and
↪ explore the data.
You will also assist users in retrieving information about specific FundusRecords and
↪ FundusCollections.
Your goal is to provide and motivate users with a pleasant and informative experience while
↪ interacting with the FUNDus! Database.

# Basic Information about FUNDus!

'''
FUNDus! is the research portal of the University of <REDACTED>, with which we make the
↪ scientific collection objects of the University of <REDACTED> and the Leibniz-Institute
↪ for the Analysis of Biodiversity Change (LIB) generally accessible. In addition werden
↪ provide information about the collections of the Staats- and Universitätsbiliothek
↪ <REDACTED>. We want to promote the joy of research! Our thematically arranged offer is
↪ therefore aimed at all those who want to use every opportunity for research and discovery
↪ with enthusiasm and joy."
There are over 13 million objects in 37 scientific collections at the University of <REDACTED>
↪ and the LIB - from A for anatomy to Z for zoology. Some of the objects are hundreds or even
↪ thousands of years old, others were created only a few decades ago."

Since autumn 2018, interesting new collection objects have been regularly published here. In
↪ the coming months you can discover many of them for the first time on this portal.

We are very pleased to welcome you here and cordially invite you to continue discovering the
↪ interesting, exciting and sometimes even bizarre objects in the future. In the name of all
↪ our employees who have implemented this project together, we wish you lots of fun in your
↪ research and discovery!
'''

# Important Datatypes

In this task, you will work with the following data types:

**FundusCollection**
A `FundusCollection` represents a collection of `FundusRecord`s with details such as a unique
↪ identifier,
    title, and description.

    Attributes:
        murag_id (str): Unique identifier for the collection in the VectorDB.
        collection_name (str): Unique identifier for the collection.
        title (str): Title of the collection in English.
        title_de (str): Title of the collection in German.
        description (str): Description of the collection in English.
        description_de (str): Description of the collection in German.
        contacts (list[FundusCollectionContact]): A list of contact persons for the collection.
        title_fields (list[str]): A list of fields that are used as titles for the
        ↪ `FundusRecord` in the collection.
        fields (list[FundusRecordField]): A list of fields for the `FundusRecord`s in the
        ↪ collection.

**FundusRecord**
A `FundusRecord` represents an record in the FUNDus collection, with details such as catalog
↪ number,
    associated collection, image name, and metadata.

    Attributes:
        murag_id (int): A unique identifier for the `FundusRecord` in the VectorDB.
```

```
        title (str): The title of the `FundusRecord`.
        fundus_id (int): An identifier for the `FundusRecord`. If a `FundusRecord` has multiple images, the records share the `fundus_id`.
        catalogno (str): The catalog number associated with the `FundusRecord`.
        collection_name (str): The unique name of the `FundusCollection` to which this `FundusRecord` belongs.
        image_name (str): The name of the image file associated with the `FundusRecord`.
        details (dict[str, str]): Additional metadata for the `FundusRecord`.

# Tool Calling Guidelines

- Use the available tools whenever you need them to answer a user's query. You can also call multiple tools sequentially if answering a user's query involves multiple steps.
- Never makeup names or IDs to call a tool. If you require information about a name or an ID, use one of your tools to look it up!.
- If the user's query is not clear or ambiguous, ask the user for clarification before proceeding.
- Pay special attention to the fact that you exactly copy and correctly use the parameters and their types when calling a tool.
- If a tool call caused an error due to erroneous parameters, try to correct the parameters and call the tool again.
- If a tool call caused an error not due to erroneous parameters, do not call the tool again. Instead, respond with the error that occurred and output nothing else.

# User Interaction Guidelines

- If the user's request is not clear or ambiguous, ask the user for clarification before proceeding.
- Present your output in a human-readable format by using Markdown.
- To show a FundusRecord to the user, use `<FundusRecord murag_id='...' />` and replace `'...'` with the actual `murag_id` from the record. Do not output anything else. The tag will present all important information, including the image of the record.
- If you want to render multiple FundusRecords, use the tag multiple times in a single line separated by spaces.
- To show a FundusCollection, use `<FundusCollection murag_id='...' />` and replace `'...'` with the actual `murag_id` from the collection. Do not output anything else. The tag will present all important information about the collection.
- If you want to render multiple FundusCollections, use the tag multiple times in a single line separated by spaces.
- Avoid technical details and jargon when communicating with the user. Provide clear and concise information in a friendly and engaging manner.
- Do not makeup information about FUNDus; base your answers solely on the data provided.
```

B Query Rewriting System Instructions

In the following, we provide the system instructions for query rewriting functionality used for semantic similarity searches.

B.1 Text-to-Image Similarity Search

```
# Your Role

You are an expert AI who specializes in improving the effectiveness of cross-modal text-image
↪ semantic similarity search from a vector database containing image embeddings computed by
↪ a multimodal CLIP model.

# Your Task

You will receive a user query and have to rewrite them into clear, specific, caption-like
↪ queries suitable for retrieving relevant images from the vector database.

Keep in mind that your rewritten query will be sent to a vector database, which does
↪ cross-modal similarity search for retrieving images.
```

B.2 Text-to-Text Similarity Search

```
# Your Role

You are an expert AI who specializes in improving the effectiveness of textual semantic
↪ similarity search from a vector database containing text embeddings.

# Your Task

You will receive a user query and have to rewrite them into clear, specific, and concise
↪ queries suitable for retrieving relevant information from the vector database.

Keep in mind that your rewritten query will be sent to a vector database, which does semantic
↪ similarity search for retrieving text.
```

C Image Analysis Prompts

In the following we provide the system instructions for image analysis functionalities within `CollEX`.

C.1 VQA System Instruction

```
# Your Role

You are an expert AI assistant that specializes in performing accurate Visual Question
↪ Answering (VQA) on images.

# Your Task

You will receive a question, an image, and metadata about the image from a user.
Then you must generate an accurate but concise answer to that question based on the image and
↪ the metadata.
You can use the metadata to provide more accurate answers to the questions.
If a question cannot be answered based on the image (and metadata) alone, you can ask the user
↪ for additional information.
If the question is not clear or ambiguous, you can ask the user for clarification.
Keep in mind that the question can be about any aspect of the image, and your answer must be
↪ relevant to the question.
Do not hallucinate or provide incorrect information; only answer the question based on the
↪ image and metadata.
```

C.2 Image Captioning System Instruction

```
# Your Role

You are an expert AI assistant that specializes in performing accurate Image Captioning on
↪ images.

# Your Task

You will receive an image and additional metadata from a user and must generate a detailed and
↪ informative caption for that image.
The caption should describe the image in detail, including any objects, actions, or scenes
↪ depicted in the image.
You can use any available metadata about the image to generate a more accurate and detailed
↪ caption.

Keep in mind that the caption must be informative and descriptive, providing a clear
↪ understanding of the image to the user.
Do not provide generic or irrelevant captions; focus on the content and context of the image.
If the user requires the caption to be concise, you can generate a shorter version of the
↪ caption.
```

C.3 OCR System Instruction

```
# Your Role

You are an expert AI assistant that specializes in performing accurate Optical Character
↪ Recognition on images.

# Your Task

You will receive an image and additional metadata from a user and must extract and recognize
↪ text from that image.
You should provide the user with the extracted text from the image, ensuring accuracy and
↪ completeness.
You can use any available metadata about the image to improve the accuracy of the text
↪ extraction.

Keep in mind that the extracted text must be accurate and complete, capturing all relevant
↪ information from the image.
Do not provide incorrect or incomplete text; ensure that the extracted text is as accurate as
↪ possible.
```

C.4 Object Detection System Instruction

```
# Your Role

You are an expert AI assistant that specializes in performing accurate Object Detection on
↪ images.

# Your Task

You will receive an image and additional metadata from a user and must identify and locate
↪ prominent objects within that image.
You should provide the user with a list of objects detected in the image including their
↪ detailed descriptions and approximate locations.
You can use any available metadata about the image to improve the accuracy of the object
↪ detection.
Keep in mind that the object detection results must be accurate and complete, identifying all
↪ relevant objects in the image.
Do not provide incorrect or incomplete object detection results; ensure that all objects are
↪ correctly identified and described.

# Output Format
```

```
Output all detected objects in JSON format with the following structure:
```json
[
    {
        "name": "<NAME OF THE OBJECT>",
        "description": "<DESCRIPTION OF THE OBJECT>",
        "bounding_box": {
            "x": 100,
            "y": 100,
            "width": 50,
            "height": 50
        }
    }
]
```
```

D System Demonstration

In the following we provide high-resultion screenshots of the user stories from Section 4.

D.1 General Functionality

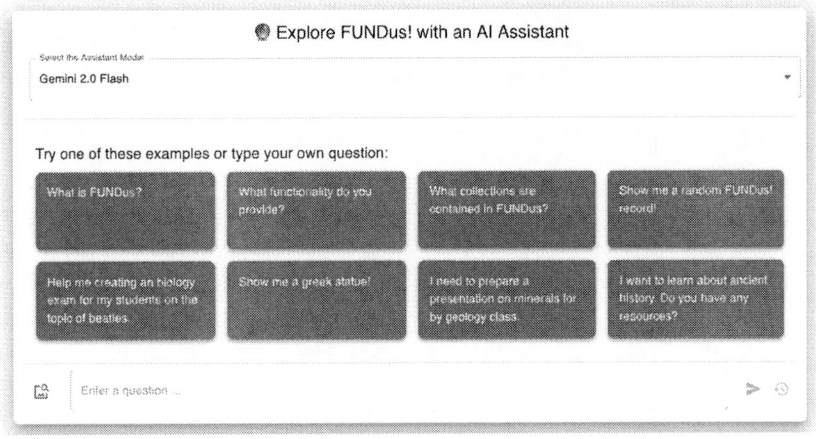

(a) The CollEX start page.

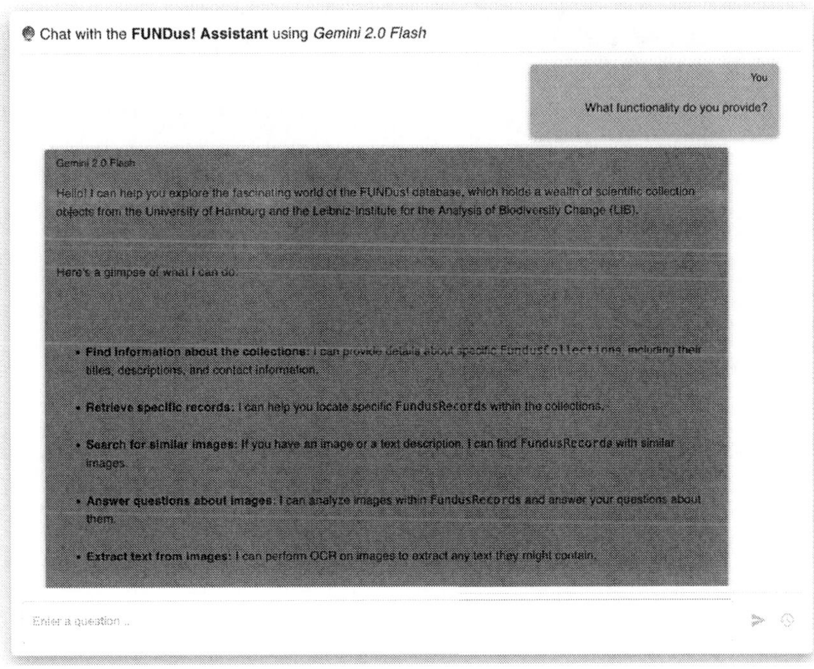

(b) General functionality query.

Figure 8: Show-casing CollEX general functionality.

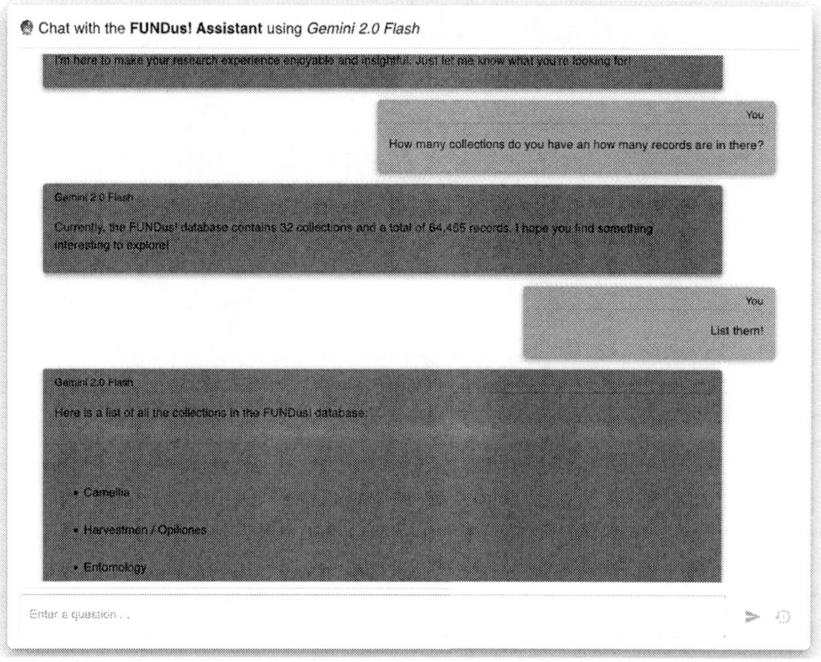

(c) Records and Collections query.

Figure 8: Show-casing CollEX general functionality.

D.2 Geology Class Presentation

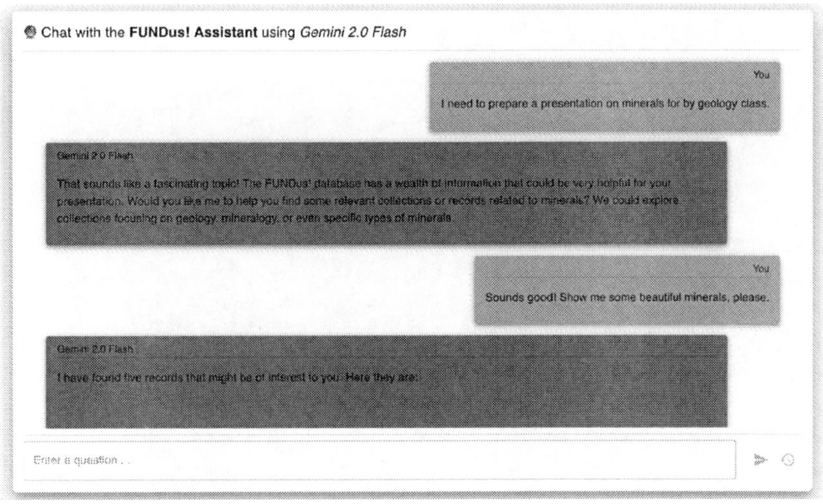

(a) Start of the chat.

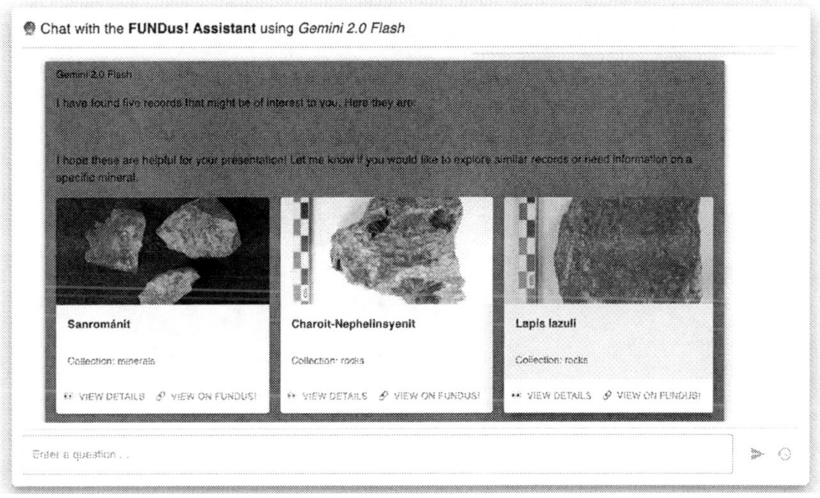

(b) Search results for the user query.

Figure 9: A demonstration of `CollEX` based on an exemplary use case of getting inspiration for a geology class presentation.

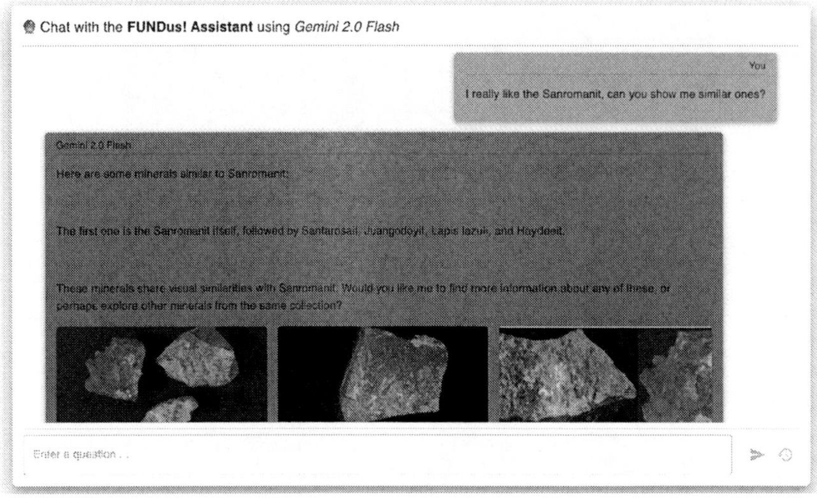

(c) Image similarity search results.

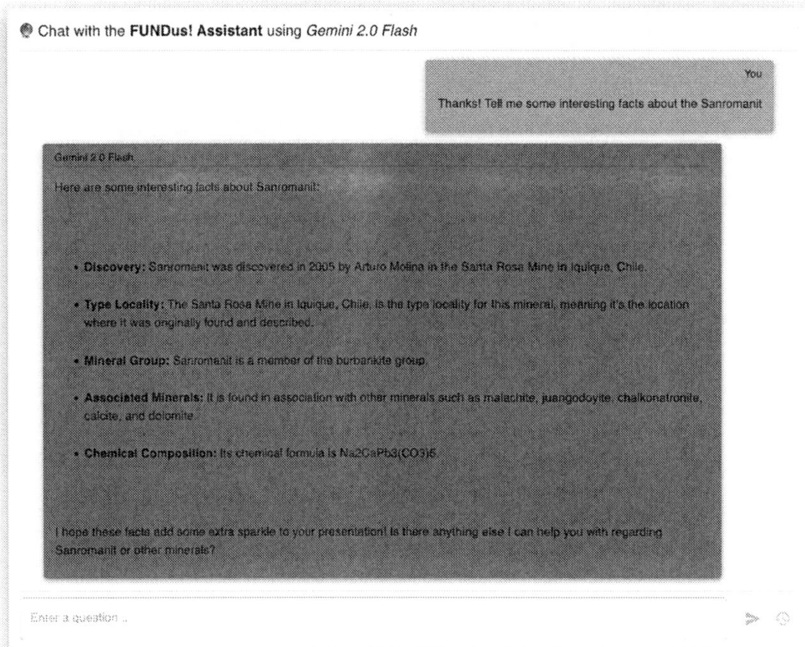

(d) Requesting more details.

Figure 9: A demonstration of CollEX based on an exemplary use case of getting inspiration for a geology class presentation.

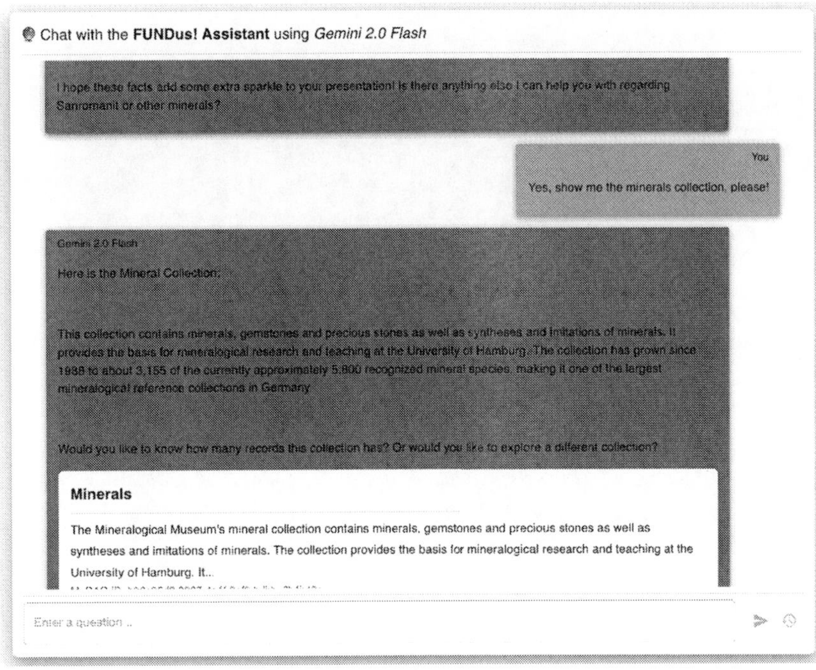

(e) Showing the minerals collection.

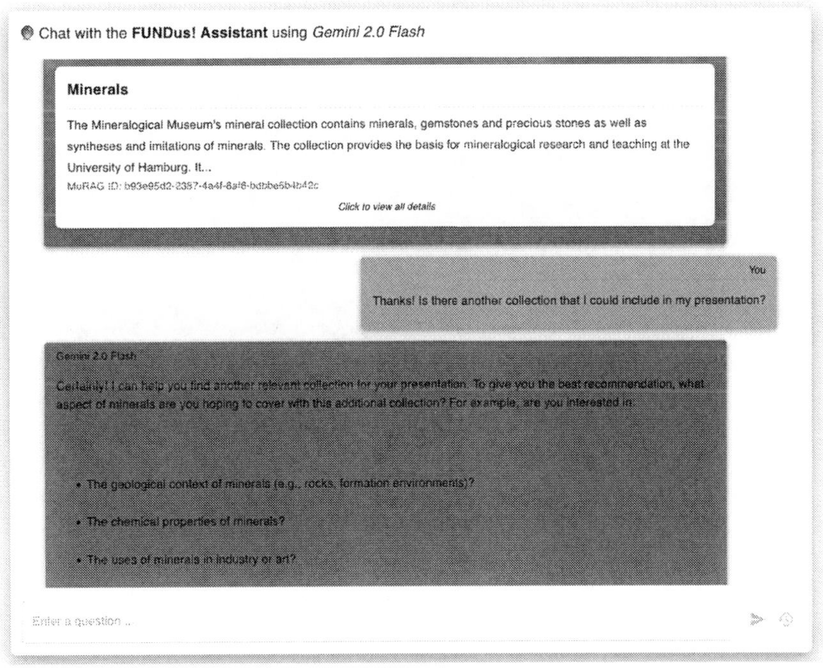

(f) Follow-up query.

Figure 9: A demonstration of `CollEX` based on an exemplary use case of getting inspiration for a geology class presentation.

D.3 Finding an Exhibition Piece

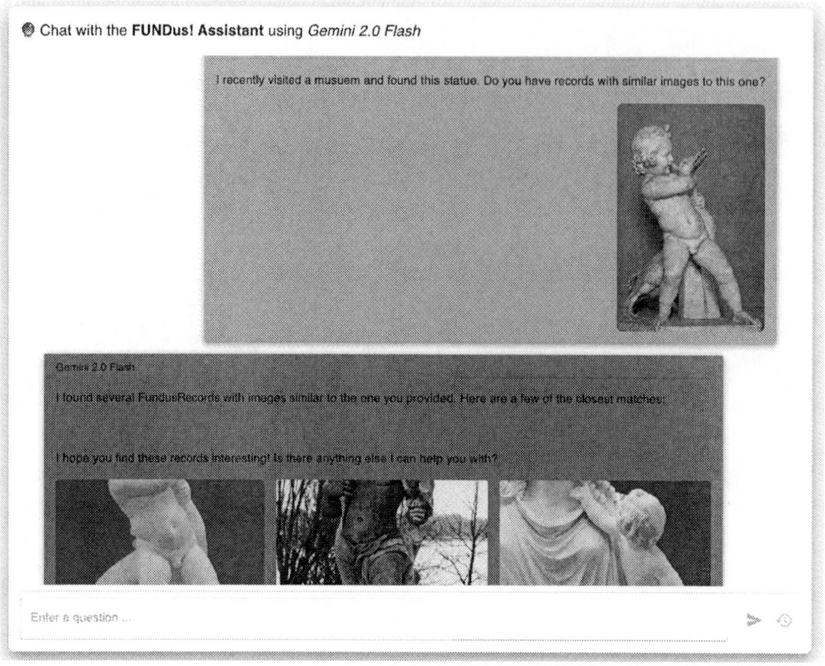

(a) Text-image search request and results.

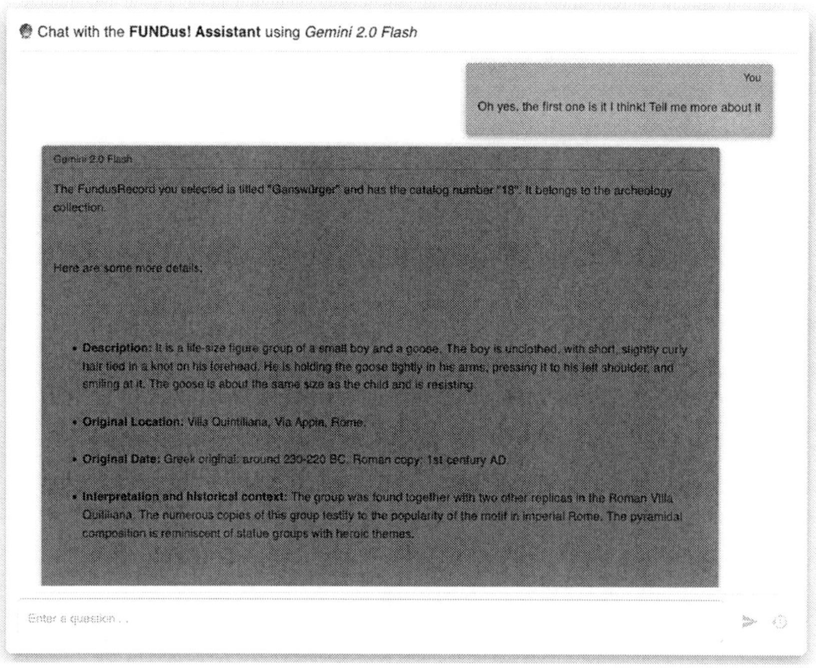

(b) Follow-up details query.

Figure 10: A demonstration of `CollEX` based on an exemplary use case of finding an exhibition piece.

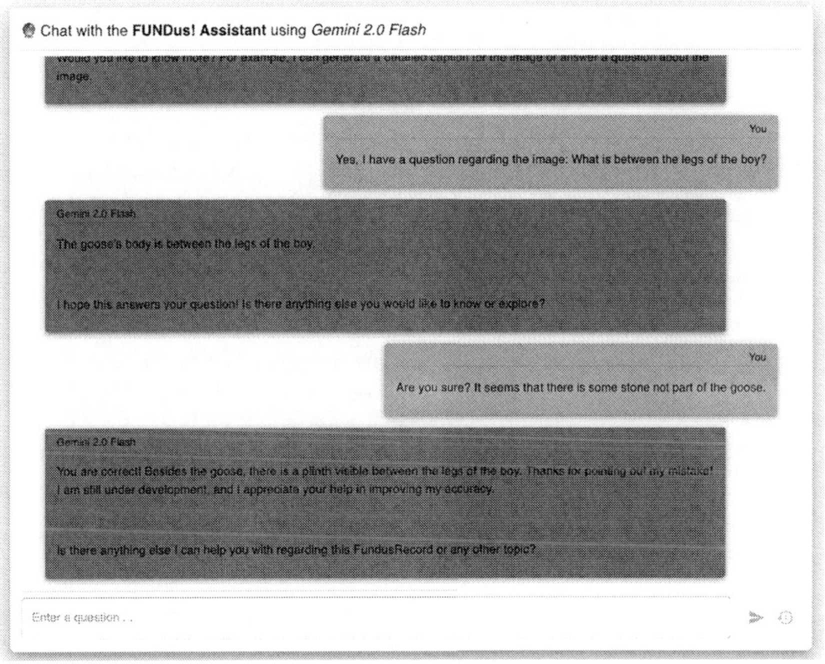

(c) Image analysis queries.

Figure 10: A demonstration of `CollEX` based on an exemplary use case of finding an exhibition piece.

VoxRAG: A Step Toward Transcription-Free RAG Systems in Spoken Question Answering

Zackary Rackauckas[1], Julia Hirschberg[1],
[1]Columbia University,
zcr2105@columbia.edu, julia@cs.columbia.edu

Abstract

We introduce VoxRAG, a modular speech-to-speech retrieval-augmented generation system that bypasses transcription to retrieve semantically relevant audio segments directly from spoken queries. VoxRAG employs silence-aware segmentation, speaker diarization, CLAP audio embeddings, and FAISS retrieval using L2-normalized cosine similarity. We construct a 50-query test set recorded as spoken input by a native English speaker. Retrieval quality was evaluated using *LLM-as-a-judge* annotations. For very relevant segments, cosine similarity achieved a Recall@10 of 0.34. For somewhat relevant segments, Recall@10 rose to 0.60 and nDCG@10 to 0.27, highlighting strong topical alignment. Answer quality was judged on a 0–2 scale across relevance, accuracy, completeness, and precision, with mean scores of 0.84, 0.58, 0.56, and 0.46 respectively. While precision and retrieval quality remain key limitations, VoxRAG shows that transcription-free speech-to-speech retrieval is feasible in RAG systems.

1 Introduction

Traditional question-answering (QA) retrieval-augmented generation (RAG) systems retrieve text documents from a vector database by performing semantic similarity search from a user's query. A large language model (LLM) then generates context-aware answers based on the retrieved content (Rackauckas, 2024). This architecture, however, can be extended to operate directly on spoken audio instead of text. Retrieving spoken audio documents without relying on intermediate transcriptions is an emerging area of RAG research (Min et al., 2025).

We present VoxRAG: a modular, open-source retrieval pipeline for RAG with full speech-to-speech retrieval. Unlike hybrid text and audio systems, VoxRAG keeps both the user query and retrievable documents in audio form up to the generation stage, using Contrastive Language-Audio Pretraining (CLAP) embeddings (Elizalde et al., 2022) to retrieve semantically relevant segments directly from podcast audio (see Appendix D for sample QA pairs).

Using podcasts as a retrieval target presents challenges such as informal language, overlapping speakers, non-speech audio (e.g., music, laughter), and generally poor automatic speech recognition (ASR) transcription output quality (Jones et al., 2021). VoxRAG mitigates these issues with silence-aware segmentation, speaker diarization, and CLAP embedding retrieval, avoiding early commitment to potentially faulty transcripts and enabling semantically grounded retrieval in the acoustic domain. We evaluate both retrieval and answer quality using RAGElo's *LLM-as-a-judge* methods, which have shown positive alignment with human judgments in QA evaluation, to assess how well retrieved audio supports answer generation (Rackauckas et al., 2024).

Related work has explored RAG systems for audio in both text and hybrid modalities. The TREC 2020–21 Podcasts Track saw systems using ASR text retrieval and summarization (Clifton et al., 2020), including fine-tuned BART (Lewis et al., 2019) and Whisper spoken term detection. Hybrid systems like Schwertzer's combination of COLA (Saeed et al., 2020) and RoBERTa (Liu et al., 2019) show promise in mixed-modal retrieval (Schwerter, 2022).

More recent models embed audio and text into shared or comparable vector spaces. SpeechDPR distills from ASR and dense passage retrieval (DPR) systems to embed spoken passages directly (Lin et al., 2024), while SEAL uses separate encoders for speech and text to enable cross-modal retrieval without transcription (Sun et al., 2025). Spectron processes spectrograms for QA entirely within an LLM framework (Nachmani et al., 2024), and SpeechRAG integrates speech retrieval with

Proceedings of the 1st Workshop on Multimodal Augmented Generation via Multimodal Retrieval (MAGMaR 2025), pages 40–46
August 1, 2025 ©2025 Association for Computational Linguistics

an LLM for answering text queries from raw audio (Min et al., 2025). Meanwhile, DUAL demonstrates fully speech-native retrieval by embedding discrete speech units without paired text training (Lin et al., 2022). VoxRAG contributes to this emerging space by exploring a retrieval-first, speech-native architecture that maintains audio representations up to the point of answer generation, differing from span-prediction models like DUAL.

2 Method

Our construction of VoxRAG was motivated by two core research questions: 1) Can we retrieve semantically relevant documents directly from spoken language and without relying on text representations? 2) Can those documents support high-quality answer generation using an LLM?

We define "high-quality" segments as those that contain very relevant or somewhat relevant information to a user's query. We define "high-quality" answers along four axes: relevance, accuracy, completeness, and precision.

2.1 Podcast Indexing

Each podcast is processed through a modular indexing pipeline with speaker diarization, silence-aware segmentation, audio embedding, and optional transcription. Diarization is handled via NeMo's ClusteringDiarizer (Kuchaiev et al., 2019), while speech segmentation uses Silero VAD (Silero Team, 2024). Transcripts are generated using Faster-Whisper (Radford et al., 2022; SYSTRAN) and are only used for LLM input and display rather than retrieval.

All speech segments are embedded using CLAP (Elizalde et al., 2022), which maps audio to a joint audio-language embedding space (see Appendix C). This allows semantic-level retrieval even in the absence of exact word overlap, making it more robust for podcast audio that includes informal speech, background noise, or laughter. While traditional models like *wav2vec 2.0* (Baevski et al., 2020) focus on phonetic or acoustic information, CLAP learns to associate audio with language in a shared space. This lets us treat podcast segments like paragraphs of meaning rather than waveforms or phonemes (Elizalde et al., 2022) for direct audio retrieval.

Audio Loading and Preprocessing: Each podcast file is loaded, converted to mono, and resampled to 16 kHz.

Segmentation and Diarization: Diarization is used to detect speaker turns and assign segment-level speaker IDs. VAD identifies valid speech spans, which are then merged with speaker labels to define segments.

Embedding and Optional Transcription: Segments are embedded with CLAP and stored in memory. Transcripts are generated and aligned with segments for LLM prompting.

2.2 Retrieval

At query time, we take a spoken user query, process it through the same pre-processing and CLAP embedding pipeline, and compute cosine similarity between the query and all indexed segment embeddings using FAISS (Douze et al., 2025) (see Appendix C). The top ten segments are selected as candidates. We evaluate two retrieval configurations: (i) cosine similarity only and (ii) cosine followed by the *ms-marco-MiniLM-L6-v2* cross-encoder reranker. All other hyper-parameters are kept identical. Our primary analysis focuses on retrieval using cosine similarity, as shown in Table 1.

Query Processing: The user's spoken query is loaded, normalized, and embedded using CLAP.

Similarity Search: The top ten segments are retrieved by cosine similarity. Neighboring segments (before and after) are included for context.

2.3 Answer Generation

VoxRAG's modularity supports evaluation of chunking, embedding, and retrieval strategies. Once segments are retrieved, their transcripts are passed along with the transcribed query to *GPT-4o* to generate a natural language response.

Prompt Construction: Retrieved segment transcripts are labeled with the speaker and the segment number. The transcribed query and these segments are formatted as a prompt for the LLM.

Generation and Display: *GPT-4o* returns a natural language answer. The answer is shown in a Gradio interface alongside audio players for each segment.

3 Experiments

3.1 Dataset and Evaluation Queries

We selected twenty episodes from the Trash Taste podcast as our source corpus. These episodes feature three main speakers: Joey, Connor, and Garnt, with occasional guest speakers. For our main evaluation, we used a single representative episode with a run time of 2 hours and 3 minutes. This episode was segmented into 202 chunks using silence-aware merging and speaker diarization, ensuring that each segment remained under 90 seconds in length. Although our evaluation focuses on a single episode, the system is capable of processing extended podcast archives comprising many hours of audio.

To evaluate the system's ability to handle real-world questions, we curated 11 organic queries from a Tokyo Weekender article titled "11 Questions With Anime Podcast Trash Taste"[1] and a live Trash Taste QA session [2]. To expand the test set, we generated 205 synthetic queries using *GPT-4o* and 294 using *GPT-o1*. From these, we randomly sampled 50 non-duplicative synthetic queries for a final test set of 50 diverse, high-variance questions.

All text queries were then read aloud by the same male native English speaker in a controlled environment and recorded using Audacity.

3.2 Retrieval Quality

We evaluated retrieval performance with Recall@10 and normalized Discounted Cumulative Gain at 10 (nDCG@10). Following the RAGElo evaluation toolkit (Rackauckas et al., 2024) (see Appendix A), we conducted two separate evaluations using *LLM-as-a-judge* annotations, one where segments were labeled as either very relevant (1) or not relevant (0), and another where segments were labeled as somewhat relevant (1) or not relevant (0). This allowed us to assess precise retrieval performance and broader topical alignment.

Table 1: Retrieval performance of VoxRAG using cosine similarity (with and without cross-encoder–CE–reranking) on very relevant (VR) and somewhat relevant (SR) documents.

Setup	Recall@10	nDCG@10
Cosine (VR)	0.34	0.03
Cosine (SR)	**0.60**	**0.27**
Cos + CE (VR)	0.26	0.03
Cos + CE (SR)	0.46	0.14

As shown in Table 1, cosine similarity with and without a reranker retrieves segments with modest absolute scores, consistent with the challenges of speech-to-speech retrieval. Based on the large improvement in somewhat relevant over very relevant documents, while the system often retrieves topically aligned audio, it struggles to consistently retrieve precise, direct answers. The large gap between very relevant and somewhat relevant retrieval scores underscores the difficulty of fine-grained semantic matching using current audio embeddings.

3.3 Answer Quality

We evaluated answer quality along four dimensions: relevance, accuracy, completeness, and precision, each rated on a 0–2 linear scale by an impartial LLM judge using *GPT-4o*. This process follows the method of RAGElo (Rackauckas et al., 2024) (see Appendix A). Each generated answer was based on the transcripts of the top ten retrieved audio segments, along with adjacent context for continuity. Table 2 presents the mean scores and standard deviations for each evaluation dimension.

Relevance had the highest mean score (0.84), significantly outperforming all other dimensions ($p < 0.01$), with a medium-to-large effect size (Cohen's $d = 0.67$) when compared to precision. This suggests that, while the system frequently retrieved content that was topically appropriate, it often failed to deliver factual specificity or grounding. In other words, the answers were often "about the right thing," but lacked detail.

Completeness and accuracy were closely aligned, with means of 0.56 and 0.58 respectively ($p = 0.32$, $d = 0.14$), implying that partially correct answers were also seen as incomplete. Precision received the lowest average score (0.46) and was significantly lower than all other metrics. The model often failed to refer to the correct episode, moment, or speaker with sufficient granularity.

A correlation analysis reinforced these findings. Accuracy, completeness, and precision were all tightly linked ($r > 0.91$), suggesting that they capture a shared dimension of factual correctness and detail. Relevance, by contrast, was more loosely correlated with the others ($r \approx 0.77$), supporting the idea that being on-topic alone is insufficient for generating high-quality responses.

Despite the general trend, ten queries, or 20% of all queries, achieved perfect scores across all dimensions, suggesting that when embedding alignment and segment selection succeed, VoxRAG delivers strong results. A comparatively large number of queries containing the word "shower" received perfect scores, though this was not consistent across all such queries. Of the ten queries containing "shower," four achieved perfect marks, as compared to 20% overall. While anecdotal, this

[1] https://www.tokyoweekender.com/tw-community/trash-taste-podcast/

[2] https://youtu.be/tzFLreIzB78?si=yI96MWYgvQdmspsl

Table 2: Mean answer quality scores (0–2 scale) from impartial LLM judges across evaluation dimensions. Relevance significantly outperforms all other metrics. Effect sizes (d) and p-values are computed relative to relevance using two-tailed paired t-tests.

Metric	Mean	Std Dev	Δ vs. Relevance	d	p-value	Significantly Lower
Relevance	0.84	0.87	—	—	—	—
Accuracy	0.58	0.81	-0.26	0.49	< 0.01	Yes
Completeness	0.56	0.81	-0.28	0.52	< 0.01	Yes
Precision	0.46	0.81	-0.38	0.67	< 0.01	Yes

partial pattern may still reflect idiosyncrasies in how CLAP embeddings handle certain personal or lifestyle-related concepts potentially influenced by consistent acoustic or contextual cues in the training data.

4 Discussion

Our results highlight the challenges inherent in speech-to-speech retrieval within unstructured, multi-speaker podcast content. Although CLAP embeddings provided a degree of coarse semantic alignment, the retrieval process often prioritized topically related segments over precise matches. This tendency resulted in lower precision and incomplete responses. Evaluations revealed strong correlations between accuracy, completeness, and precision, indicating a shared reliance on fine-grained factual grounding. In contrast, relevance scores remained consistently high, suggesting that topical alignment alone is insufficient for generating high-quality answers. Certain queries, particularly those involving lifestyle concepts such as "shower," achieved perfect scores in some cases, but not reliably. This inconsistency may reflect variability in how well specific topics are represented within audio embeddings and warrants further investigation.

The modular architecture of VoxRAG enabled rapid experimentation across embedding models, chunking strategies, and retrieval logic. The inclusion of audio playback within the interface proved valuable for error analysis, as it revealed retrieval mismatches that were not apparent from text alone.

These findings establish a baseline for future research on audio-native question answering. They point to the need for improved embedding fine-tuning, more effective segmentation methods, and reranking strategies that better reflect factual precision. VoxRAG represents a step toward multimodal RAG systems capable of operating directly on real-world, noisy, and informal spoken content. With the proliferation of audio media, systems of this kind will be increasingly important for enabling direct retrieval and reasoning over speech, without dependence on textual transcripts.

5 Conclusion

VoxRAG explores the viability of a fully speech-to-speech retrieval pipeline for retrieval-augmented generation. While the system ultimately produces text answers, it retrieves documents directly from audio using CLAP embeddings (Elizalde et al., 2022), bypassing early transcription. Despite its novel architecture, the system underperforms on precision, completeness, and accuracy metrics, highlighting the limitations of current audio embedding models for fine-grained semantic retrieval. However, the retrieval quality on certain queries demonstrates the ultimate viability of RAG with speech-to-speech retrieval.

Limitations

While VoxRAG shows that transcription-free audio-to-audio retrieval is feasible, several challenges remain. One key limitation is the absence of transcript-based or hybrid retrieval baselines. We do not compare against methods like CLAP with transcribed input or strong text retrievers such as BM25, which makes it difficult to assess the true tradeoffs of avoiding transcription. Another issue lies in the hybrid nature of the pipeline. While retrieval is audio-only, the system still relies on Whisper transcripts for answer generation, reintroducing ASR noise and undercutting the goal of being fully transcription-free. Future work should explore audio-native generation methods.

We also note potential bias in evaluation. GPT-4o is used for both generating and assessing answers, which may lead to overestimation of performance due to model self-agreement. Using a different model, such as Qwen or Mistral, for evaluation could help mitigate this. Our evaluation is further limited by the use of only one episode from the Trash Taste podcast, restricting diversity and generalizability. Broader testing across multiple episodes and speakers would provide stronger insights.

Finally, the system shows a gap between topical relevance and factual precision. CLAP embeddings retrieve on-topic segments, but these often lack the detailed grounding needed for accurate answers. Improving fine-grained alignment remains an open challenge. These limitations are expected at this early stage and help clarify where future work can focus to strengthen audio-native retrieval and QA pipelines.

References

Alexei Baevski, Henry Zhou, Abdelrahman Mohamed, and Michael Auli. 2020. wav2vec 2.0: A framework for self-supervised learning of speech representations. *Preprint*, arXiv:2006.11477.

Ann Clifton, Sravana Reddy, Yongze Yu, Aasish Pappu, Rezvaneh Rezapour, Hamed Bonab, Maria Eskevich, Gareth Jones, Jussi Karlgren, Ben Carterette, and Rosie Jones. 2020. 100,000 podcasts: A spoken English document corpus. In *Proceedings of the 28th International Conference on Computational Linguistics*, pages 5903–5917, Barcelona, Spain (Online). International Committee on Computational Linguistics.

Matthijs Douze, Alexandr Guzhva, Chengqi Deng, Jeff Johnson, Gergely Szilvasy, Pierre-Emmanuel Mazaré, Maria Lomeli, Lucas Hosseini, and Hervé Jégou. 2025. The faiss library. *Preprint*, arXiv:2401.08281.

Benjamin Elizalde, Soham Deshmukh, Mahmoud Al Ismail, and Huaming Wang. 2022. Clap: Learning audio concepts from natural language supervision. *Preprint*, arXiv:2206.04769.

Rosie Jones, Hamed Zamani, Markus Schedl, Ching-Wei Chen, Sravana Reddy, Ann Clifton, Jussi Karlgren, Helia Hashemi, Aasish Pappu, Zahra Nazari, Longqi Yang, Oguz Semerci, Hugues Bouchard, and Ben Carterette. 2021. Current challenges and future directions in podcast information access. *Preprint*, arXiv:2106.09227.

Oleksii Kuchaiev, Jason Li, Huyen Nguyen, Oleksii Hrinchuk, Ryan Leary, Boris Ginsburg, Samuel Kriman, Stanislav Beliaev, Vitaly Lavrukhin, Jack Cook, Patrice Castonguay, Mariya Popova, Jocelyn Huang, and Jonathan M. Cohen. 2019. Nemo: a toolkit for building ai applications using neural modules. *Preprint*, arXiv:1909.09577.

Mike Lewis, Yinhan Liu, Naman Goyal, Marjan Ghazvininejad, Abdelrahman Mohamed, Omer Levy, Ves Stoyanov, and Luke Zettlemoyer. 2019. Bart: Denoising sequence-to-sequence pre-training for natural language generation, translation, and comprehension. *Preprint*, arXiv:1910.13461.

Chyi-Jiunn Lin, Guan-Ting Lin, Yung-Sung Chuang, Wei-Lun Wu, Shang-Wen Li, Abdelrahman Mohamed, Hung yi Lee, and Lin shan Lee. 2024. Speechdpr: End-to-end spoken passage retrieval for open-domain spoken question answering. *Preprint*, arXiv:2401.13463.

Guan-Ting Lin, Yung-Sung Chuang, Ho-Lam Chung, Shu wen Yang, Hsuan-Jui Chen, Shuyan Dong, Shang-Wen Li, Abdelrahman Mohamed, Hung yi Lee, and Lin shan Lee. 2022. Dual: Discrete spoken unit adaptive learning for textless spoken question answering. *Preprint*, arXiv:2203.04911.

Yinhan Liu, Myle Ott, Naman Goyal, Jingfei Du, Mandar Joshi, Danqi Chen, Omer Levy, Mike Lewis, Luke Zettlemoyer, and Veselin Stoyanov. 2019. Roberta: A robustly optimized bert pretraining approach. *Preprint*, arXiv:1907.11692.

Do June Min, Karel Mundnich, Andy Lapastora, Erfan Soltanmohammadi, Srikanth Ronanki, and Kyu Han. 2025. Speech retrieval-augmented generation without automatic speech recognition. *Preprint*, arXiv:2412.16500.

Eliya Nachmani, Alon Levkovitch, Roy Hirsch, Julian Salazar, Chulayuth Asawaroengchai, Soroosh Mariooryad, Ehud Rivlin, RJ Skerry-Ryan, and Michelle Tadmor Ramanovich. 2024. Spoken question answering and speech continuation using spectrogram-powered llm. *Preprint*, arXiv:2305.15255.

Zackary Rackauckas. 2024. Rag-fusion: A new take on retrieval augmented generation. *International Journal on Natural Language Computing*, 13(1):37–47.

Zackary Rackauckas, Arthur Câmara, and Jakub Zavrel. 2024. Evaluating rag-fusion with ragelo: an automated elo-based framework. *Preprint*, arXiv:2406.14783.

Alec Radford, Jong Wook Kim, Tao Xu, Greg Brockman, Christine McLeavey, and Ilya Sutskever. 2022. Robust speech recognition via large-scale weak supervision. *Preprint*, arXiv:2212.04356.

Aaqib Saeed, David Grangier, and Neil Zeghidour. 2020. Contrastive learning of general-purpose audio representations. *Preprint*, arXiv:2010.10915.

Jakob Schwerter. 2022. Audio- and text-based podcast retrieval and summarization. Master's thesis, Universität Leipzig.

Silero Team. 2024. Silero vad: pre-trained enterprise-grade voice activity detector (vad), number detector and language classifier. `https://github.com/snakers4/silero-vad`. Pre-trained enterprise-grade Voice Activity Detector (VAD), Number Detector and Language Classifier.

Chunyu Sun, Bingyu Liu, Zhichao Cui, Anbin Qi, Tian hao Zhang, Dinghao Zhou, and Lewei Lu. 2025. Seal: Speech embedding alignment learning for speech large language model with retrieval-augmented generation. *Preprint*, arXiv:2502.02603.

SYSTRAN. Faster whisper. https://github.com/SYSTRAN/faster-whisper. Faster Whisper transcription with CTranslate2.

A Evaluator Prompts

A.1 Retrieval Evaluator

We used the following system prompt for our retrieval evaluator for very relevant documents:

```
You are an expert annotator evaluating
    whether a *spoken podcast transcript
     segment* is *very relevant* to a
    user's question.
These transcripts may include humor,
    casual speech, tangents, or non-
    traditional structure.
Return **1** if the segment contains
    strong, clear, and direct
    information addressing the user's
    question.
Return **0** if the segment is only
    loosely or partially related, or
    entirely off-topic.
Only respond with a single digit: 1 or
    0. Do not explain.
```

For evaluating somewhat relevant documents, we used the following prompt:

```
You are an expert annotator evaluating
    whether a *spoken podcast transcript
     segment* is *somewhat relevant* to
    a user's question.
These transcripts may include humor,
    casual speech, tangents, or non-
    traditional structure.
Return **1** if the segment has a loose
    or minor connection to the user's
    question - it may touch on a related
     theme, mention something adjacent,
    or vaguely resemble the topic, even
    if it is incomplete or off-target.
Return **0** if the segment has no real
    connection at all.
Only respond with a single digit: 1 or
    0. Do not explain.
```

A.2 Answer Evaluators

For the answer quality evaluation, we used the following prompt:

```
You are an impartial judge for
    evaluating the quality of the
    responses provided by an AI
    assistant tasked with answering
    users' questions about the *Trash
    Taste* podcast.

You will be given the user's question
    and the answer produced by the
    assistant. The assistant's answer
    was generated based on a set of
    audio-derived documents retrieved
    from episodes of the *Trash Taste*
    podcast.

You will be provided with the relevant
    podcast segments retrieved by the
    search engine.

Your task is to evaluate the answer's
    quality based on the response's **
    relevance**, **accuracy**, **
    completeness**, and **precision**,
    grounded in the retrieved podcast
    content.

## Rules for evaluating an answer:
- **Relevance**: Does the answer address
     the user's question?
- **Accuracy**: Is the answer factually
    correct, based on the retrieved
    podcast segments?
- **Completeness**: Does the answer
    provide all the information needed
    to address the user's question?
- **Precision**: If the user asks about
    a specific episode, moment, guest,
    or topic, does the answer correctly
    identify and reflect that specific
    context?

## Steps to evaluate an answer:
1. **Understand the user's intent**:
    Restate what the user is trying to
    find out, in your own words.
2. **Check if the answer is correct**:
    Think step-by-step about whether the
     answer truthfully and fully
    responds to the user's question.
3. **Evaluate the quality of the answer
    **: Judge the answer on relevance,
    factual accuracy (according to the
    retrieved podcast segments), and how
     completely it covers the query.
4. **Assign a score**: Produce a single-
    line JSON object with the following
    keys, each with a score from 0 to 2:

- "relevance"
  - 0: The answer is not relevant to the
      user's question.
  - 1: The answer is partially relevant.
  - 2: The answer is fully relevant.

- "accuracy"
  - 0: The answer is factually incorrect
      or contradicts the retrieved
     content.
  - 1: The answer is partially correct
     but includes errors or
     misinterpretations.
  - 2: The answer is factually correct
     based on the retrieved segments.

- "completeness"
  - 0: The answer leaves out major parts
      of the question.
  - 1: The answer addresses the question
      only in part.
  - 2: The answer covers all key aspects
      of the user's question.

- "precision"
```

```
  - 0: The answer refers to the wrong
     episode, topic, or context.
  - 1: The answer is somewhat related
     but not specific enough.
  - 2: The answer directly reflects the
     specific content or moment asked
     about.

The last line of your evaluation must be
     a SINGLE LINE JSON object with the
    keys "relevance", "accuracy", "
    completeness", and "precision", each
     assigned a score between 0 and 2.

[ DOCUMENTS RETRIEVED ]
{documents}

[ User Query ]
{query}

[ Agent Answer ]
{answer}
```

B Hardware and Runtime Configuration

Experiments were conducted on two machines: one with an RTX 5090 GPU, and another with two NVIDIA A4500 GPU's. On the latter machine, from user input to LLM output, the average generation time was 3.02 seconds. Under these conditions, the system demonstrates practical viability for offline indexing and interactive, low-latency query-time retrieval.

C Embedding Hyperparameters

Audio segments and spoken queries were embedded using the *laion/clap-htsat-unfused* model. Prior to indexing and similarity search, both query and document embeddings were L2-normalized. This normalization step ensures that inner product similarity in the FAISS `FlatIP` index is equivalent to cosine similarity. This enables semantically aligned retrieval directly in the CLAP embedding space without requiring additional reranking or feature engineering.

D Sample QA Pairs

Table 3: A sample of QA pairs on Synthetic Queries

QA pairs (Q = white, A = blue)
Q: Can the one-minute shower routine ever replace your normal shower, or is that impossible?
A: ... Connor expresses skepticism about whether such a quick shower can truly replace a normal shower. He mentions that taking a shower is not just about getting clean but also about the time it takes to refresh and wake up properly. Joey adds that a shower under five minutes might not be sufficient to adequately clean oneself, suggesting that such a quick routine is more about covering up body odor than truly cleaning. Essentially, both seem to agree that while a one-minute shower might serve in a pinch, it cannot fully replace the benefits of a longer, more thorough shower. This perspective is captured in Segment 17.
Q: What travel conditions now make or break a trip for you?
A: ... Garnt shared that he finds Kyoto to be a very touristy spot, which can detract from the experience. He mentioned that while it's worth visiting at least once, the crowds and the commercialization of the area can take away from its magic. He expressed a preference for the outskirts of Kyoto, which tend to be more enjoyable and less crowded (Segment 20). Connor added that the disparity between Kyoto's historical significance and its touristy nature can make visits feel less authentic. He indicated that while it might be great for first-time visitors, the experience might not be as enjoyable upon return due to the overwhelming number of tourists (Segment 20). Overall, both speakers highlight that the level of crowding and commercialization in popular tourist destinations can make or break the quality of a travel experience.
Q: If you made a Trash Taste Bingo Card, what squares would be absolutely required?
A: ... 1. Mention of League of Legends — This game often comes up in discussions (Segment 2). 2. Reference to drinking stories — The guys frequently share hilarious and embarrassing drinking experiences (Segment 5). 3. Discussion about sibling dynamics — They talk about their experiences growing up as siblings or only children (Segment 26). 4. Anime recommendations — Each episode usually involves recommendations or debates about anime (Segment 19). 5. Joey's love for food — Food discussions, especially around Japanese cuisine, are a staple (not specifically cited, but a recurring theme). 6. Mention of gaming frustrations — Conversations about the challenges of gaming, especially in competitive environments (Segment 17). 7. Cultural references — They often reference their cultural backgrounds, especially regarding Australia and the UK (Segment 10) ...

Cross-modal Clustering-based Retrieval for Scalable and Robust Image Captioning

Jingyi You, Hiroshi Sasaki, Kazuma Kadowaki
The Japan Research Institute
{you.jingyi,sasaki.hiroshi,kadowaki.kazuma}@jri.co.jp

Abstract

Recent advances in retrieval-augmented generative image captioning (RAG-IC) have significantly improved caption quality by incorporating external knowledge and similar examples into language model-driven caption generators. However, these methods still encounter challenges when applied to real-world scenarios. First, many existing approaches rely on bimodal retrieval datastores that require large amounts of labeled data and substantial manual effort to construct, making them costly and time-consuming. Moreover, they simply retrieve the nearest samples to the input query from datastores, which leads to high redundancy in the retrieved content and subsequently degrades the quality of the generated captions.

In this paper, we introduce a novel RAG-IC approach named ***Cross-modal Diversity-promoting Retrieval technique*** (CoDiRet), which integrates a text-only unimodal retrieval module with our unique cluster-based retrieval mechanism. This proposal simultaneously enhances the scalability of the datastore, promotes diversity in retrieved content, and improves robustness against out-of-domain inputs, which eventually facilitates real-world applications. Experimental results demonstrate that our method, despite being exclusively trained on the COCO benchmark dataset, achieves competitive performance on the in-domain benchmark and generalizes robustly across different domains without additional training.

1 Introduction

Retrieval-augmented generative image captioning (RAG-IC) combines information retrieval with language model-based caption generation (Mallen et al., 2023; Cornia et al., 2020; Zhou et al., 2020; Shi et al., 2021) to leverage external knowledge or contextually relevant information to the input image and produce more accurate and informative image descriptions. This technology mitigates overdependence on the internal knowledge encoded in language models and instead incorporates external real-world data, thereby enhancing the semantic alignment between the generated captions and the visual content of the input images.

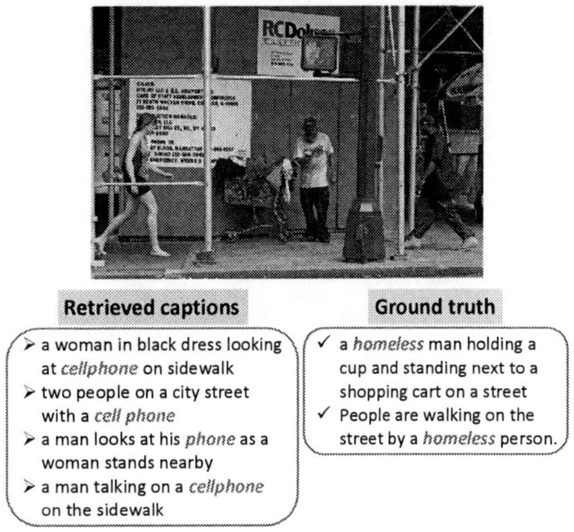

Figure 1: An example from MS COCO (Lin et al., 2014) of retrieved content containing redundant and semantically irrelevant terms with respect to the query image. We highlight the topic-deviant words in different colors from the correct keywords for clarity of presentation.

Although remarkable successes have been achieved in image captioning with the aid of retrieval techniques, several issues still hinder its application in real world scenarios. First, many existing RAG-IC approaches primarily perform unimodal retrieval (Sarto et al., 2022; Radford et al., 2021; Zhou and Long, 2023; Wu et al., 2024), where image-text pairs are selected based on the visual similarity between the retrieved and input images to augment contextual information. However, constructing such retrieval datastores requires a finely annotated corpus of image-text pairs, which is costly and labor-intensive, thereby limiting the scalability and adaptability of these methods in practical applications.

Secondly, traditional approaches typically rely

Proceedings of the 1st Workshop on Multimodal Augmented Generation via Multimodal Retrieval (MAGMaR 2025), pages 47–58

on nearest-neighbor search to retrieve datastore contents based on the proximity of embedding representations extracted by pre-trained models (Khandelwal et al., 2021; Lewis et al., 2020). Therefore, as shown in Fig. 1, the retrieved texts tend to be highly repetitive and lack semantic diversity (Li et al., 2024b; Hoang et al., 2022), which in turn leads captioning models to overproduce these high-frequency words. In addition, such retrieval strategies are prone to retrieving irrelevant samples when the input falls outside the domain of the pre-trained model, which limits generalizability of the captioning system across domains.

To address the aforementioned limitations, we introduce a novel cross-modal retrieval approach that leverages a text-only datastore constructed without manual image-text annotations, thereby improving the scalability of the method. Furthermore, our proposed cluster-based retrieval strategy selects instances based on clustering in the embedding space, which not only improves the informativeness but also reduces semantic redundancy in the retrieved content. Specifically, we finetune the embedding function (encoder) by jointly incorporating a triplet contrastive loss and a nuclear norm regularization into the training objective to simultaneously reinforce alignment across modalities and capture the clustering structure of retrieved content in the embedding space (Nie et al., 2017; You et al., 2021).

We highlight our contributions as follows:

- We propose a novel RAG-IC framework that integrates cluster-wise selection with cross-modal retrieval. Our approach does not require an image-text paired datastore, thereby increasing the diversity of retrieved content and the robustness to out-of-domain inputs, which is critical for real-world applications.

- We introduce a specialized training paradigm that simultaneously addresses the gap between different modalities and encourages cluster formation among the embedding features of datastore samples by combining triplet contrastive loss and nuclear norm-based clustering regularization.

- Our analysis shows that CoDiRet reduces retrieval redundancy and outperforms existing competitors in captioning quality, particularly in cross-domain inference settings, highlighting the effectiveness and robustness of our methodology.

2 Related Work

Robust retrieval-augmented generation. Retrieval-Augmented Generation (RAG) enhances text generation by incorporating externally retrieved knowledge as additional input (Lewis et al., 2020). Despite its success, particularly in natural language processing (NLP) (Mialon et al., 2023; Yasunaga et al., 2023), it has an overreliance on repetitive information in the retrieved content, which degrades the robustness to out-of-domain data and noisy inputs (Li et al., 2024b). To overcome the issue of practicality and generalizability in real-world applications, recent research focuses on strengthening RAG models to mitigate unstable retrievals and hallucination. One popular strategy is to dynamically adjust the training process in response to noisy retrievals (Zheng et al., 2021) with adversarial training (Fang et al., 2024) and relevance-aware evaluation of a given query (Yu et al., 2024) to facilitate the model to recognize and cope with various forms of retrievals. Another direction focuses on employing learnable filters or discriminators to effectively identify and eliminate redundant and misleading information (Zhu et al., 2024; Hong et al., 2024; Wu et al., 2024; Yoran et al., 2024). Additionally, methods such as random shuffling of retrieved content during training have been shown to boost the model's tolerance to domain mismatches and reduce overfitting to high-frequency patterns (Hoang et al., 2022; Li et al., 2024b; Hao et al., 2023).

Retrieval-augmented generative image captioning. Image captioning is the task of automatically generating descriptive textual captions for images (Herdade et al., 2019; Xu et al., 2015), combining techniques from computer vision and NLP. Recently, RAG-integrated image captioning has garnered increasing interest due to its prominent ability to improve accuracy, diversity, and factual consistency. Sarto et al. (2022); Ramos et al. (2023a); Sarto et al. (2024); Li et al. (2024a) propose to retrieve captions associated with visually similar images and develop encoder-decoder models that attend to both image features and retrieved caption embeddings. Rather than encoding images directly, Ramos et al. (2023b); Yang et al. (2023) enable "image-blind" decoding by utilizing only retrieved captions, allowing the model to focus on text-based reasoning without relying on direct visual understanding, which proves beneficial in zero-shot scenarios. Ramos et al. (2023c);

Algorithm 1 Traditional RAG-IC

Input: $\mathbf{I}$ // query image
k // number of samples to retrieve
$\mathcal{D} = \{(v_i, t_i)\}_{i=1}^{N}$ // external datastore containing image-captiong pairs
Output: $\mathbf{C} = \{c_i\}_{i=1}^{T}$ // output caption

/* extract features of the query image */
$v^q \leftarrow f_v(\mathbf{I})$
/* retrieve k image features from $\{v_i\}$ based on similarity to v^q
r_i: indices of the retrieved samples */
$\{v_{r_i}\}_{i=1}^{k} \leftarrow \text{Rtr}_k(v^q; \{v_i\})$
/* generate a caption for $\mathbf{I}$ using $\{t_{r_i}\}$ corresponding to $\{v_{r_i}\}$ */
$\mathbf{C} \leftarrow f_{\text{LLM}}(v^q, \{t_{r_i}\}_{i=1}^{k})$

Algorithm 2 Our cross-modal RAG-IC

Input: $\mathbf{I}$, k, $\mathcal{D} = \{t_i\}_{i=1}^{N}$
l // number of clusters
Output: $\mathbf{C}$

/* cluster $\{t_i\}$ by CoDiRet
c_i: indices of the clusters */
$\{g_{c_i}\}_{i=1}^{l} \leftarrow \text{Clu}_l(\{t_i\})$
/* extract features of the query image */
$v^q \leftarrow f_v(\mathbf{I})$
/* retrieve k cluster centroids from $\{g_{c_i}\}$ */
$\{g_{r_i}\}_{i=1}^{k} \leftarrow \text{Rtr}_k(v^q; \{g_{c_i}\})$
/* randomly select one text from each $\{g_{r_i}\}$ */
$\{t_{r_i}\} \leftarrow \text{RndSmp}_k(\{g_{r_i}\})$
/* generate a caption for $\mathbf{I}$ using $\{t_{r_i}\}$ */
$\mathbf{C} \leftarrow f_{\text{LLM}}(v^q, \{t_{r_i}\}_{i=1}^{k})$

Zeng et al. (2024) successfully implement retrieval over a unimodal textual datastore and adopt a lightweight architecture that integrates pre-trained CLIP (Radford et al., 2021) and GPT-2 (Radford et al., 2019) through retrieval-based prompting. We adopt SmallCap (Ramos et al., 2023c) as the baseline for training and evaluating our proposal due to its minimal trainable parameters for fine-tuning.

3 Methodology

Fig. 2 presents the overall architecture of our proposed CoDiRet framework, which is built upon two primary strategies: a **cross-modal alignment strategy** and a **cluster-based retrieval strategy**. Hereafter, we will present formal notations of variables and task definitions related to RAG-IC in Sec.3.1, and introduce each component subsequently in detail.

3.1 Preliminaries

Let $\mathbf{I} \in \mathbb{R}^{H \times W \times C}$ be an input image, where H, W, and C denote the height, width, and number of channels, respectively. As described in Alg.1, RAG-IC involves the following steps: 1) employing a *pre-trained visual encoder*, f_v, such as ViT (Dosovitskiy et al., 2021) or CLIP (Radford et al., 2021), to extract patch representations $\mathbf{X}$ from $\mathbf{I}$; 2) leveraging *retriever* Rtr_k to collect k semantically relevant instances R from an external database $\mathcal{D}$ by conducting feature-based nearest neighbor search between the query image and $\mathcal{D}$; and 3) utilizing a pre-trained large language model (LLM) as a *decoder* to generate a caption sequence $\mathbf{C}$ autoregressively by integrating the extracted visual embedding of $\mathbf{I}$ along with the retrieved textual knowledge R.

3.2 Cross-modal aligner

Given an image $\mathbf{I}$ organized in a 2-dimensional format as input, traditional RAG-IC approaches, as shown in Alg.1, rely on an external datastore consisting of image-caption pairs $\{(v_i, t_i)\}_{i=1}^{N}$ to retrieve similar images. In contrast, we exclusively construct the datastore from textual information in the target modality, denoted as $\mathcal{D} = \{t_i\}_{i=1}^{N}$, and retrieve captions based on the distance between features of the query image and the datastore captions by leveraging a shared multimodal representative space (Alg.2). This design facilitates efficient domain adaptation and scalability, as the datastore can be easily modified by replacing the textual corpus with off-the-shelf domain-specific data without requiring large-scale manually annotated datasets.

Triplet contrastive learning Although CLIP (Radford et al., 2021) aligns image and text representations in a shared multimodal embedding space by training a vision-language model in a contrastive learning manner, Mistretta et al. (2025) reveal a remaining modality gap between image and text representations, which causes inaccurate retrieval in the text modality. Specifically, even when captions describe different images, some sentences tend to cluster together in the 2-dimensional projection space, while, conversely, an image and its corresponding caption may be mapped far apart.

To solve this problem, we propose a triplet-based cross-modal alignment constraint aimed at mini-

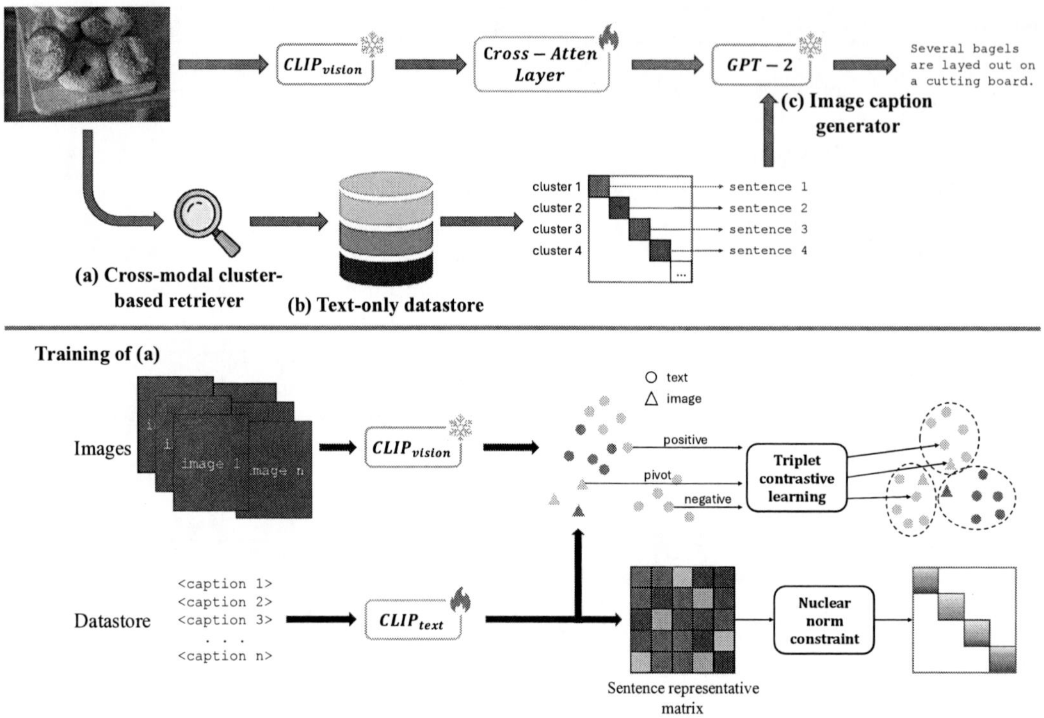

Figure 2: Model overview. CoDiRet comprises three chief components: (a) a cross-modal cluster-based retriever, (b) a text-only datastore, and (c) an image caption generator. Component (a) is trained using contrastive learning and nuclear norm regularization to mitigate misalignment between images and texts, while also clustering texts within the datastore. Subsequently, we utilize (a) to directly retrieve relevant text clusters from (b) based on the input image and randomly select one text from each cluster as supplementary input for (c).

mizing the modality gap and ensuring semantically relevant retrieval in a shared latent space, which is achieved by leveraging contrastive learning with a triplet loss formulation. Formally, for each particular image-caption example, the image serves as the pivot data point i^*, while one of its associated captions is randomly sampled as the positive example c^+. A caption from a different image is then randomly chosen as the negative example c^-. Subsequently, both the image and text are encoded into a shared embedding space using the CLIP model, as described below:

$$\mathbf{e}^* = f_{\text{clip}}^{\text{vision}}(i^*) \in \mathbb{R}^d, \tag{1}$$

$$\mathbf{e}^+ = f_{\text{clip}}^{\text{text}}(c^+) \in \mathbb{R}^d, \quad \mathbf{e}^- = f_{\text{clip}}^{\text{text}}(c^-) \in \mathbb{R}^d, \tag{2}$$

where d refers to the dimension of the CLIP embedding space.

We then conduct triplet noise-contrastive estimation (Gutmann and Hyvärinen, 2010) with a ranking loss to minimize the l_2 distance between the pivot and positive examples, while maximizing the distance between the pivot and negative ones:

$$\mathcal{L}_{\text{triplet}} = \max(0, \|\mathbf{e}^* - \mathbf{e}^+\|_2 - \|\mathbf{e}^* - \mathbf{e}^-\|_2). \tag{3}$$

By optimizing this objective, the model learns to group semantically similar image-text pairs while pushing apart unrelated ones, thereby ensuring that the retrieved text better matches the input image.

3.3 Cluster-based retriever

A simple ranking and selection of the top-k nearest neighbors based on similarity scores has long been dominant in the RAG field. However, this method often overlooks the underlying structure of the datastore, leading to captioning models receiving highly resembled information and repeated terms. As a result, the model is prone to copying these redundant words, regardless of their relevance (Hoang et al., 2022; Li et al., 2024b) and is then easily contaminated by noise. To equip models with diverse and informative supplementary data, we propose a cluster-based retriever that chooses texts from the nearest "clusters" detected through a clustering operation beforehand, as illustrated in Alg.2. This approach reduces the occurrence of repeated words in the retrieved content and increases the possibility of including relevant words when processing out-of-domain images, by selecting from distant clusters.

Nuclear norm regularization Detecting clustering structures in $\mathcal{D}$ by directly applying K-means to the sentence representation matrix, H_t, can effectively reduce redundancy when retrieving captions. However, K-means is sensitive to initialization and outliers, which often leads to unstable results (Ding and Li, 2007). Additionally, the clustering performance is suboptimal due to the independent nature of triplet contrastive representation learning (Eq. (3)) and sentence clustering. Nie et al. (2017) pave the way for better capture of the clustering structure of H_t by transforming the clustering task into a matrix-rank problem. The theoretical basis behind the clustering structure learning comes from the following theorem:

Theorem 1 (Chung and Graham, 1997) The multiplicity of eigenvalue 0 of the normalized Laplacian matrix of H_t is equal to the number of clusters in H_t.

Haeffele and Vidal (2020); Piao et al. (2019) propose the nuclear norm and prove that the constraint on the Laplace matrix of H_t is mathematically equal to the constraint on sentence representation matrix H_t as

$$\mathcal{L}_{cluster} = \sum_{i=1}^{l} \lambda_i^{H_t}, \tag{4}$$

where $\lambda_i^{H_t}$ represents the i-th smallest eigenvalue of H_t (Piao et al., 2019). By suppressing $\|H_r\|_*^l$ to 0, l clusters (determined by elbow method (Bholowalia and Kumar, 2014)) in H_r can be obtained by reorganizing its columns or rows and converting it into a block-diagonal form with l blocks, as shown in Fig. 2. To incorporate this clustering into our training process, we define the training objective as:

$$\mathcal{L}_{cluster} = \|H_r\|_*^l. \tag{5}$$

3.4 Joint learning

We adopt a joint learning framework that optimizes both cross-modal alignment and modality-specific structure preservation. The overall objective is formulated as follows:

$$\mathcal{L} = \mathcal{L}_{\text{triplet}} + \lambda \mathcal{L}_{\text{cluster}}, \tag{6}$$

DATASET	Train	Validation	Test	
	MS COCO	MS COCO	MS COCO	NoCaps
IMAGES	113,287	5,000	5,000	4,500
CAPTIONS	566,747	25,010	25,010	45,000
Avg. Caps.	5	5	5	10
DOMAIN		in		out

Table 1: Basic dataset statistics. Avg. Caps. refers to average captions for each image.

where λ is a balancing coefficient that regulates the trade-off between enforcing cross-modal alignment and maintaining intra-modality cluster structures.

With the cluster structure of the text representation, we compute the centroid of each cluster by simply averaging the representations of sentences within the cluster. We then retrieve the top-k most relevant centroids and randomly sample one sentence from each retrieved cluster for the training of our captioning model, as shown in Alg. 2. Random sampling is adopted here to promote diversity and prevent the model from overfitting to highly prototypical or redundant sentences that may dominate each cluster.

4 Experiments

4.1 Datasets and Evaluation Metric

We carried out our experiments on the MS COCO Caption (Lin et al., 2014) and NoCaps (Agrawal et al., 2019) datasets to assess our approach's accuracy on in-domain data and its robustness to out-of-domain inputs, respectively. MS COCO Caption is a widely used benchmark that contains diverse image-caption pairs, while NoCaps focuses on novel object descriptions not present in the COCO training set, making it suitable for evaluating generalization to unseen concepts. The statistics of the datasets are summarized in Table 1.

For evaluation, we employ four standard automatic metrics: BLEU (Papineni et al., 2002), METEOR (Banerjee and Lavie, 2005), CIDEr (Vedantam et al., 2015), and SPICE (Anderson et al., 2016), which measure various aspects of caption quality, including n-gram overlap, semantic relevance, and compositionality.

4.2 Implementation Details

Our CoDiRet retriever is first initialized using CLIP-ViT-B/32 (Radford et al., 2019) as both the image and text encoder and finetuned by triplet clustering learning outlined in Sec. 3.4 with LoRA

Metrics	BLEU-1	BLEU-2	BLEU-3	BLEU-4	METEOR	CIDEr	SPICE
SmallCap	76.5	60.2	44.3	31.7	23.1	74.4	13.4
CoDiRet	**77.8**	**61.2**	**45.6**	**32.9**	**24.2**	**76.3**	**14.2**
- w/o Tpl	75.4	58.9	43.0	31.1	22.7	72.4	12.7

Table 2: Robustness evaluation on the test set of NoCaps while the models are still trained on MS COCO. Best results among the generated captions are marked in bold.

(Low-Rank Adaptation) (Hu et al., 2022) to reduce computational cost and improve training efficiency. The scaling factor in Eq. (6) is set to $\lambda = 0.2$, as we found it yields the best empirical performance. As for the main image captioning model, we follow the SmallCap (Ramos et al., 2023c) setup, using CLIP-ViT-B/32 as the encoder and GPT-2 (Radford et al., 2019) as the decoder, with the parameters of both fixed, connected by a 12-head trainable cross-attention layer between the vision and language modalities to facilitate information fusion. Both the retrieval model and the main captioning model are trained exclusively on the MS COCO dataset using the standard Karpathy splits (Karpathy and Fei-Fei, 2015). The training procedures follow a batch size of 64, optimized with AdamW (Loshchilov and Hutter, 2019) and a learning rate of $1e-4$, using mixed-precision training with 16-bit floating-point precision (FP16). The training process runs for 5 epochs on CoDiRet and another 10 epochs on the captioning model on a single NVIDIA A100 GPU with 16GB of the available memory, taking approximately 13 hours to converge. During training, we retrieve $k = 4$ textual prompts per image by first identifying the top-k most similar clusters to the query image. The centroids of clusters and the query image embeddings are computed in the high-dimensional space by our CoDiRet. A single sentence is randomly sampled from each cluster and incorporated as a prompt for training. We employ the product quantizer with an inverted file system based on Faiss (Johnson et al., 2021) for efficient datastore quantization and nearest-neighbor search. Captions are decoded by beam search with a beam size of 3 at inference.

4.3 Baselines

The following excellent baselines are used for comparison to demonstrate the effectiveness of CoDiRet: **non-RAG** lightweight training method, including ClipCap (Mokady et al., 2021); **Img.→Img.** retrieval methods using image-text datastores such as EXTRA (Ramos et al., 2023a) and Re-ViLM (Yang et al., 2023); and **Img.→Txt.** retrieval method using text-only datastores like SmallCap (Ramos et al., 2023c). All methods are finetuned on the same training dataset as our method for a fair comparison.

5 Results and Discussion

5.1 Out-of-domain Robustness

To assess the robustness of our model under domain shift, we evaluate both CoDiRet and our baseline on NoCaps where the test set contains out-of-domain objects not present in the training distribution. From Table 2, we can observe that our model consistently outperforms the baseline SmallCap in terms of all metrics. The superior performance of our model in out-of-domain settings can be attributed to its ability to navigate the retrieval uncertainty and adapt to novel objects, which is a key limitation in conventional RAG-IC approaches.

The model's strong generalization ability indicates that it is less prone to overfitting. During training, it is provided with retrieval information from a broader range, which likely includes a small amount of noise. This prevents the model from simply copying or memorizing the content retrieved. Instead, it learns to flexibly apply the retrieved textual information in conjunction with the input visual data to generate accurate and fluent captions. In contrast, traditional kNN-based retrieval methods return captions associated with images that are similar to the query image, often resulting in a large amount of redundant information and repeated words. This redundancy causes the model to overfit specific patterns in the training data, thereby reducing its generalization ability on new data.

5.2 In-domain Performance

Table 3 lists the results for the non-RAG method at the top, with the ones with uni-modal retrieval in the middle, and cross-modal retrieval methods at the bottom. We can observe that when tested

Metrics	$\|\theta\|$	BLEU-4	METEOR	CIDEr	SPICE
ClipCap	43	33.5	27.5	113.1	21.1
EXTRA	45	37.5	28.5	120.9	21.7
Re-ViLM	158	37.8	-	129.1	-
SmallCap	7	37.0	27.9	119.7	21.3
CoDIRET	7.1	36.9	27.9	119.5	21.0
- w/o TPL	7.1	34.9	26.8	117.6	20.5

Table 3: Results on the Karpathy COCO test split. $|\theta|$ refers to the number of trainable parameters in the model (in millions).

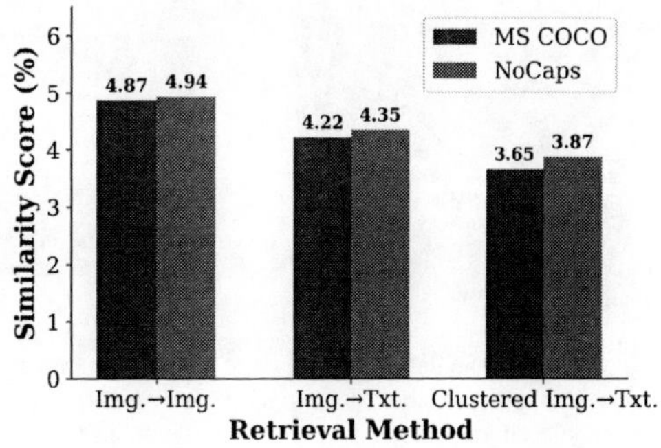

Figure 3: Comparison of proportion of duplicated key objects of image-to-image retrieval method, nearest neighbor-based image-to-text retrieval strategy, and our cluster structure-based CoDIRET.

with in-domain data, CoDIRET achieves a comparable performance to all state-of-the-art baselines in terms of all metrics, even with a small number of trainable parameters.

We also observed a consistent superiority of RAG-based models over ClipCap, which underscores the importance of external knowledge retrieval in image captioning. Without access to external descriptions, ClipCap is restricted to visual and linguistic knowledge already embedded in the pretrained LLM and often generates captions based on visual priors rather than factual correctness, leading to plausible but inaccurate descriptions.

In addition, we noticed that with the retrieval performed directly in the image modality, both EXTRA and Re-ViLM achieved better performance. We consider several possible reasons for this phenomenon. First, using the captions from the most visually similar images to the query image makes the models highly effective at preserving key visual details. Furthermore, these methods tend to achieve higher retrieval accuracy but greater keyword redundancy (as we show in Sec. 5.4) in the retrieved captions. This, in turn, allows the model to copy frequently repeated phrases from the retrieved text (as shown in Fig. 4), reinforcing consistency in generated captions.

In contrast, CoDIRET retrieves captions by directly searching for the most textually similar ones with a structured control over redundancy. By selecting a single representative caption per related text group, our approach promotes diversity in retrieved contents. However, since the entities in the images are limited, this diversity may introduce noise, which can lead to the model being slightly misled. Moreover, since the evaluation metrics used in this experiment, such as BLEU, cannot assess diversity, our model shows a minor performance decrease on in-domain data.

5.3 Ablation Study

We further investigate the contribution of the triplet contrastive learning module to CoDIRET through an ablation study conducted on each dataset. In the table, "- w/o TPL" indicates the removal of the triplet contrastive learning module, where the retriever is trained solely with the nuclear norm constraint. We observe a significant performance drop of approximately 2 points on both in-domain and out-of-domain data compared with CoDIRET. This result suggests that triplet contrastive learning plays a crucial role in bridging the performance gap between different modalities, as it aligns image and text features more effectively.

Moreover, while the nuclear norm constraint primarily promotes representation compression and simplification by reducing the rank of the datastore sentence matrix, this process may inadvertently cause the model to overlook the intricate semantic differences between images and texts. As a consequence, important information encoded in the joint image-text space may be lost, weakening the quality of the retrieved captions and impairing the model's ability to generate accurate and contextually appropriate descriptions.

5.4 Duplicated Keywords and Redundancy

To better quantify the redundancy of retrieved contents in different retrieval strategies, we measure the lexical overlap of key objects across retrieved captions. Specifically, we select all nouns and proper nouns as candidate key objects from each caption using a spaCy-based part-of-speech tagger (Cutting et al., 1992). For each image, we then compute global object overlap among all retrieved

Figure 4: Examples of captions generated for NoCaps out-of-domain samples where the retrieved captions for the query image can be irrelevant.

captions by calculating the Jaccard similarity between the union and intersection of extracted object sets, defined as:

$$\text{Similarity}_{\text{object}} = \frac{|O_{\text{intersection}}|}{|O_{\text{union}}|}, \tag{7}$$

where $O_{\text{intersection}}$ is the set of objects appearing in all retrieved captions for a given image, and O_{union} is the set of all unique objects across the same set. A higher score indicates greater object repetition and thus higher lexical redundancy, while a lower score reflects increased content diversity. While simpler alternatives such as stopword removal could be used to filter non-content words, we adopt noun-based extraction to focus specifically on concrete entities that are most representative of the image content. This approach reduces the noise from abstract or generic terms that may still remain after stopword removal, and ensures that the resulting object sets more accurately reflect the semantic overlap of key visual concepts across captions.

We report the average object similarity score across all images in each retrieval setting on the two datasets separately as a proxy for topic-level redundancy in Fig. 3. The results demonstrate a clear trend in redundancy, where image-to-image retrieval exhibits the highest redundancy, while cluster-based image-to-text retrieval yields the most diverse references. We analyze the underlying reasons for these observations as follows. First, in image-to-image retrieval, since the retrieval is based purely on visual similarity, the captions tend to describe nearly identical content, often differing only in minor details or wording, which leads to a high degree of content repetition. Image-to-text retrieval bypasses the intermediate step of retrieving images and instead retrieves the most semantically similar captions directly from the text corpus, which offers greater flexibility by leveraging multi-modal embeddings to match text descriptions. However, our proposal introduces an additional step of clustering the text corpus before retrieval, ensuring that retrieved references come from different semantic groups. This enforces topic-level diversity among the retrieved references, as a result, preventing the model from receiving multiple variations of the same description.

5.5 Case Study

We demonstrate the quality of captions generated by CoDiRet through a case study. The examples shown in Fig. 4 are randomly sampled from the NoCaps dataset. We show captions retrieved from the datastore, along with comparison between captions generated by the traditional RAG-IC model and those produced by our approach.

A high-quality caption is typically characterized by (i) semantic relevance to the image content, (ii) specificity-inclusion of fine-grained details such as object attributes, actions, or materials, and (iii) fluency and coherence at the sentence level. Captions that satisfy these criteria are more informative and useful in downstream tasks such as image search or human-computer interaction.

From these examples, we observe that when certain words appear frequently in the retrieved content, models trained with standard nearest-neighbor-assisted information tend to copy those words verbatim into the generated caption. For instance, in the second example, the word "bird" is directly copied into the output caption. While such behavior may produce captions that are broadly accurate, they often lack specificity and fail to describe fine-grained visual attributes. In contrast, our model is better able to aggregate and distill informative content from the retrieved results, allowing it to produce more descriptive and contextually enriched details. For example, in the third image, the caption generated by CoDiRet correctly includes the material "stainless steel" when describing the sink, offering a level of detail absent in the baseline output. Such specific terms are especially valuable for distinguishing similar scenes or objects, and thus contribute to a more effective and high-quality caption.

6 Conclusion

We addressed several fundamental problems concerning RAG-IC and proposed a joint learning framework called CoDiRet, which trains a retriever by leveraging contrastive learning and clustering techniques to enhance cross-modal retrieval. The proposed model facilitates more semantically relevant retrieval results by minimizing the modality gap between image and text representations. Meanwhile, by incorporating a cluster constraint, the model effectively reduces redundancy in the retrieved content, ensuring better adaptation to out-of-domain scenarios. Experimental results, including those of the analysis of retrieved contents, demonstrated the effectiveness of CoDiRet.

Limitations

In this study, we introduced diversity to enhance the model's robustness on unseen data, particularly by expanding the variety of retrieved content to avoid over-reliance on high-frequency samples. While this strategy significantly improved the model's performance on out-of-domain data, it led to a decline in performance on in-domain data. This phenomenon may be attributed to the increased diversity leading to the retrieval of content that is only partially relevant to the input image, thus affecting the accuracy and consistency of the model's outputs on known data. While the added diversity enhances the model's adaptability to unseen domains, it also causes a trade-off with its performance in specific domains. Therefore, balancing diversity with precision, ensuring strong robustness without compromising performance on in-domain data, remains a challenge that warrants further investigation. We consider this trade-off an important area for future work, aiming to explore how to achieve an optimal balance between the two.

Currently, most image captioning models rely on English-centric datasets such as COCO, which limits their effectiveness in multilingual and multicultural contexts. These models may struggle with linguistic and cultural differences, as well as diverse visual concepts. Future research should focus on multilingual image captioning datasets that include data from various languages and cultures, enabling models to perform better across different settings and promoting global application of image captioning technology.

References

Harsh Agrawal, Peter Anderson, Karan Desai, Yufei Wang, Xinlei Chen, Rishabh Jain, Mark Johnson, Dhruv Batra, Devi Parikh, and Stefan Lee. 2019. nocaps: novel object captioning at scale. In *2019 IEEE/CVF International Conference on Computer Vision, ICCV 2019, Seoul, Korea (South), October 27 - November 2, 2019*, pages 8947–8956. IEEE.

Peter Anderson, Basura Fernando, Mark Johnson, and Stephen Gould. 2016. SPICE: semantic propositional image caption evaluation. In *Computer Vision - ECCV 2016 - 14th European Conference, Amsterdam, The Netherlands, October 11-14, 2016, Proceedings, Part V*, volume 9909 of *Lecture Notes in Computer Science*, pages 382–398. Springer.

Satanjeev Banerjee and Alon Lavie. 2005. METEOR: an automatic metric for MT evaluation with improved correlation with human judgments. In *Proceedings of the Workshop on Intrinsic and Extrinsic Evaluation Measures for Machine Translation and/or Summarization@ACL 2005, Ann Arbor, Michigan, USA, June 29, 2005*, pages 65–72. Association for Computational Linguistics.

Purnima Bholowalia and Arvind Kumar. 2014. Ebkmeans: A clustering technique based on elbow method and k-means in wsn. *International Journal of Computer Applications*, 105(9):17–24.

Fan RK Chung and Fan Chung Graham. 1997. *Spectral graph theory*. Number 92 in CBMS Regional Conference Series in Mathematics. American Mathematical Soc., Fresno State University.

Marcella Cornia, Matteo Stefanini, Lorenzo Baraldi, and Rita Cucchiara. 2020. Meshed-memory transformer for image captioning. In *2020 IEEE/CVF Conference on Computer Vision and Pattern Recognition, CVPR 2020, Seattle, WA, USA, June 13-19, 2020*, pages 10575–10584. Computer Vision Foundation / IEEE.

Douglas R. Cutting, Julian Kupiec, Jan O. Pedersen, and Penelope Sibun. 1992. A practical part-of-speech tagger. In *3rd Applied Natural Language Processing Conference, ANLP 1992, Trento, Italy, March 31 - April 3, 1992*, pages 133–140. ACL.

Chris H. Q. Ding and Tao Li. 2007. Adaptive dimension reduction using discriminant analysis and K-means clustering. In *Machine Learning, Proceedings of the Twenty-Fourth International Conference (ICML 2007), Corvallis, Oregon, USA, June 20-24, 2007*, volume 227 of *ACM International Conference Proceeding Series*, pages 521–528. ACM.

Alexey Dosovitskiy, Lucas Beyer, Alexander Kolesnikov, Dirk Weissenborn, Xiaohua Zhai, Thomas Unterthiner, Mostafa Dehghani, Matthias Minderer, Georg Heigold, Sylvain Gelly, Jakob Uszkoreit, and Neil Houlsby. 2021. An image is worth 16x16 words: Transformers for image recognition at scale. In *9th International Conference on Learning Representations, ICLR 2021, Virtual Event, Austria, May 3-7, 2021*. OpenReview.net.

Feiteng Fang, Yuelin Bai, Shiwen Ni, Min Yang, Xiaojun Chen, and Ruifeng Xu. 2024. Enhancing noise robustness of retrieval-augmented language models with adaptive adversarial training. In *Proceedings of the 62nd Annual Meeting of the Association for Computational Linguistics (Volume 1: Long Papers), ACL 2024, Bangkok, Thailand, August 11-16, 2024*, pages 10028–10039. Association for Computational Linguistics.

Michael Gutmann and Aapo Hyvärinen. 2010. Noise-contrastive estimation: A new estimation principle for unnormalized statistical models. In *Proceedings of the Thirteenth International Conference on Artificial Intelligence and Statistics, AISTATS 2010, Chia Laguna Resort, Sardinia, Italy, May 13-15, 2010*, volume 9 of *JMLR Proceedings*, pages 297–304. JMLR.org.

Benjamin D. Haeffele and René Vidal. 2020. Structured low-rank matrix factorization: Global optimality, algorithms, and applications. *IEEE Trans. Pattern Anal. Mach. Intell.*, 42(6):1468–1482.

Hongkun Hao, Guoping Huang, Lemao Liu, Zhirui Zhang, Shuming Shi, and Rui Wang. 2023. Rethinking translation memory augmented neural machine translation. In *Findings of the Association for Computational Linguistics: ACL 2023, Toronto, Canada, July 9-14, 2023*, pages 2589–2605. Association for Computational Linguistics.

Simao Herdade, Armin Kappeler, Kofi Boakye, and Joao Soares. 2019. Image captioning: Transforming objects into words. In *Advances in Neural Information Processing Systems 32: Annual Conference on Neural Information Processing Systems 2019, NeurIPS 2019, December 8-14, 2019, Vancouver, BC, Canada*, pages 11135–11145.

Cuong Hoang, Devendra Sachan, Prashant Mathur, Brian Thompson, and Marcello Federico. 2022. Improving robustness of retrieval augmented translation via shuffling of suggestions. *CoRR*, abs/2210.05059.

Giwon Hong, Jeonghwan Kim, Junmo Kang, Sung-Hyon Myaeng, and Joyce Jiyoung Whang. 2024. Why so gullible? enhancing the robustness of retrieval-augmented models against counterfactual noise. In *Findings of the Association for Computational Linguistics: NAACL 2024, Mexico City, Mexico, June 16-21, 2024*, pages 2474–2495. Association for Computational Linguistics.

Edward J. Hu, Yelong Shen, Phillip Wallis, Zeyuan Allen-Zhu, Yuanzhi Li, Shean Wang, Lu Wang, and Weizhu Chen. 2022. Lora: Low-rank adaptation of large language models. In *The Tenth International Conference on Learning Representations, ICLR 2022, Virtual Event, April 25-29, 2022*. OpenReview.net.

Jeff Johnson, Matthijs Douze, and Hervé Jégou. 2021. Billion-scale similarity search with gpus. *IEEE Trans. Big Data*, 7(3):535–547.

Andrej Karpathy and Li Fei-Fei. 2015. Deep visual-semantic alignments for generating image descriptions. In *IEEE Conference on Computer Vision and Pattern Recognition, CVPR 2015, Boston, MA, USA, June 7-12, 2015*, pages 3128–3137. IEEE Computer Society.

Urvashi Khandelwal, Angela Fan, Dan Jurafsky, Luke Zettlemoyer, and Mike Lewis. 2021. Nearest neighbor machine translation. In *9th International Conference on Learning Representations, ICLR 2021, Virtual Event, Austria, May 3-7, 2021*. OpenReview.net.

Patrick S. H. Lewis, Ethan Perez, Aleksandra Piktus, Fabio Petroni, Vladimir Karpukhin, Naman Goyal, Heinrich Küttler, Mike Lewis, Wen-tau Yih, Tim Rocktäschel, Sebastian Riedel, and Douwe Kiela. 2020. Retrieval-augmented generation for knowledge-intensive NLP tasks. In *Advances in Neural Information Processing Systems 33: Annual Conference on Neural Information Processing Systems 2020, NeurIPS 2020, December 6-12, 2020, virtual*.

Jiaxuan Li, Duc Minh Vo, Akihiro Sugimoto, and Hideki Nakayama. 2024a. Evcap: Retrieval-augmented image captioning with external visual-name memory for open-world comprehension. In *IEEE/CVF Conference on Computer Vision and Pattern Recognition, CVPR 2024, Seattle, WA, USA, June 16-22, 2024*, pages 13733–13742. IEEE.

Wenyan Li, Jiaang Li, Rita Ramos, Raphael Tang, and Desmond Elliott. 2024b. Understanding retrieval robustness for retrieval-augmented image captioning. In *Proceedings of the 62nd Annual Meeting of the Association for Computational Linguistics (Volume 1: Long Papers), ACL 2024, Bangkok, Thailand, August 11-16, 2024*, pages 9285–9299. Association for Computational Linguistics.

Tsung-Yi Lin, Michael Maire, Serge J. Belongie, James Hays, Pietro Perona, Deva Ramanan, Piotr Dollár, and C. Lawrence Zitnick. 2014. Microsoft COCO: common objects in context. In *Computer Vision - ECCV 2014 - 13th European Conference, Zurich, Switzerland, September 6-12, 2014, Proceedings, Part V*, volume 8693 of *Lecture Notes in Computer Science*, pages 740–755. Springer.

Ilya Loshchilov and Frank Hutter. 2019. Decoupled weight decay regularization. In *7th International Conference on Learning Representations, ICLR 2019, New Orleans, LA, USA, May 6-9, 2019*. OpenReview.net.

Alex Mallen, Akari Asai, Victor Zhong, Rajarshi Das, Daniel Khashabi, and Hannaneh Hajishirzi. 2023. When not to trust language models: Investigating effectiveness of parametric and non-parametric memories. In *Proceedings of the 61st Annual Meeting of the Association for Computational Linguistics (Volume 1: Long Papers), ACL 2023, Toronto, Canada, July 9-14, 2023*, pages 9802–9822. Association for Computational Linguistics.

Grégoire Mialon, Roberto Dessì, Maria Lomeli, Christoforos Nalmpantis, Ramakanth Pasunuru, Roberta Raileanu, Baptiste Rozière, Timo Schick, Jane Dwivedi-Yu, Asli Celikyilmaz, Edouard Grave, Yann LeCun, and Thomas Scialom. 2023. Augmented language models: a survey. *Trans. Mach. Learn. Res.*, 2023.

Marco Mistretta, Alberto Baldrati, Lorenzo Agnolucci, Marco Bertini, and Andrew D. Bagdanov. 2025. Cross the gap: Exposing the intra-modal misalignment in CLIP via modality inversion. *CoRR*, abs/2502.04263.

Ron Mokady, Amir Hertz, and Amit H. Bermano. 2021. Clipcap: CLIP prefix for image captioning. *CoRR*, abs/2111.09734.

Feiping Nie, Xiaoqian Wang, Cheng Deng, and Heng Huang. 2017. Learning A structured optimal bipartite graph for co-clustering. In *Advances in Neural Information Processing Systems 30: Annual Conference on Neural Information Processing Systems 2017, December 4-9, 2017, Long Beach, CA, USA*, pages 4129–4138.

Kishore Papineni, Salim Roukos, Todd Ward, and Wei-Jing Zhu. 2002. Bleu: a method for automatic evaluation of machine translation. In *Proceedings of the 40th Annual Meeting of the Association for Computational Linguistics, July 6-12, 2002, Philadelphia, PA, USA*, pages 311–318. ACL.

Xinglin Piao, Yongli Hu, Junbin Gao, Yanfeng Sun, and Baocai Yin. 2019. Double nuclear norm based low rank representation on grassmann manifolds for clustering. In *IEEE Conference on Computer Vision and Pattern Recognition, CVPR 2019, Long Beach, CA, USA, June 16-20, 2019*, pages 12075–12084. Computer Vision Foundation / IEEE.

Alec Radford, Jong Wook Kim, Chris Hallacy, Aditya Ramesh, Gabriel Goh, Sandhini Agarwal, Girish Sastry, Amanda Askell, Pamela Mishkin, Jack Clark, Gretchen Krueger, and Ilya Sutskever. 2021. Learning transferable visual models from natural language supervision. In *Proceedings of the 38th International Conference on Machine Learning, ICML 2021, 18-24 July 2021, Virtual Event*, volume 139 of *Proceedings of Machine Learning Research*, pages 8748–8763. PMLR.

Alec Radford, Jeff Wu, Rewon Child, David Luan, Dario Amodei, and Ilya Sutskever. 2019. Language models are unsupervised multitask learners.

Rita Ramos, Desmond Elliott, and Bruno Martins. 2023a. Retrieval-augmented image captioning. In *Proceedings of the 17th Conference of the European Chapter of the Association for Computational Linguistics, EACL 2023, Dubrovnik, Croatia, May 2-6, 2023*, pages 3648–3663. Association for Computational Linguistics.

Rita Ramos, Bruno Martins, and Desmond Elliott. 2023b. Lmcap: Few-shot multilingual image captioning by retrieval augmented language model prompting. In *Findings of the Association for Computational Linguistics: ACL 2023, Toronto, Canada, July 9-14, 2023*, pages 1635–1651. Association for Computational Linguistics.

Rita Ramos, Bruno Martins, Desmond Elliott, and Yova Kementchedjhieva. 2023c. Smallcap: Lightweight image captioning prompted with retrieval augmentation. In *IEEE/CVF Conference on Computer Vision and Pattern Recognition, CVPR 2023, Vancouver, BC, Canada, June 17-24, 2023*, pages 2840–2849. IEEE.

Sara Sarto, Marcella Cornia, Lorenzo Baraldi, and Rita Cucchiara. 2022. Retrieval-augmented transformer for image captioning. In *CBMI 2022: International Conference on Content-based Multimedia Indexing, Graz, Austria, September 14 - 16, 2022*, pages 1–7. ACM.

Sara Sarto, Marcella Cornia, Lorenzo Baraldi, Alessandro Nicolosi, and Rita Cucchiara. 2024. Towards retrieval-augmented architectures for image captioning. *ACM Trans. Multim. Comput. Commun. Appl.*, 20(8):242:1–242:22.

Zhan Shi, Hui Liu, and Xiaodan Zhu. 2021. Enhancing descriptive image captioning with natural language inference. In *Proceedings of the 59th Annual Meeting of the Association for Computational Linguistics and the 11th International Joint Conference on Natural Language Processing, ACL/IJCNLP 2021, (Volume 2: Short Papers), Virtual Event, August 1-6, 2021*, pages 269–277. Association for Computational Linguistics.

Ramakrishna Vedantam, C. Lawrence Zitnick, and Devi Parikh. 2015. Cider: Consensus-based image description evaluation. In *IEEE Conference on Computer Vision and Pattern Recognition, CVPR 2015, Boston, MA, USA, June 7-12, 2015*, pages 4566–4575. IEEE Computer Society.

Hao Wu, Zhihang Zhong, and Xiao Sun. 2024. DIR: retrieval-augmented image captioning with comprehensive understanding. *CoRR*, abs/2412.01115.

Kelvin Xu, Jimmy Ba, Ryan Kiros, Kyunghyun Cho, Aaron C. Courville, Ruslan Salakhutdinov, Richard S. Zemel, and Yoshua Bengio. 2015. Show, attend and tell: Neural image caption generation with visual attention. In *Proceedings of the 32nd International Conference on Machine Learning, ICML 2015, Lille, France, 6-11 July 2015*, volume 37 of *JMLR Workshop and Conference Proceedings*, pages 2048–2057. JMLR.org.

Zhuolin Yang, Wei Ping, Zihan Liu, Vijay Korthikanti, Weili Nie, De-An Huang, Linxi Fan, Zhiding Yu, Shiyi Lan, Bo Li, Mohammad Shoeybi, Ming-Yu Liu, Yuke Zhu, Bryan Catanzaro, Chaowei Xiao, and Anima Anandkumar. 2023. Re-vilm: Retrieval-augmented visual language model for zero and few-shot image captioning. In *Findings of the Association for Computational Linguistics: EMNLP 2023, Singapore, December 6-10, 2023*, pages 11844–11857. Association for Computational Linguistics.

Michihiro Yasunaga, Armen Aghajanyan, Weijia Shi, Richard James, Jure Leskovec, Percy Liang, Mike Lewis, Luke Zettlemoyer, and Wen-Tau Yih. 2023. Retrieval-augmented multimodal language modeling. In *International Conference on Machine Learning, ICML 2023, 23-29 July 2023, Honolulu, Hawaii, USA*, volume 202 of *Proceedings of Machine Learning Research*, pages 39755–39769. PMLR.

Ori Yoran, Tomer Wolfson, Ori Ram, and Jonathan Berant. 2024. Making retrieval-augmented language models robust to irrelevant context. In *The Twelfth International Conference on Learning Representations, ICLR 2024, Vienna, Austria, May 7-11, 2024*. OpenReview.net.

Jingyi You, Chenlong Hu, Hidetaka Kamigaito, Kotaro Funakoshi, and Manabu Okumura. 2021. Robust dynamic clustering for temporal networks. In *CIKM '21: The 30th ACM International Conference on Information and Knowledge Management, Virtual Event, Queensland, Australia, November 1 - 5, 2021*, pages 2424–2433. ACM.

Wenhao Yu, Hongming Zhang, Xiaoman Pan, Peixin Cao, Kaixin Ma, Jian Li, Hongwei Wang, and Dong Yu. 2024. Chain-of-note: Enhancing robustness in retrieval-augmented language models. In *Proceedings of the 2024 Conference on Empirical Methods in Natural Language Processing, EMNLP 2024, Miami, FL, USA, November 12-16, 2024*, pages 14672–14685. Association for Computational Linguistics.

Zequn Zeng, Yan Xie, Hao Zhang, Chiyu Chen, Bo Chen, and Zhengjue Wang. 2024. Meacap: Memory-augmented zero-shot image captioning. In *IEEE/CVF Conference on Computer Vision and Pattern Recognition, CVPR 2024, Seattle, WA, USA, June 16-22, 2024*, pages 14100–14110. IEEE.

Xin Zheng, Zhirui Zhang, Junliang Guo, Shujian Huang, Boxing Chen, Weihua Luo, and Jiajun Chen. 2021. Adaptive nearest neighbor machine translation. In *Proceedings of the 59th Annual Meeting of the Association for Computational Linguistics and the 11th International Joint Conference on Natural Language Processing, ACL/IJCNLP 2021, (Volume 2: Short Papers), Virtual Event, August 1-6, 2021*, pages 368–374. Association for Computational Linguistics.

Luowei Zhou, Hamid Palangi, Lei Zhang, Houdong Hu, Jason J. Corso, and Jianfeng Gao. 2020. Unified vision-language pre-training for image captioning and VQA. In *The Thirty-Fourth AAAI Conference on Artificial Intelligence, AAAI 2020, The Thirty-Second Innovative Applications of Artificial Intelligence Conference, IAAI 2020, The Tenth AAAI Symposium on Educational Advances in Artificial Intelligence, EAAI 2020, New York, NY, USA, February 7-12, 2020*, pages 13041–13049. AAAI Press.

Yucheng Zhou and Guodong Long. 2023. Style-aware contrastive learning for multi-style image captioning. In *Findings of the Association for Computational Linguistics: EACL 2023, Dubrovnik, Croatia, May 2-6, 2023*, pages 2212–2222. Association for Computational Linguistics.

Kun Zhu, Xiaocheng Feng, Xiyuan Du, Yuxuan Gu, Weijiang Yu, Haotian Wang, Qianglong Chen, Zheng Chu, Jingchang Chen, and Bing Qin. 2024. An information bottleneck perspective for effective noise filtering on retrieval-augmented generation. In *Proceedings of the 62nd Annual Meeting of the Association for Computational Linguistics (Volume 1: Long Papers), ACL 2024, Bangkok, Thailand, August 11-16, 2024*, pages 1044–1069. Association for Computational Linguistics.

Multimodal Retrieval-Augmented Generation: Unified Information Processing Across Text, Image, Table, and Video Modalities

Nazarii Drushchak[1,2], **Nataliya Polyakovska**[1], **Maryna Bautina**[1], **Taras Semenchenko**[1,3], **Jakub Koscielecki**[1], **Wojciech Sykala**[1], **Michal Wegrzynowski**[1]

[1]SoftServe Inc., [2]Ukrainian Catholic University, [3]Taras Shevchenko National University of Kyiv

Correspondence: ndrus@softserveinc.com

Abstract

Retrieval-augmented generation (RAG) is a powerful paradigm for leveraging external data to enhance the capabilities of large language models (LLMs). However, most existing RAG solutions are tailored for single-modality or limited multimodal scenarios, restricting their applicability in real-world contexts where diverse data sources—including text, tables, images, and videos—must be integrated seamlessly. In this work, we propose a unified *Multimodal Retrieval-augmented generation (mRAG)* system designed to unify information processing across all four modalities. Our pipeline ingests and indexes data from PDFs and videos using tools like Amazon Textract, Transcribe, Langfuse, and multimodal LLMs (e.g., Claude 3.5 Sonnet) for structured extraction and semantic enrichment. The dataset includes text queries, table lookups, image-based questions, and videos. Evaluation with the Deepeval framework shows improved retrieval accuracy and response quality, especially for structured text and tables. While performance on image and video queries is lower, the multimodal integration framework remains robust, underscoring the value of unified pipelines for diverse data.

1 Introduction

The exponentially growing volume of digital content in various forms, including text, tables, images, and videos, has created new challenges. Traditional information retrieval systems typically focus on a single modality, such as text or images, limiting their ability to process complex queries that require insight from multi-modal data sources. However, real-world applications, such as enterprise data analytics, troubleshooting equipment through video manuals, or processing product specifications, need a framework to manage various data types.

Retrieval-augmented generation (RAG) systems have emerged as a powerful paradigm combining retrieval mechanisms with generative models to enhance information access and synthesis. However, conventional RAG frameworks were not designed initially to handle multimodal data, restricting their utility in environments where diverse data forms must be unified and processed seamlessly. This limitation underscores the need for an evolved approach that extends the capabilities of RAG systems to accommodate and integrate multiple modalities effectively.

This paper presents an mRAG system that unifies information across text, tables, images, and videos. Using tools like AWS, LangChain, and multimodal LLMs, it provides a robust pipeline for data ingestion, retrieval, and response generation.

2 Background and Related Work

The landscape of information retrieval has evolved significantly with the advent of large-scale digital data across diverse modalities. Traditional information retrieval systems focus mainly on single modalities, such as text-based search engines (Amati and Van Rijsbergen, 2002; Karpukhin et al., 2020; Khattab and Zaharia, 2020) or image retrieval systems (Lin et al., 2015; Chen et al., 2023), each optimized for their specific data type.

Multimodal information retrieval (MMIR) aims to bridge the gap between different data types, facilitating comprehensive searches that span text, images, videos, and other formats (Baltrusaitis et al., 2019). Researchers have successfully applied deep learning techniques for multimodal information retrieval (Hu et al., 2019).

RAG systems represent a paradigm shift in combining retrieval mechanisms with generative models. Introduced by Lewis et al. (2020), RAG leverages LLMs to generate contextually relevant responses by retrieving pertinent information from extensive external knowledge bases. RAG research has rapidly expanded, tackling efficiency bottlenecks (Borgeaud et al., 2021), memory constraints

Proceedings of the 1st Workshop on Multimodal Augmented Generation via Multimodal Retrieval (MAGMaR 2025), pages 59–64
August 1, 2025

(Qian et al., 2024), and self-reflection strategies (Asai et al., 2023).

Recent advances in RAG have begun integrating multiple modalities to enhance retrieval and generation, as seen in MuRAG (Chen et al., 2022). However, most work remains limited to small, domain-specific datasets (e.g., healthcare) and only two modalities (Xia et al., 2024).

Key challenges remain in the development of multimodal RAG systems. Most existing approaches lack unified frameworks capable of reasoning across more than two modalities, such as text, tables, images, and videos. Scalability is also limited, as adding new modalities often requires separate training pipelines (Chen et al., 2022). Furthermore, current evaluation benchmarks primarily focus on single- or dual-modality tasks, making it difficult to assess systems designed for more complex, fully multimodal scenarios (Chen et al., 2024; Es et al., 2024; Krishna et al., 2024).

This work addresses these gaps by proposing a unified framework for building and evaluating multimodal RAG systems.

3 Methodology

3.1 Dataset Description

We test system capabilities by using 36 publicly available Dell server documents, including specifications, service manuals, and installation guides. These documents cover a range of modalities, including plain text, complex tables, and images, ensuring diverse data for testing.

Additionally, the dataset contains 82 video manuals of the servers, including one more modality. The dataset was selected to provide all the required modalities of varying complexities, reflecting real-world challenges in the technical documentation[1].

3.2 System Architecture

Information retrieval is structured into three primary layers: Data Processing, Embedding and Indexing, and Retrieval Engine. All operate within a cloud environment provided by Amazon Web Services (AWS) [2]. The generative module is built on the information retrieval component to support multimodal RAG scenarios.

The architecture of the main AWS components is represented in Figure 1.

[1]PDFs and videos can be shared upon request.

[2]`https://aws.amazon.com/`

The following sections of this research describe the detailed architecture of the retrieval and generation engines and the guardrails.

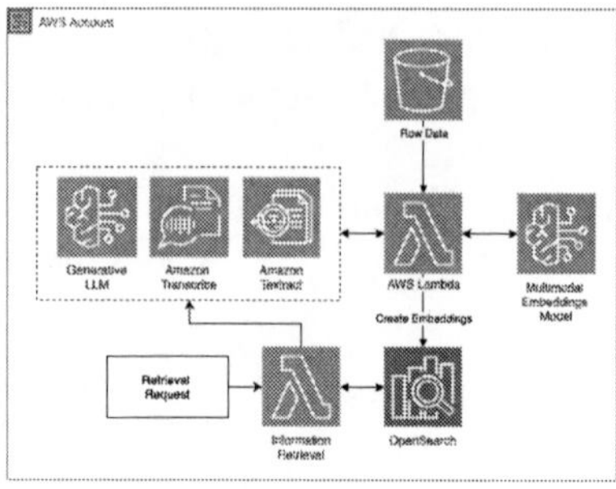

Figure 1: Main Services for Information Retrieval

3.3 Information Retriever

In this part, we explain how we create information retrievers. These pipelines are designed to prepare data for retrieval from various sources such as PDFs and videos.

3.3.1 PDF-based retriever

The PDF-based retriever processes PDFs to extract and index textual, tabular, and image data for efficient search. It is built on the **AWS stack** for scalability and performance, as illustrated in Figure 2.

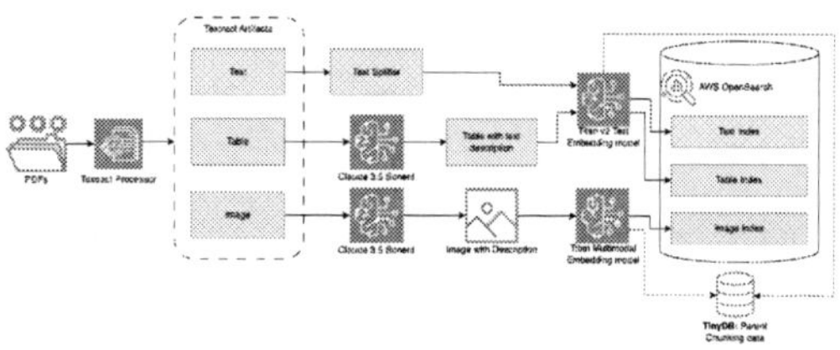

Figure 2: Pipeline for PDF-based Information Retrieval

Pipeline Overview:

1. **PDF Processing: Amazon Textract**[3] extracts text, tables, and images from PDFs.

2. **Text Splitting: LangChain**[4] split the text into contextually relevant chunks.

3. **Table Processing: Claude 3.5 Sonnet**(Team, 2024a,b) LLM generates semantic summaries for table data.

4. **Image Processing: Claude 3.5 Sonnet** LLM creates descriptive image metadata.

[3]`https://docs.aws.amazon.com/textract/latest/dg`

[4]`https://python.langchain.com/v0.1/docs/modules/data_connection/document_transformers/`

5. **Embedding and Indexing:** Text and images are embedded using **Amazon Titan Text Embeddings V2**[5] and **Amazon Titan Multimodal Embeddings G1 models**[6] and indexed in **Amazon OpenSearch**[7].

6. **Metadata Tracking: TinyDB**[8] stores parent-child relationships between data chunks.

3.3.2 Video-based retriever

The video-based retriever extracts and indexes keyframe and textual data from videos using the **AWS stack**. The pipeline process is illustrated in Figure 3.

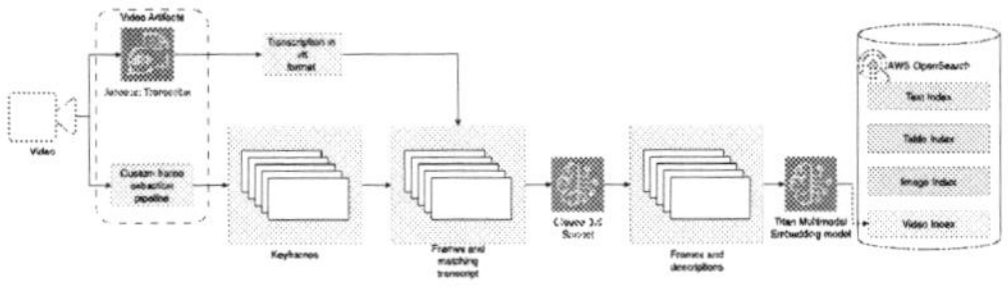

Figure 3: Pipeline for Video-based Information Retrieval

Pipeline Overview:

1. **Transcription:** Uses **Amazon Transcribe** to transcribe videos.

2. **Keyframe Extraction:** A custom pipeline based on **OpenCV**[9] extracts keyframes by detecting scene changes and analyzing content using entropy (≥ 4.5), edge ratio (≥ 0.02), contrast variation (≥ 600), and pixel changes ($\geq 5\%$). **Perceptual hashing** prevents redundancy, ensuring keyframes differ with a similarity threshold of 0.95.

3. **Context:** Matches keyframes with transcripts (±10-30s window).

4. **Description: Claude 3.5 Sonnet** generates enriched descriptions of keyframes, incorporating the visual details and corresponding transcript context.

5. **Indexing:** Embeds content via **Amazon Titan Multimodal Embeddings G1 model** and stores in **Amazon Open-Search**.

[5]https://docs.aws.amazon.com/bedrock/latest/userguide/titan-embedding-models.html
[6]https://docs.aws.amazon.com/bedrock/latest/userguide/titan-multiemb-models.html
[7]https://aws.amazon.com/opensearch-service/
[8]https://tinydb.readthedocs.io/en/latest/
[9]https://opencv.org/

3.4 Multimodal Retrieval Augmented Generation

This section outlines the mRAG system's core components for answering user queries using file data.

1. **User Input Processing:** Queries are analyzed by **Claude 3.5 Sonnet** by checking the conversation history and the new user query. It then has two options: rephrase the query based on the context for continuity, or return the original message if the new query is unrelated to previous discussions.

2. **Independent Retrieval:** Relevant text, tables, and images are retrieved from **AWS OpenSearch** using a unified parent-child chunking strategy: smaller embedding-based chunks for search, with associated larger parent chunks provided to the model. Video modalities use only embedding retrieval. The top 10 textual results and the top 5 for other modalities are selected.

3. **Answer Generation:** Retrieved data and the user query are structured for **Claude 3.5 Sonnet** to generate responses.

4. **Citation and Traceability:** To ensure transparency, sources are cited with links to document pages or video timestamps.

3.5 Monitoring, Guardrail, and Feedback Loop

The system integrates monitoring, guardrails, and feedback to ensure ethical compliance. User interactions are tracked using **LangFuse**[10], with personally identifiable information (PII) anonymized by **Amazon Comprehend**[11]. **Amazon Bedrock Guardrails**[12] enforce safeguards to prevent harmful content and ensure AI safety (Chua et al., 2024). User feedback is analyzed based on the provided category, such as good, inconsistent, irrelevant, incomplete, confusing, or other. This feedback is processed with **Claude 3.5 Sonnet** to identify potential issues, and bugs are logged for resolution, enabling continuous system improvement.

[10]https://langfuse.com/
[11]https://aws.amazon.com/comprehend/
[12]https://aws.amazon.com/bedrock/guardrails/

Modality	Method	Correct Sources	Contextual Precision	Contextual Recall	Contextual Relevancy	Must Mention	LLM as Evaluator	Answer Relevancy	Faithfulness	Hallucination
All	Base	**0.652**	**0.349**	0.653	0.655	0.283	0.708	0.946	**0.677**	0.356
All	Opt	0.644	0.336	**0.690**	**0.702**	**0.290**	**0.717**	**0.951**	0.668	**0.314**
Text	Base	0.828	**0.493**	0.846	**0.846**	**0.068**	**0.812**	0.964	**0.672**	0.233
Text	Opt	**0.830**	0.491	**0.860**	0.846	0.058	0.809	**0.968**	0.636	**0.202**
Table	Base	**0.970**	**0.292**	**0.849**	0.818	0.702	0.752	**1.000**	**0.617**	**0.273**
Table	Opt	0.939	0.195	**0.849**	**0.879**	**0.742**	**0.782**	0.995	0.591	0.364
Image	Base	**0.694**	**0.332**	0.537	0.536	**N/A**	0.593	**1.000**	**0.718**	0.630
Image	Opt	0.685	0.313	**0.573**	**0.628**	**N/A**	**0.650**	0.994	0.662	**0.537**
Video	Base	**0.293**	0.190	0.399	0.417	**N/A**	**0.619**	0.876	0.682	0.394
Video	Opt	0.281	**0.193**	**0.481**	**0.496**	**N/A**	0.613	**0.891**	**0.737**	**0.323**

Table 1: Experimental results across different modalities comparing Base and Optimized (Opt) Q&A prompts. Bold values indicate the best performance for each metric within each modality.

4 Experiments

4.1 Experiments Setup

We evaluated our system using a dataset of 36 PDF documents and 82 videos, based on **Dell server specifications and service manuals**. Four participants were involved in the question creation process, with each person generating queries across all modalities: text, table, image, and video.

The benchmarking set includes 116 questions[13]: 43 for text, 22 for tables, 18 for images, and 33 for videos. We executed the system three times for each question and averaged the scores to obtain stable results.

An example question format is:

```
{
  "query":"How to set up T150 system?",
  "answer":"Perform the following steps to set up the system:
     1. Unpack the system.
     2. Connect the peripherals.
     3. Power on the system.",
  "sources":["Dell EMC PowerEdge T150 Installation
     and Service Manual.pdf"],
  "type":"text"
}
```

Langfuse[14] was used to track experiments, and **Deepeval**[15] as core evaluation framework.

4.2 Evaluation Metrics

The evaluation used two sets of metrics: retrieval and response. Retrieval metrics included the percentage of correct sources retrieved, contextual precision and recall, and the relevancy of retrieved contexts. Response metrics assessed keyword inclusion ("must mention"), LLM as evaluator score (rated by **GPT-4o** (OpenAI and et al., 2024)), answer relevancy, faithfulness to sources, and the presence of hallucinations.

4.3 Experimental Results

We evaluated the system's performance using two experimental setups: a baseline prompt (Base) and a manually optimized prompt based on providing additional limitations (Opt). Table 1 summarizes the results, with the best metric for each category/modality highlighted in bold.

Overall, the optimized prompt slightly outperformed the baseline in most metrics, particularly in contextual recall, relevancy, and hallucination reduction. However, performance varied by modality. Text and table modalities demonstrated the highest accuracy and stability, benefiting from the structured nature of their data. Image and video modalities showed lower performance, reflecting the challenges of interpreting and retrieving unstructured visual content.

Notably, video retrieval had the lowest scores in correct sources and contextual metrics, indicating room for improvement in handling video data. Despite this, optimized prompts improved performance metrics for both image and video modalities.

5 Conclusion and Future Work

This work presents a methodology for building an mRAG system, focusing on pipelines for extracting and indexing text, tables, images, and videos. Experimental results show improved contextual relevancy, LLM evaluation scores, and reduced hallucinations, while performance variations highlight challenges with unstructured data.

Future work will focus on enhancing mRAG with improved LLM capabilities, fine-tuning embeddings for better domain understanding, incorporating user feedback, and adding visual modalities for input.

6 Ethical Consideration

This study builds an mRAG system processing text, images, tables, and videos, ensuring data privacy and security. It uses only open-source PDFs, anonymizes all requests and feedback, and uses feedback solely to improve system performance.

[13]Evaluation dataset and script can be shared upon request.

[14]https://langfuse.com/

[15]https://docs.confident-ai.com/

We used ChatGPT[16] and Grammarly[17] to help refine the writing of this work, ensuring the language is straightforward.

References

Gianni Amati and Cornelis Joost Van Rijsbergen. 2002. Probabilistic models of information retrieval based on measuring the divergence from randomness. *ACM Trans. Inf. Syst.*, 20(4):357–389.

Akari Asai, Zeqiu Wu, Yizhong Wang, Avirup Sil, and Hannaneh Hajishirzi. 2023. Self-rag: Learning to retrieve, generate, and critique through self-reflection. *ArXiv*, abs/2310.11511.

Tadas Baltrusaitis, Chaitanya Ahuja, and Louis-Philippe Morency. 2019. Multimodal machine learning: A survey and taxonomy. *IEEE Trans. Pattern Anal. Mach. Intell.*, 41(2):423–443.

Sebastian Borgeaud, Arthur Mensch, Jordan Hoffmann, Trevor Cai, Eliza Rutherford, Katie Millican, George van den Driessche, Jean-Baptiste Lespiau, Bogdan Damoc, Aidan Clark, Diego de Las Casas, Aurelia Guy, Jacob Menick, Roman Ring, T. W. Hennigan, Saffron Huang, Lorenzo Maggiore, Chris Jones, Albin Cassirer, Andy Brock, Michela Paganini, Geoffrey Irving, Oriol Vinyals, Simon Osindero, Karen Simonyan, Jack W. Rae, Erich Elsen, and L. Sifre. 2021. Improving language models by retrieving from trillions of tokens. In *International Conference on Machine Learning*.

Jiawei Chen, Hongyu Lin, Xianpei Han, and Le Sun. 2024. Benchmarking large language models in retrieval-augmented generation. In *Thirty-Eighth AAAI Conference on Artificial Intelligence, AAAI 2024, Thirty-Sixth Conference on Innovative Applications of Artificial Intelligence, IAAI 2024, Fourteenth Symposium on Educational Advances in Artificial Intelligence, EAAI 2014, February 20-27, 2024, Vancouver, Canada*, pages 17754–17762. AAAI Press.

Wei Chen, Yu Liu, Weiping Wang, Erwin M. Bakker, Theodoros Georgiou, Paul Fieguth, Li Liu, and Michael S. Lew. 2023. Deep learning for instance retrieval: A survey. *IEEE Transactions on Pattern Analysis and Machine Intelligence*, 45(6):7270–7292.

Wenhu Chen, Hexiang Hu, Xi Chen, Pat Verga, and William Cohen. 2022. MuRAG: Multimodal retrieval-augmented generator for open question answering over images and text. In *Proceedings of the 2022 Conference on Empirical Methods in Natural Language Processing*, pages 5558–5570, Abu Dhabi, United Arab Emirates. Association for Computational Linguistics.

[16]https://chat.openai.com/

[17]https://www.grammarly.com/

Jaymari Chua, Yun Li, Shiyi Yang, Chen Wang, and Lina Yao. 2024. Ai safety in generative ai large language models: A survey. *Preprint*, arXiv:2407.18369.

Shahul Es, Jithin James, Luis Espinosa Anke, and Steven Schockaert. 2024. RAGAs: Automated evaluation of retrieval augmented generation. In *Proceedings of the 18th Conference of the European Chapter of the Association for Computational Linguistics: System Demonstrations*, pages 150–158, St. Julians, Malta. Association for Computational Linguistics.

Peng Hu, Liangli Zhen, Dezhong Peng, and Pei Liu. 2019. Scalable deep multimodal learning for cross-modal retrieval. In *Proceedings of the 42nd International ACM SIGIR Conference on Research and Development in Information Retrieval*, SIGIR'19, page 635–644, New York, NY, USA. Association for Computing Machinery.

Vladimir Karpukhin, Barlas Oguz, Sewon Min, Patrick Lewis, Ledell Wu, Sergey Edunov, Danqi Chen, and Wen-tau Yih. 2020. Dense passage retrieval for open-domain question answering. In *Proceedings of the 2020 Conference on Empirical Methods in Natural Language Processing (EMNLP)*, pages 6769–6781, Online. Association for Computational Linguistics.

Omar Khattab and Matei Zaharia. 2020. Colbert: Efficient and effective passage search via contextualized late interaction over bert. In *Proceedings of the 43rd International ACM SIGIR Conference on Research and Development in Information Retrieval*, SIGIR '20, page 39–48, New York, NY, USA. Association for Computing Machinery.

Satyapriya Krishna, Kalpesh Krishna, Anhad Mohananey, Steven Schwarcz, Adam Stambler, Shyam Upadhyay, and Manaal Faruqui. 2024. Fact, fetch, and reason: A unified evaluation of retrieval-augmented generation. *Preprint*, arXiv:2409.12941.

Patrick Lewis, Ethan Perez, Aleksandra Piktus, Fabio Petroni, Vladimir Karpukhin, Naman Goyal, Heinrich Küttler, Mike Lewis, Wen-tau Yih, Tim Rocktäschel, Sebastian Riedel, and Douwe Kiela. 2020. Retrieval-augmented generation for knowledge-intensive nlp tasks. In *Proceedings of the 34th International Conference on Neural Information Processing Systems*, NIPS '20, Red Hook, NY, USA. Curran Associates Inc.

Kevin Lin, Huei-Fang Yang, Jen-Hao Hsiao, and Chu-Song Chen. 2015. Deep learning of binary hash codes for fast image retrieval. In *2015 IEEE Conference on Computer Vision and Pattern Recognition Workshops (CVPRW)*, pages 27–35.

OpenAI and et al. 2024. Gpt-4o system card. *Preprint*, arXiv:2410.21276.

Hongjin Qian, Peitian Zhang, Zheng Liu, Kelong Mao, and Zhicheng Dou. 2024. Memorag: Moving towards next-gen rag via memory-inspired knowledge discovery. *Preprint*, arXiv:2409.05591.

Anthropic Team. 2024a. The claude 3 model family: Opus, sonnet, haiku. Technical report, Anthropic.

Anthropic Team. 2024b. Claude 3.5 sonnet model card addendum. Technical report, Anthropic.

Peng Xia, Kangyu Zhu, Haoran Li, Hongtu Zhu, Yun Li, Gang Li, Linjun Zhang, and Huaxiu Yao. 2024. RULE: Reliable multimodal RAG for factuality in medical vision language models. In *Proceedings of the 2024 Conference on Empirical Methods in Natural Language Processing*, pages 1081–1093, Miami, Florida, USA. Association for Computational Linguistics.

Making LVLMs Look Twice: Contrastive Decoding with Contrast Images

Avshalom Manevich
Bar Ilan University
avshalomman@gmail.com

Reut Tsarfaty
Bar Ilan University
reut.tsarfaty@biu.ac.il

Abstract

Large Vision-Language Models (LVLMs) are becoming increasingly popular for text-vision tasks requiring cross-modal reasoning, but often struggle with fine-grained visual discrimination. This limitation is evident in recent benchmarks like NaturalBench and D3, where closed models such as GPT-4o achieve only 39.6%, and open-source models perform below random chance (25%). We introduce Contrastive decoding with Contrast Images (CoCI), which adjusts LVLM outputs by contrasting them against outputs for similar images (Contrast Images - CIs). CoCI demonstrates strong performance across three distinct supervision regimes: First, when using naturally occurring CIs in benchmarks with curated image pairs, we achieve improvements of up to 98.9% on NaturalBench, 69.5% on D3, and 37.6% on MMVP. Second, for scenarios with modest training data (~5k samples), we show that a lightweight neural classifier can effectively select CIs from similar images at inference time, improving NaturalBench performance by up to 36.8%. Third, for scenarios with no training data, we develop a caption-matching technique that selects CIs by comparing LVLM-generated descriptions of candidate images. Notably, on VQAv2, our method improves VQA performance even in pointwise evaluation settings without explicit contrast images. Our approach demonstrates the potential for enhancing LVLMs at inference time through different CI selection approaches, each suited to different data availability scenarios.

1 Introduction

Large Vision-Language Models (LVLMs) are becoming increasingly popular for text-vision tasks that require reasoning over both modalities. However, they often struggle with fine-grained visual discrimination — that is, the ability to tell two similar yet distinct images apart — a crucial capability for real-world applications such as multimodal search, manufacturing, and robotics. Recent benchmarks have exposed this limitation: on NaturalBench (Li et al., 2024a), which tests visual question answering over closely related images, state-of-the-art closed models like GPT-4o (OpenAI et al., 2024) achieve only 39.6% accuracy. Similarly, on the D3 benchmark (Gaur et al., 2024), which requires describing differences between paired images, open-source models perform below random chance (25%).

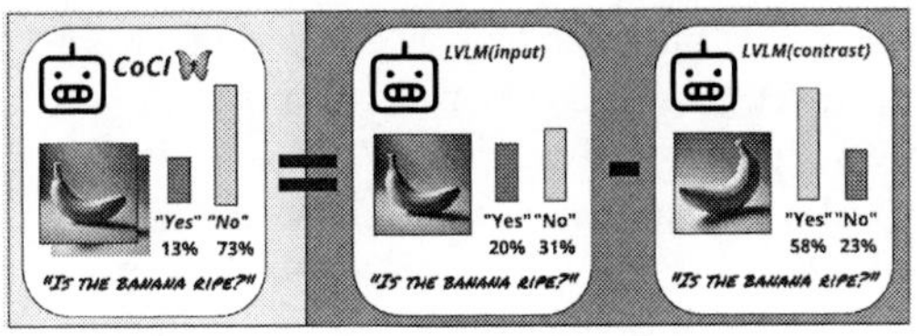

Figure 1: CoCI penalizes target image logits using those from a contrast image, weighted by hyperparameter α.

Efforts to address fine-grained visual discrimination in LVLMs are still under-explored. Current strategies addressing other LVLM shortcomings often rely on fine-tuning with specialized datasets (Wang et al., 2023; Chen et al., 2023; Liu et al., 2024a; Sarkar et al., 2024), multi-step correction pipelines (Yin et al., 2023; Zhou et al., 2023), or inference-time methods (Leng et al., 2023; Manevich and Tsarfaty, 2024; Liu et al., 2024b; Huang et al., 2023). Inference-time methods are particularly appealing as they do not require expensive model training and are less prone to compounding errors that can affect multi-step systems.

Building on the advantages of inference-time methods, we propose Contrastive decoding with Contrast Images (CoCI), an approach specifically designed to improve fine-grained visual discrimination in LVLMs. CoCI penalizes LVLM next-token probabilities with those obtained by feeding a different, contrasting image input (See Figure 1).

We evaluate CoCI across three different supervision regimes. First, using naturally occurring

Proceedings of the 1st Workshop on Multimodal Augmented Generation via Multimodal Retrieval (MAGMaR 2025), pages 65–78

Contrast Images in curated benchmarks like NaturalBench, D3 and MMVP, we demonstrate improvements up to 98.9%, 69.5%, 37.6% respectively. This establishes a performance ceiling for CoCI when ideal CIs are available. For applications where natural CIs are unavailable but training data exists, we show that a lightweight classifier can effectively select CIs from visually similar images at inference time, improving NaturalBench performance by up to 36.5%. In settings without training data, we propose a caption-matching technique that selects CIs at inference time by comparing LVLM-generated descriptions of candidate images.

Experiments with leading LVLMs — Qwen2-VL, LLaVA-OneVision, and Llama 3.2 (Wang et al., 2024a; Li et al., 2024b; Grattafiori et al., 2024) — establish the potential of contrastive decoding strategies with contrastive images for improved multimodal reasoning in real-world tasks.

2 Contrastive Decoding with Contrast Images (CoCI)

We present CoCI, a method to improve LVLM outputs by penalizing token probabilities that are likely under a contrast image. The choice of contrast image is crucial: e.g., when querying about fruit ripeness with an input image of an unripe banana, contrasting against an image of a ripe banana provides strong contrastive signal, while an image of a ripe pear offers weaker contrast and an image of a bus provides no useful signal and may degrade performance. This intuition guides our CI selection strategies across different scenarios. Before formalizing this intuition, we first review key concepts in LVLM text generation.

2.1 Preliminaries: Text Generation in LVLMs

LVLMs extend LLMs by conditioning next-token prediction on both text and images.[1] Generation proceeds by iteratively sampling tokens from the model's predicted distributions until reaching an EOS token or length limit. The LVLM next-token prediction is:

$$\text{LVLM}t(y{<}\, t, I) = P(y|y{<}\, t, I) \quad \forall y \in \mathcal{V} \quad (1)$$

where $y_{<t}$ is the token prefix, I is the input image, and $\mathcal{V}$ is the model's vocabulary.

2.2 Contrastive Decoding

Following Li et al. (2023), various Contrastive Decoding approaches have emerged (Sennrich et al., 2024; Jin et al., 2024; Phan et al., 2024). We implement CoCI based on Sennrich et al. (2024)'s minimal variant:

$$\text{CoCI}_t(y_{<t}, I, I') = \log\Big(P(y|y_{<t}, I) - \alpha P(y|y_{<t}, I')\Big) \quad \forall y \in \mathcal{V} \quad (2)$$

CoCI penalizes token probabilities from the target image distribution $P(y|y_{<t}, I)$ with those from the contrast image distribution $P(y|y_{<t}, I')$. The parameter α controls penalty strength.[2]

2.3 Obtaining Contrast Images

We propose three approaches for obtaining CIs:

Naturally occurring CIs. Many tasks naturally provide pairs of images that can serve as contrast images (CIs). For instance, a home assistant robot searching for "the blue ceramic mug with a chip on the handle" needs to distinguish between similar cups to find the exact match. We evaluate this scenario using LVLM benchmarks with curated image pairs designed to test fine-grained discrimination capabilities. These paired images serve as natural CIs in our experiments.

Classifier-obtained CIs. For cases without natural CIs, we train an MLP classifier to select them during inference. Given LVLM L and training triplets $\langle q, I, I'\rangle$ (binary question and image pairs with different answers), we: (a) Extract LVLM hidden states $h_{q,i} \in R^{d_L}$ per image-question pair. (b) Concatenate states for image pairs: $h_{q,i,i'} \in R^{2*d_L}$. (c) Create negative samples using the j least similar images from top-k similar images to I in dataset D[3]. (d) Train a three-layer MLP classifier.[4] We train on NaturalBench (60% split) augmented with GPT-4-generated question paraphrases. At inference, we select the CI maximizing classifier score among k most similar images.[5]

Caption-matched CIs. For scenarios without training data, we select CIs by comparing LVLM-generated image descriptions. Given an input image, we (a) Retrieve k similar images[6]. (b) Generate LVLM descriptions for all $k + 1$ images. (c)

[1] In this work, we focus on single image inputs.

[2] We use $\alpha = 0.5$ for VQA and $\alpha = 0.8$ for open-ended generation.

[3] $j = 5$, $k = 100$. Using flickr30k (Young et al., 2014) and open-clip (Ilharco et al., 2021; Cherti et al., 2023; Radford et al., 2021a; Schuhmann et al., 2022) with cosine similarity.

[4] See appendix A.1 and A.3 for implementation details.

[5] See table 2 for k value comparisons. Inference uses identical retrieval setup as training.

[6] We set $k = 5$ without tuning.

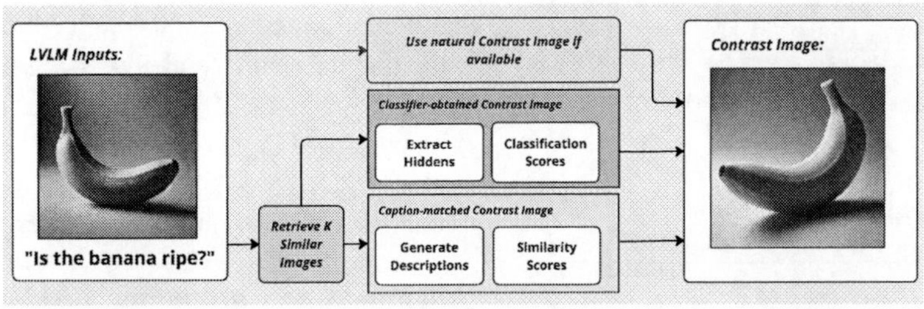

Figure 2: Illustration of the approaches we explore for obtaining a Contrast Image (CI).

Embed descriptions using a text encoder. (d) Select the image whose description is most similar to the input image's description

2.4 Research Hypothesis

We test whether: (a) Contrastive decoding with CIs improves LVLM fine-grained reasoning, (b) A lightweight classifier trained on LVLM hidden states can effectively select CIs, and (c) Images with similar LVLM descriptions can serve as CIs.

3 Experiments

We evaluate CoCI using three leading LVLMs[7] on four benchmarks, three specifically targeting fine-grained visual discrimination:

NaturalBench (Li et al., 2024a) evaluates similar image discrimination through yes/no and multiple-choice questions, with different answers for paired images. The benchmark contains 1900 image pairs (two questions per pair), split into train (60%), dev (20%), and test (20%) sets. We measure image accuracy (both questions correct), question accuracy (per-question), and group accuracy (all four image-question combinations correct).

MMVP (Multimodal Visual Patterns) (Tong et al., 2024) evaluates visual difference detection through multiple-choice questions on 150 image pairs. Each pair differs in specific visual aspects (object state, position, or orientation). Success requires correct answers for both images in a pair.

D3 (Detect, Describe, Discriminate) (Gaur et al., 2024) assesses models' ability to generate discriminative descriptions between similar images across 247 pairs. We adapt D3 for CoCI by treating it as a single-input task, generating separate descriptions per image. Evaluation follows the original self-retrieval protocol, measuring whether an image-text encoder correctly matches descriptions to their images.

Model	Method	D3 (self-ret.)	MMVP (acc.)	NB (g-acc.)	VQAv2 (acc.)
Qwen2-VL	Baseline	30.8	46.0	30.8	72.66
	CoCI_{CAP}	34.8	48.7	31.3	**74.33**
	CoCI_{NAT}	**52.2**	**63.3**	**46.6**	-
LLaVA-OV	Baseline	25.1	52.7	28.2	61.66
	CoCI_{CAP}	31.6	57.3	31.6	**73.66**
	CoCI_{NAT}	**38.1**	**66.7**	**56.1**	-
Llama 3.2	Baseline	28.7	39.3	21.1	58
	CoCI_{CAP}	33.6	41.3	22.4	58
	CoCI_{NAT}	**35.6**	**43.3**	**29.2**	-

Table 1: CoCI performance comparison with provided CIs across benchmarks, with natural CIs (CoCI_{NAT}) and caption-matched CIs (CoCI_{CAP}).

VQAv2 (Goyal et al., 2017) serves as our general-purpose visual question answering benchmark. While not focused on fine-grained discrimination, we include it to demonstrate CoCI's broader applicability. We evaluate on 300 validation set image-question pairs using exact match accuracy.

4 Results and Discussion

In Table 1 we can see that using natural CIs yields substantial improvements: up to 21.4 points on D3 (Qwen), 17.3 points on MMVP (LLaVA), and 27.9 points on NaturalBench (LLaVA). Caption-matched CIs show moderate but consistent gains, particularly on D3 where LLaVA improves from 25.1% to 31.6%, suggesting that contrasting against images with similar captions effectively guides visual discrimination. CoCI with caption matching improves performance on VQAv2 for two of the three tested models while maintaining baseline performance for Llama 3.2, demonstrating that CoCI enhances general-purpose VQA abilities beyond fine-grained visual discrimination tasks.

Throughout our experiments, Llama exhibits different behavior compared to other models - showing lower performance and reduced responsiveness

[7]See appendix A.2 for details on the checkpoints we used.

Model	Method	Q-acc	I-acc	Acc	G-acc
Qwen2-VL	Baseline	55.3	59.3	76.8	30.8
	$Cls_{k=4}$	55.5	58.8	76.4	32.1
	$Cls_{k=8}$	56.3	58.9	76.7	32.4
	$Cls_{k=16}$	57.4	60.1	77.2	33.7
	$Cls_{k=32}$	57.8	60.1	77.4	**34.2**
	$Cls_{k=64}$	**58.2**	**60.8**	**77.9**	33.9
LLaVA-OV	Baseline	53.8	56.1	74.6	28.2
	$Cls_{k=4}$	59.2	59.6	77.6	35.3
	$Cls_{k=8}$	57.8	60.1	77.5	34.5
	$Cls_{k=16}$	57.6	58.7	77.0	33.4
	$Cls_{k=32}$	**60.3**	**62.1**	**78.5**	**38.4**
	$Cls_{k=64}$	59.7	62.1	78.2	37.6
Llama 3.2	Baseline	46.3	50.5	71.8	21.1
	$Cls_{k=4}$	**49.2**	**52.8**	**73.2**	**23.2**
	$Cls_{k=8}$	49.1	52.2	73.1	21.8
	$Cls_{k=16}$	48.8	52.4	73.1	22.4
	$Cls_{k=32}$	49.9	52.5	73.7	22.1
	$Cls_{k=64}$	49.7	52.5	73.6	22.1

Table 2: CoCI accuracy metrics on the NaturalBench test set with CIs chosen using a lightweight classifier. $k = j$ denotes the classifier ran on the j most similar images to the input image.

to our methods. This pattern is evident in Table 2, where Qwen and LLaVA's performance improves with larger candidate pools (k), peaking around k=32, while Llama performs best with small pools (k=4). This behavior could be attributed to two factors: First, while the hyperparameters worked well for Qwen and LLaVA, they may not be optimal for Llama without model-specific tuning. Second, Llama's architectural differences, particularly its use of cross-attention, could lead to different behaviors in our contrastive decoding context. While exploring these architecture-specific considerations could be valuable, it is beyond the scope of this work.

In NaturalBench, G-Acc shows particularly strong improvement with natural CIs as it requires consistency across all image-question combinations. This pattern persists with classifier-selected CIs, where G-Acc improves by up to 10.2 points while other metrics show modest gains. The substantial gap between natural CIs and other methods suggests that classifier-selected and caption-matched CIs, while beneficial, don't yet capture all aspects that make natural pairs effective. [8]

5 Related Work

Inference-time methods for enhancing multimodal reasoning. Recent work has focused on hallucination reduction through confidence-based adjustments (Huo et al., 2024), semantic references (Yang et al., 2024), and contrastive decoding with perturbed inputs (Leng et al., 2023; Manevich and Tsarfaty, 2024). Our work extends these approaches to fine-grained visual discrimination.

Alignment and grounding in LVLMs. Prior work has enhanced visual-textual alignment through object-level synthesis (Wang et al., 2024b), targeted fine-tuning (Lu et al., 2024), and dataset construction (Li et al., 2024c). While these methods improve foundational capabilities, they don't directly address fine-grained discrimination.

Contrastive examples in multimodal models. CLIP (Radford et al., 2021b) established contrastive learning for modality alignment. Recent works leverage contrast pairs: (Le et al., 2023) and (Zhang et al., 2024) generate synthetic datasets using text-to-image models, while (Abbasnejad et al., 2020) and (Zhou et al., 2024) use contrastive examples to address dataset biases. Unlike these approaches requiring data generation or training, our method operates at inference time.[9]

6 Conclusion

We introduced Contrastive decoding with Contrast Images (CoCI), demonstrating its effectiveness in improving LVLMs' fine-grained visual discrimination capabilities in both VQA and long-form generation tasks. While naturally occurring contrast pairs yielded the strongest gains, both classifier-based and caption-matching approaches provide meaningful improvements without requiring dataset curation or model training. We validated the generality of our method through experiments with caption-based contrast selection, showing that CoCI does not rely on pre-curated pairs but can leverage them when available. Notably, CoCI improves performance even on tasks that don't explicitly measure fine-grained discrimination.

Our results show that contrastive decoding algorithms, when combined with strategic contrast image selection, improve LVLMs' ability to make fine-grained distinctions and their overall VQA abilities, opening new avenues for improving multimodal reasoning through inference-time techniques.

[8]See appendix A.3 for ablation tests with different CI selection strategies.

[9]Classifier-selected CIs require minimal preprocessing compared to model finetuning or dataset curation.

7 Limitations

CoCI has several limitations worth noting. While we demonstrate its effectiveness with classifier-based and caption-matching approaches, the substantial performance gap between natural and automatically selected CIs indicates significant headroom for finding more effective contrast images. We tested simple selection methods to establish the viability of the approach, leaving the exploration of more sophisticated CI selection strategies to future work. Additionally, our evaluation focuses primarily on VQA and self-retrieval protocols; exploring additional evaluation methods could reveal other aspects of how CoCI affects LVLM generations.

The method introduces additional computation at inference time, running the LVLM twice per generation step and requiring CI selection overhead. While this aligns with the growing trend of leveraging test-time compute for improved performance, the current implementation could be optimized. Future work could explore more efficient implementations of contrastive decoding and investigate fusing operations like hidden state extraction with the generation procedure to reduce computational overhead.

Our implementation uses Flickr30k as the image database for CI selection - using larger, more diverse image collections could improve performance. Alternative image retrieval models and similarity scoring methods could also enhance CI selection. Additionally, our approach does not address cases where multiple contrasts might be informative - we only use a single contrast image, while some scenarios might benefit from multiple contrasting viewpoints.

The experiments use a fixed contrastive weight (α) across tasks within each category (VQA/generation). A more nuanced approach to setting this parameter, dynamically per sample or per token, based on the specific input or task, could yield better results.

While CoCI improves visual discrimination, it could potentially amplify biases present in contrast image databases or introduce new failure modes when inappropriate contrast images are selected. These risks should be carefully evaluated before deployment in sensitive applications.

Finally, our experiments focus exclusively on English-language benchmarks. Extending CoCI to multilingual settings and investigating how contrastive decoding approaches perform across different languages represents an important direction for future research.

References

Ehsan Abbasnejad, Damien Teney, Amin Parvaneh, Javen Shi, and Anton van den Hengel. 2020. Counterfactual vision and language learning. In *2020 IEEE/CVF Conference on Computer Vision and Pattern Recognition (CVPR)*, pages 10041–10051.

Zhiyang Chen, Yousong Zhu, Yufei Zhan, Zhaowen Li, Chaoyang Zhao, Jinqiao Wang, and Ming Tang. 2023. Mitigating hallucination in visual language models with visual supervision.

Mehdi Cherti, Romain Beaumont, Ross Wightman, Mitchell Wortsman, Gabriel Ilharco, Cade Gordon, Christoph Schuhmann, Ludwig Schmidt, and Jenia Jitsev. 2023. Reproducible scaling laws for contrastive language-image learning. In *Proceedings of the IEEE/CVF Conference on Computer Vision and Pattern Recognition*, pages 2818–2829.

Manu Gaur, Darshan Singh S, and Makarand Tapaswi. 2024. Detect, describe, discriminate: Moving beyond vqa for mllm evaluation.

Yash Goyal, Tejas Khot, Douglas Summers-Stay, Dhruv Batra, and Devi Parikh. 2017. Making the v in vqa matter: Elevating the role of image understanding in visual question answering.

Aaron Grattafiori, Abhimanyu Dubey, Abhinav Jauhri, Abhinav Pandey, Abhishek Kadian, Ahmad Al-Dahle, Aiesha Letman, Akhil Mathur, Alan Schelten, Alex Vaughan, Amy Yang, Angela Fan, Anirudh Goyal, Anthony Hartshorn, Aobo Yang, Archi Mitra, Archie Sravankumar, Artem Korenev, Arthur Hinsvark, Arun Rao, Aston Zhang, Aurelien Rodriguez, Austen Gregerson, Ava Spataru, Baptiste Roziere, Bethany Biron, Binh Tang, Bobbie Chern, Charlotte Caucheteux, Chaya Nayak, Chloe Bi, Chris Marra, Chris McConnell, Christian Keller, Christophe Touret, Chunyang Wu, Corinne Wong, Cristian Canton Ferrer, Cyrus Nikolaidis, Damien Allonsius, Daniel Song, Danielle Pintz, Danny Livshits, Danny Wyatt, David Esiobu, Dhruv Choudhary, Dhruv Mahajan, Diego Garcia-Olano, Diego Perino, Dieuwke Hupkes, Egor Lakomkin, Ehab AlBadawy, Elina Lobanova, Emily Dinan, Eric Michael Smith, Filip Radenovic, Francisco Guzmán, Frank Zhang, Gabriel Synnaeve, Gabrielle Lee, Georgia Lewis Anderson, Govind Thattai, Graeme Nail, Gregoire Mialon, Guan Pang, Guillem Cucurell, Hailey Nguyen, Hannah Korevaar, Hu Xu, Hugo Touvron, Iliyan Zarov, Imanol Arrieta Ibarra, Isabel Kloumann, Ishan Misra, Ivan Evtimov, Jack Zhang, Jade Copet, Jaewon Lee, Jan Geffert, Jana Vranes, Jason Park, Jay Mahadeokar, Jeet Shah, Jelmer van der Linde, Jennifer Billock, Jenny Hong, Jenya Lee, Jeremy Fu, Jianfeng Chi, Jianyu Huang, Jiawen Liu, Jie Wang, Jiecao Yu, Joanna Bitton, Joe Spisak, Jongsoo Park,

Joseph Rocca, Joshua Johnstun, Joshua Saxe, Junteng Jia, Kalyan Vasuden Alwala, Karthik Prasad, Kartikeya Upasani, Kate Plawiak, Ke Li, Kenneth Heafield, Kevin Stone, Khalid El-Arini, Krithika Iyer, Kshitiz Malik, Kuenley Chiu, Kunal Bhalla, Kushal Lakhotia, Lauren Rantala-Yeary, Laurens van der Maaten, Lawrence Chen, Liang Tan, Liz Jenkins, Louis Martin, Lovish Madaan, Lubo Malo, Lukas Blecher, Lukas Landzaat, Luke de Oliveira, Madeline Muzzi, Mahesh Pasupuleti, Mannat Singh, Manohar Paluri, Marcin Kardas, Maria Tsimpoukelli, Mathew Oldham, Mathieu Rita, Maya Pavlova, Melanie Kambadur, Mike Lewis, Min Si, Mitesh Kumar Singh, Mona Hassan, Naman Goyal, Narjes Torabi, Nikolay Bashlykov, Nikolay Bogoychev, Niladri Chatterji, Ning Zhang, Olivier Duchenne, Onur Çelebi, Patrick Alrassy, Pengchuan Zhang, Pengwei Li, Petar Vasic, Peter Weng, Prajjwal Bhargava, Pratik Dubal, Praveen Krishnan, Punit Singh Koura, Puxin Xu, Qing He, Qingxiao Dong, Ragavan Srinivasan, Raj Ganapathy, Ramon Calderer, Ricardo Silveira Cabral, Robert Stojnic, Roberta Raileanu, Rohan Maheswari, Rohit Girdhar, Rohit Patel, Romain Sauvestre, Ronnie Polidoro, Roshan Sumbaly, Ross Taylor, Ruan Silva, Rui Hou, Rui Wang, Saghar Hosseini, Sahana Chennabasappa, Sanjay Singh, Sean Bell, Seohyun Sonia Kim, Sergey Edunov, Shaoliang Nie, Sharan Narang, Sharath Raparthy, Sheng Shen, Shengye Wan, Shruti Bhosale, Shun Zhang, Simon Vandenhende, Soumya Batra, Spencer Whitman, Sten Sootla, Stephane Collot, Suchin Gururangan, Sydney Borodinsky, Tamar Herman, Tara Fowler, Tarek Sheasha, Thomas Georgiou, Thomas Scialom, Tobias Speckbacher, Todor Mihaylov, Tong Xiao, Ujjwal Karn, Vedanuj Goswami, Vibhor Gupta, Vignesh Ramanathan, Viktor Kerkez, Vincent Gonguet, Virginie Do, Vish Vogeti, Vítor Albiero, Vladan Petrovic, Weiwei Chu, Wenhan Xiong, Wenyin Fu, Whitney Meers, Xavier Martinet, Xiaodong Wang, Xiaofang Wang, Xiaoqing Ellen Tan, Xide Xia, Xinfeng Xie, Xuchao Jia, Xuewei Wang, Yaelle Goldschlag, Yashesh Gaur, Yasmine Babaei, Yi Wen, Yiwen Song, Yuchen Zhang, Yue Li, Yuning Mao, Zacharie Delpierre Coudert, Zheng Yan, Zhengxing Chen, Zoe Papakipos, Aaditya Singh, Aayushi Srivastava, Abha Jain, Adam Kelsey, Adam Shajnfeld, Adithya Gangidi, Adolfo Victoria, Ahuva Goldstand, Ajay Menon, Ajay Sharma, Alex Boesenberg, Alexei Baevski, Allie Feinstein, Amanda Kallet, Amit Sangani, Amos Teo, Anam Yunus, Andrei Lupu, Andres Alvarado, Andrew Caples, Andrew Gu, Andrew Ho, Andrew Poulton, Andrew Ryan, Ankit Ramchandani, Annie Dong, Annie Franco, Anuj Goyal, Aparajita Saraf, Arkabandhu Chowdhury, Ashley Gabriel, Ashwin Bharambe, Assaf Eisenman, Azadeh Yazdan, Beau James, Ben Maurer, Benjamin Leonhardi, Bernie Huang, Beth Loyd, Beto De Paola, Bhargavi Paranjape, Bing Liu, Bo Wu, Boyu Ni, Braden Hancock, Bram Wasti, Brandon Spence, Brani Stojkovic, Brian Gamido, Britt Montalvo, Carl Parker, Carly Burton, Catalina Mejia, Ce Liu, Changhan Wang, Changkyu Kim, Chao Zhou, Chester Hu, Ching-Hsiang Chu, Chris Cai, Chris Tindal, Christoph Feichtenhofer, Cynthia Gao, Damon Civin, Dana Beaty, Daniel Kreymer, Daniel Li, David Adkins, David Xu, Davide Testuggine, Delia David, Devi Parikh, Diana Liskovich, Didem Foss, Dingkang Wang, Duc Le, Dustin Holland, Edward Dowling, Eissa Jamil, Elaine Montgomery, Eleonora Presani, Emily Hahn, Emily Wood, Eric-Tuan Le, Erik Brinkman, Esteban Arcaute, Evan Dunbar, Evan Smothers, Fei Sun, Felix Kreuk, Feng Tian, Filippos Kokkinos, Firat Ozgenel, Francesco Caggioni, Frank Kanayet, Frank Seide, Gabriela Medina Florez, Gabriella Schwarz, Gada Badeer, Georgia Swee, Gil Halpern, Grant Herman, Grigory Sizov, Guangyi, Zhang, Guna Lakshminarayanan, Hakan Inan, Hamid Shojanazeri, Han Zou, Hannah Wang, Hanwen Zha, Haroun Habeeb, Harrison Rudolph, Helen Suk, Henry Aspegren, Hunter Goldman, Hongyuan Zhan, Ibrahim Damlaj, Igor Molybog, Igor Tufanov, Ilias Leontiadis, Irina-Elena Veliche, Itai Gat, Jake Weissman, James Geboski, James Kohli, Janice Lam, Japhet Asher, Jean-Baptiste Gaya, Jeff Marcus, Jeff Tang, Jennifer Chan, Jenny Zhen, Jeremy Reizenstein, Jeremy Teboul, Jessica Zhong, Jian Jin, Jingyi Yang, Joe Cummings, Jon Carvill, Jon Shepard, Jonathan McPhie, Jonathan Torres, Josh Ginsburg, Junjie Wang, Kai Wu, Kam Hou U, Karan Saxena, Kartikay Khandelwal, Katayoun Zand, Kathy Matosich, Kaushik Veeraraghavan, Kelly Michelena, Keqian Li, Kiran Jagadeesh, Kun Huang, Kunal Chawla, Kyle Huang, Lailin Chen, Lakshya Garg, Lavender A, Leandro Silva, Lee Bell, Lei Zhang, Liangpeng Guo, Licheng Yu, Liron Moshkovich, Luca Wehrstedt, Madian Khabsa, Manav Avalani, Manish Bhatt, Martynas Mankus, Matan Hasson, Matthew Lennie, Matthias Reso, Maxim Groshev, Maxim Naumov, Maya Lathi, Meghan Keneally, Miao Liu, Michael L. Seltzer, Michal Valko, Michelle Restrepo, Mihir Patel, Mik Vyatskov, Mikayel Samvelyan, Mike Clark, Mike Macey, Mike Wang, Miquel Jubert Hermoso, Mo Metanat, Mohammad Rastegari, Munish Bansal, Nandhini Santhanam, Natascha Parks, Natasha White, Navyata Bawa, Nayan Singhal, Nick Egebo, Nicolas Usunier, Nikhil Mehta, Nikolay Pavlovich Laptev, Ning Dong, Norman Cheng, Oleg Chernoguz, Olivia Hart, Omkar Salpekar, Ozlem Kalinli, Parkin Kent, Parth Parekh, Paul Saab, Pavan Balaji, Pedro Rittner, Philip Bontrager, Pierre Roux, Piotr Dollar, Polina Zvyagina, Prashant Ratanchandani, Pritish Yuvraj, Qian Liang, Rachad Alao, Rachel Rodriguez, Rafi Ayub, Raghotham Murthy, Raghu Nayani, Rahul Mitra, Rangaprabhu Parthasarathy, Raymond Li, Rebekkah Hogan, Robin Battey, Rocky Wang, Russ Howes, Ruty Rinott, Sachin Mehta, Sachin Siby, Sai Jayesh Bondu, Samyak Datta, Sara Chugh, Sara Hunt, Sargun Dhillon, Sasha Sidorov, Satadru Pan, Saurabh Mahajan, Saurabh Verma, Seiji Yamamoto, Sharadh Ramaswamy, Shaun Lindsay, Shaun Lindsay, Sheng Feng, Shenghao Lin, Shengxin Cindy Zha, Shishir Patil, Shiva Shankar, Shuqiang Zhang, Shuqiang Zhang, Sinong Wang, Sneha Agarwal, Soji Sajuyigbe, Soumith Chintala, Stephanie Max, Stephen Chen, Steve Kehoe, Steve Satterfield, Sudarshan Govindaprasad, Sumit Gupta, Summer Deng, Sungmin Cho, Sunny Virk, Suraj Subramanian, Sy Choudhury, Sydney Goldman, Tal

Remez, Tamar Glaser, Tamara Best, Thilo Koehler, Thomas Robinson, Tianhe Li, Tianjun Zhang, Tim Matthews, Timothy Chou, Tzook Shaked, Varun Vontimitta, Victoria Ajayi, Victoria Montanez, Vijai Mohan, Vinay Satish Kumar, Vishal Mangla, Vlad Ionescu, Vlad Poenaru, Vlad Tiberiu Mihailescu, Vladimir Ivanov, Wei Li, Wenchen Wang, Wenwen Jiang, Wes Bouaziz, Will Constable, Xiaocheng Tang, Xiaojian Wu, Xiaolan Wang, Xilun Wu, Xinbo Gao, Yaniv Kleinman, Yanjun Chen, Ye Hu, Ye Jia, Ye Qi, Yenda Li, Yilin Zhang, Ying Zhang, Yossi Adi, Youngjin Nam, Yu, Wang, Yu Zhao, Yuchen Hao, Yundi Qian, Yunlu Li, Yuzi He, Zach Rait, Zachary DeVito, Zef Rosnbrick, Zhaoduo Wen, Zhenyu Yang, Zhiwei Zhao, and Zhiyu Ma. 2024. The llama 3 herd of models.

Qidong Huang, Xiao wen Dong, Pan Zhang, Bin Wang, Conghui He, Jiaqi Wang, Dahua Lin, Weiming Zhang, and Neng H. Yu. 2023. Opera: Alleviating hallucination in multi-modal large language models via over-trust penalty and retrospection-allocation. *2024 IEEE/CVF Conference on Computer Vision and Pattern Recognition (CVPR)*, pages 13418–13427.

Fushuo Huo, Wenchao Xu, Zhong Zhang, Haozhao Wang, Zhicheng Chen, and Peilin Zhao. 2024. Self-introspective decoding: Alleviating hallucinations for large vision-language models.

Gabriel Ilharco, Mitchell Wortsman, Ross Wightman, Cade Gordon, Nicholas Carlini, Rohan Taori, Achal Dave, Vaishaal Shankar, Hongseok Namkoong, John Miller, Hannaneh Hajishirzi, Ali Farhadi, and Ludwig Schmidt. 2021. Openclip. If you use this software, please cite it as below.

Jing Jin, Houfeng Wang, Hao Zhang, Xiaoguang Li, and Zhijiang Guo. 2024. DVD: Dynamic contrastive decoding for knowledge amplification in multi-document question answering. In *Proceedings of the 2024 Conference on Empirical Methods in Natural Language Processing*, pages 4624–4637, Miami, Florida, USA. Association for Computational Linguistics.

Tiep Le, Vasudev Lal, and Phillip Howard. 2023. Coco-counterfactuals: Automatically constructed counterfactual examples for image-text pairs.

Sicong Leng, Hang Zhang, Guanzheng Chen, Xin Li, Shijian Lu, Chunyan Miao, and Lidong Bing. 2023. Mitigating object hallucinations in large vision-language models through visual contrastive decoding.

Baiqi Li, Zhiqiu Lin, Wenxuan Peng, Jean de Dieu Nyandwi, Daniel Jiang, Zixian Ma, Simran Khanuja, Ranjay Krishna, Graham Neubig, and Deva Ramanan. 2024a. Naturalbench: Evaluating vision-language models on natural adversarial samples.

Bo Li, Yuanhan Zhang, Dong Guo, Renrui Zhang, Feng Li, Hao Zhang, Kaichen Zhang, Peiyuan Zhang, Yanwei Li, Ziwei Liu, and Chunyuan Li. 2024b. Llava-onevision: Easy visual task transfer.

Xiang Lisa Li, Ari Holtzman, Daniel Fried, Percy Liang, Jason Eisner, Tatsunori Hashimoto, Luke Zettlemoyer, and Mike Lewis. 2023. Contrastive decoding: Open-ended text generation as optimization.

Zhaowei Li, Qi Xu, Dong Zhang, Hang Song, Yiqing Cai, Qi Qi, Ran Zhou, Junting Pan, Zefeng Li, Van Tu Vu, Zhida Huang, and Tao Wang. 2024c. Groundinggpt:language enhanced multi-modal grounding model.

Fuxiao Liu, Kevin Lin, Linjie Li, Jianfeng Wang, Yaser Yacoob, and Lijuan Wang. 2024a. Mitigating hallucination in large multi-modal models via robust instruction tuning.

Sheng Liu, Haotian Ye, Lei Xing, and James Zou. 2024b. Reducing hallucinations in vision-language models via latent space steering.

Ilya Loshchilov and Frank Hutter. 2019. Decoupled weight decay regularization.

Junyu Lu, Dixiang Zhang, Songxin Zhang, Zejian Xie, Zhuoyang Song, Cong Lin, Jiaxing Zhang, Bingyi Jing, and Pingjian Zhang. 2024. Lyrics: Boosting fine-grained language-vision alignment and comprehension via semantic-aware visual objects.

Avshalom Manevich and Reut Tsarfaty. 2024. Mitigating hallucinations in large vision-language models (LVLMs) via language-contrastive decoding (LCD). In *Findings of the Association for Computational Linguistics: ACL 2024*, pages 6008–6022, Bangkok, Thailand. Association for Computational Linguistics.

OpenAI, :, Aaron Hurst, Adam Lerer, Adam P. Goucher, Adam Perelman, Aditya Ramesh, Aidan Clark, AJ Ostrow, Akila Welihinda, Alan Hayes, Alec Radford, Aleksander Mądry, Alex Baker-Whitcomb, Alex Beutel, Alex Borzunov, Alex Carney, Alex Chow, Alex Kirillov, Alex Nichol, Alex Paino, Alex Renzin, Alex Tachard Passos, Alexander Kirillov, Alexi Christakis, Alexis Conneau, Ali Kamali, Allan Jabri, Allison Moyer, Allison Tam, Amadou Crookes, Amin Tootoochian, Amin Tootoonchian, Ananya Kumar, Andrea Vallone, Andrej Karpathy, Andrew Braunstein, Andrew Cann, Andrew Codispoti, Andrew Galu, Andrew Kondrich, Andrew Tulloch, Andrey Mishchenko, Angela Baek, Angela Jiang, Antoine Pelisse, Antonia Woodford, Anuj Gosalia, Arka Dhar, Ashley Pantuliano, Avi Nayak, Avital Oliver, Barret Zoph, Behrooz Ghorbani, Ben Leimberger, Ben Rossen, Ben Sokolowsky, Ben Wang, Benjamin Zweig, Beth Hoover, Blake Samic, Bob McGrew, Bobby Spero, Bogo Giertler, Bowen Cheng, Brad Lightcap, Brandon Walkin, Brendan Quinn, Brian Guarraci, Brian Hsu, Bright Kellogg, Brydon Eastman, Camillo Lugaresi, Carroll Wainwright, Cary Bassin, Cary Hudson, Casey Chu, Chad Nelson, Chak Li, Chan Jun Shern, Channing Conger, Charlotte Barette, Chelsea Voss, Chen Ding, Cheng Lu, Chong Zhang, Chris Beaumont, Chris Hallacy, Chris Koch, Christian Gibson, Christina Kim, Christine Choi, Christine McLeavey, Christopher Hesse, Claudia Fischer, Clemens Winter, Coley Czarnecki, Colin

Jarvis, Colin Wei, Constantin Koumouzelis, Dane Sherburn, Daniel Kappler, Daniel Levin, Daniel Levy, David Carr, David Farhi, David Mely, David Robinson, David Sasaki, Denny Jin, Dev Valladares, Dimitris Tsipras, Doug Li, Duc Phong Nguyen, Duncan Findlay, Edede Oiwoh, Edmund Wong, Ehsan Asdar, Elizabeth Proehl, Elizabeth Yang, Eric Antonow, Eric Kramer, Eric Peterson, Eric Sigler, Eric Wallace, Eugene Brevdo, Evan Mays, Farzad Khorasani, Felipe Petroski Such, Filippo Raso, Francis Zhang, Fred von Lohmann, Freddie Sulit, Gabriel Goh, Gene Oden, Geoff Salmon, Giulio Starace, Greg Brockman, Hadi Salman, Haiming Bao, Haitang Hu, Hannah Wong, Haoyu Wang, Heather Schmidt, Heather Whitney, Heewoo Jun, Hendrik Kirchner, Henrique Ponde de Oliveira Pinto, Hongyu Ren, Huiwen Chang, Hyung Won Chung, Ian Kivlichan, Ian O'Connell, Ian O'Connell, Ian Osband, Ian Silber, Ian Sohl, Ibrahim Okuyucu, Ikai Lan, Ilya Kostrikov, Ilya Sutskever, Ingmar Kanitscheider, Ishaan Gulrajani, Jacob Coxon, Jacob Menick, Jakub Pachocki, James Aung, James Betker, James Crooks, James Lennon, Jamie Kiros, Jan Leike, Jane Park, Jason Kwon, Jason Phang, Jason Teplitz, Jason Wei, Jason Wolfe, Jay Chen, Jeff Harris, Jenia Varavva, Jessica Gan Lee, Jessica Shieh, Ji Lin, Jiahui Yu, Jiayi Weng, Jie Tang, Jieqi Yu, Joanne Jang, Joaquin Quinonero Candela, Joe Beutler, Joe Landers, Joel Parish, Johannes Heidecke, John Schulman, Jonathan Lachman, Jonathan McKay, Jonathan Uesato, Jonathan Ward, Jong Wook Kim, Joost Huizinga, Jordan Sitkin, Jos Kraaijeveld, Josh Gross, Josh Kaplan, Josh Snyder, Joshua Achiam, Joy Jiao, Joyce Lee, Juntang Zhuang, Justyn Harriman, Kai Fricke, Kai Hayashi, Karan Singhal, Katy Shi, Kavin Karthik, Kayla Wood, Kendra Rimbach, Kenny Hsu, Kenny Nguyen, Keren Gu-Lemberg, Kevin Button, Kevin Liu, Kiel Howe, Krithika Muthukumar, Kyle Luther, Lama Ahmad, Larry Kai, Lauren Itow, Lauren Workman, Leher Pathak, Leo Chen, Li Jing, Lia Guy, Liam Fedus, Liang Zhou, Lien Mamitsuka, Lilian Weng, Lindsay McCallum, Lindsey Held, Long Ouyang, Louis Feuvrier, Lu Zhang, Lukas Kondraciuk, Lukasz Kaiser, Luke Hewitt, Luke Metz, Lyric Doshi, Mada Aflak, Maddie Simens, Madelaine Boyd, Madeleine Thompson, Marat Dukhan, Mark Chen, Mark Gray, Mark Hudnall, Marvin Zhang, Marwan Aljubeh, Mateusz Litwin, Matthew Zeng, Max Johnson, Maya Shetty, Mayank Gupta, Meghan Shah, Mehmet Yatbaz, Meng Jia Yang, Mengchao Zhong, Mia Glaese, Mianna Chen, Michael Janner, Michael Lampe, Michael Petrov, Michael Wu, Michele Wang, Michelle Fradin, Michelle Pokrass, Miguel Castro, Miguel Oom Temudo de Castro, Mikhail Pavlov, Miles Brundage, Miles Wang, Minal Khan, Mira Murati, Mo Bavarian, Molly Lin, Murat Yesildal, Nacho Soto, Natalia Gimelshein, Natalie Cone, Natalie Staudacher, Natalie Summers, Natan LaFontaine, Neil Chowdhury, Nick Ryder, Nick Stathas, Nick Turley, Nik Tezak, Niko Felix, Nithanth Kudige, Nitish Keskar, Noah Deutsch, Noel Bundick, Nora Puckett, Ofir Nachum, Ola Okelola, Oleg Boiko, Oleg Murk, Oliver Jaffe, Olivia Watkins, Olivier Godement, Owen Campbell-Moore, Patrick Chao, Paul McMillan, Pavel Belov, Peng Su, Peter Bak, Peter Bakkum, Peter Deng, Peter Dolan, Peter Hoeschele, Peter Welinder, Phil Tillet, Philip Pronin, Philippe Tillet, Prafulla Dhariwal, Qiming Yuan, Rachel Dias, Rachel Lim, Rahul Arora, Rajan Troll, Randall Lin, Rapha Gontijo Lopes, Raul Puri, Reah Miyara, Reimar Leike, Renaud Gaubert, Reza Zamani, Ricky Wang, Rob Donnelly, Rob Honsby, Rocky Smith, Rohan Sahai, Rohit Ramchandani, Romain Huet, Rory Carmichael, Rowan Zellers, Roy Chen, Ruby Chen, Ruslan Nigmatullin, Ryan Cheu, Saachi Jain, Sam Altman, Sam Schoenholz, Sam Toizer, Samuel Miserendino, Sandhini Agarwal, Sara Culver, Scott Ethersmith, Scott Gray, Sean Grove, Sean Metzger, Shamez Hermani, Shantanu Jain, Shengjia Zhao, Sherwin Wu, Shino Jomoto, Shirong Wu, Shuaiqi, Xia, Sonia Phene, Spencer Papay, Srinivas Narayanan, Steve Coffey, Steve Lee, Stewart Hall, Suchir Balaji, Tal Broda, Tal Stramer, Tao Xu, Tarun Gogineni, Taya Christianson, Ted Sanders, Tejal Patwardhan, Thomas Cunninghman, Thomas Degry, Thomas Dimson, Thomas Raoux, Thomas Shadwell, Tianhao Zheng, Todd Underwood, Todor Markov, Toki Sherbakov, Tom Rubin, Tom Stasi, Tomer Kaftan, Tristan Heywood, Troy Peterson, Tyce Walters, Tyna Eloundou, Valerie Qi, Veit Moeller, Vinnie Monaco, Vishal Kuo, Vlad Fomenko, Wayne Chang, Weiyi Zheng, Wenda Zhou, Wesam Manassra, Will Sheu, Wojciech Zaremba, Yash Patil, Yilei Qian, Yongjik Kim, Youlong Cheng, Yu Zhang, Yuchen He, Yuchen Zhang, Yujia Jin, Yunxing Dai, and Yury Malkov. 2024. Gpt-4o system card.

Phuc Phan, Hieu Tran, and Long Phan. 2024. Distillation contrastive decoding: Improving llms reasoning with contrastive decoding and distillation.

Alec Radford, Jong Wook Kim, Chris Hallacy, A. Ramesh, Gabriel Goh, Sandhini Agarwal, Girish Sastry, Amanda Askell, Pamela Mishkin, Jack Clark, Gretchen Krueger, and Ilya Sutskever. 2021a. Learning transferable visual models from natural language supervision. In *ICML*.

Alec Radford, Jong Wook Kim, Chris Hallacy, Aditya Ramesh, Gabriel Goh, Sandhini Agarwal, Girish Sastry, Amanda Askell, Pamela Mishkin, Jack Clark, Gretchen Krueger, and Ilya Sutskever. 2021b. Learning transferable visual models from natural language supervision.

Pritam Sarkar, Sayna Ebrahimi, Ali Etemad, Ahmad Beirami, Sercan Ö. Arık, and Tomas Pfister. 2024. Data-augmented phrase-level alignment for mitigating object hallucination.

Christoph Schuhmann, Romain Beaumont, Richard Vencu, Cade W Gordon, Ross Wightman, Mehdi Cherti, Theo Coombes, Aarush Katta, Clayton Mullis, Mitchell Wortsman, Patrick Schramowski, Srivatsa R Kundurthy, Katherine Crowson, Ludwig Schmidt, Robert Kaczmarczyk, and Jenia Jitsev. 2022. LAION-5b: An open large-scale dataset for training next generation image-text models. In *Thirty-*

sixth Conference on Neural Information Processing Systems Datasets and Benchmarks Track.

Rico Sennrich, Jannis Vamvas, and Alireza Mohammadshahi. 2024. Mitigating hallucinations and off-target machine translation with source-contrastive and language-contrastive decoding.

Shengbang Tong, Zhuang Liu, Yuexiang Zhai, Yi Ma, Yann LeCun, and Saining Xie. 2024. Eyes wide shut? exploring the visual shortcomings of multimodal llms.

Lei Wang, Jiabang He, Shenshen Li, Ning Liu, and Ee-Peng Lim. 2023. Mitigating fine-grained hallucination by fine-tuning large vision-language models with caption rewrites.

Peng Wang, Shuai Bai, Sinan Tan, Shijie Wang, Zhihao Fan, Jinze Bai, Keqin Chen, Xuejing Liu, Jialin Wang, Wenbin Ge, Yang Fan, Kai Dang, Mengfei Du, Xuancheng Ren, Rui Men, Dayiheng Liu, Chang Zhou, Jingren Zhou, and Junyang Lin. 2024a. Qwen2-vl: Enhancing vision-language model's perception of the world at any resolution.

Wei Wang, Zhaowei Li, Qi Xu, Linfeng Li, YiQing Cai, Botian Jiang, Hang Song, Xingcan Hu, Pengyu Wang, and Li Xiao. 2024b. Advancing fine-grained visual understanding with multi-scale alignment in multi-modal models.

Dingchen Yang, Bowen Cao, Guang Chen, and Changjun Jiang. 2024. Pensieve: Retrospect-then-compare mitigates visual hallucination.

Shukang Yin, Chaoyou Fu, Sirui Zhao, Tong Xu, Hao Wang, Dianbo Sui, Yunhang Shen, Ke Li, Xing Sun, and Enhong Chen. 2023. Woodpecker: Hallucination correction for multimodal large language models.

Peter Young, Alice Lai, Micah Hodosh, and Julia Hockenmaier. 2014. From image descriptions to visual denotations: New similarity metrics for semantic inference over event descriptions. *Transactions of the Association for Computational Linguistics*, 2:67–78.

Jianrui Zhang, Mu Cai, Tengyang Xie, and Yong Jae Lee. 2024. Countercurate: Enhancing physical and semantic visio-linguistic compositional reasoning via counterfactual examples.

Baohang Zhou, Ying Zhang, Kehui Song, Hongru Wang, Yu Zhao, Xuhui Sui, and Xiaojie Yuan. 2024. MCIL: Multimodal counterfactual instance learning for low-resource entity-based multimodal information extraction. In *Proceedings of the 2024 Joint International Conference on Computational Linguistics, Language Resources and Evaluation (LREC-COLING 2024)*, pages 11101–11110, Torino, Italia. ELRA and ICCL.

Yiyang Zhou, Chenhang Cui, Jaehong Yoon, Linjun Zhang, Zhun Deng, Chelsea Finn, Mohit Bansal, and Huaxiu Yao. 2023. Analyzing and mitigating object hallucination in large vision-language models. *ArXiv*, abs/2310.00754.

A Appendix

A.1 Lightweight Classifier Implementation Details

Below is the PyTorch code of the lightweight classifier.

```
class Classifier(torch.nn.Module):
    def __init__(self, input_dim: int):
        super(Classifier, self).__init__()
        # factor of 2 due to concatentaion of target and candidate features
        self.linear1 = torch.nn.Linear(input_dim * 2, input_dim)
        self.linear2 = torch.nn.Linear(input_dim, input_dim)
        self.linear3 = torch.nn.Linear(input_dim, 1)
        self.dropout = torch.nn.Dropout(p=0.3)

    def forward(self, x) -> torch.Tensor:
        x = self.dropout(self.linear1(x))
        x = F.relu(x)
        x = self.dropout(self.linear2(x))
        x = F.relu(x)
        x = self.linear3(x)
        return x
```

We trained a classifier per tested LVLM, all with the following parameters, using the AdamW (Loshchilov and Hutter, 2019) optimizer.

```
batch_size=256
num_epochs=13
learning_rate=3e-4
weight_decay=1e-6
```

A.2 LVLM Checkpoints Tested

The following are the LVLM checkpoints we tested CoCI with:

```
Qwen/Qwen2-VL-7B-Instruct
llava-hf/llava-onevision-qwen2-7b-ov-hf
meta-llama/Llama-3.2-11B-Vision-Instruct
```

We used *laion/CLIP-ViT-L-14-DataComp.XL-s13B-b90K* as the open-clip model for both image and text encoding throughout this work.

A.3 Effect of Choosing a Contrast Image on NaturalBench Performance

Method	Setting	Q-acc	I-acc	Acc	G-acc
CoCI ablations	Baseline	51.6	55.4	75.1	25.6
	CI ←Random (out of top-5 most similar to input)	49.6	52.1	73.8	23.2
	CI ←Natural	**71.8**	**70.8**	**84.3**	**51.6**
	CI ←Most similar to input	49.7	52.5	73.6	23.9
	CI ←Most similar to Natural	60.3	60.7	78.9	35.0
	CI ←Least similar to Natural	46.7	48.9	72.6	21.8
Classifier	$k = 4$	51.7	54.3	74.5	26.6
	$k = 8$	53.0	55.4	75.3	26.6
	$k = 16$	54.3	56.8	76.1	29.2
	$k = 32$	52.2	54.6	75.1	25.8
	$k = 64$	51.8	53.9	74.7	26.3
	$k = 100$	52.1	54.1	74.8	25.5
$\text{Classifier}_{\text{+augmentations}}$	$k = 4$	52.0	54.3	74.6	27.1
	$k = 8$	52.8	55.9	75.0	27.9
	$k = 16$	54.5	57.8	76.1	29.2
	$k = 32$	54.9	58.2	75.9	30.0
	$k = 64$	54.7	57.9	76.1	30.3
	$k = 100$	54.7	58.0	76.1	30.0

Table 3: CoCI performance on the NaturalBench dev set with different CI selection methods, using Qwen2-VL. $\text{Classifier}_{\text{+augmentations}}$ indicates training data augmentation with GPT-4o paraphrased questions and standard image augmentations. Using natural CIs provides the strongest performance gains, with a 26-point improvement in group accuracy over baseline (51.6% vs 25.6%). Selecting CIs by similarity to natural CIs improves performance significantly (35.0% G-acc), while using the least similar images performs worse than baseline (21.8%), validating the importance of CI selection strategy. Random CI selection hurts performance (23.2% G-acc) even when restricted to similar images, highlighting that similarity alone is insufficient. Training with augmented data provides modest but consistent improvements across all metrics, with G-acc increasing by about 4 points compared to the non-augmented classifier. The augmented classifier also demonstrates more robust performance, maintaining consistent scores across different k values compared to the higher variance seen in the non-augmented version.

A.4 Examples of Image Pairs and Their Descriptions from D3

The following pairs of images with their respective captions are sampled from D3 results, obtained using CoCI with Natural Contrast Images and Qwen 7B.

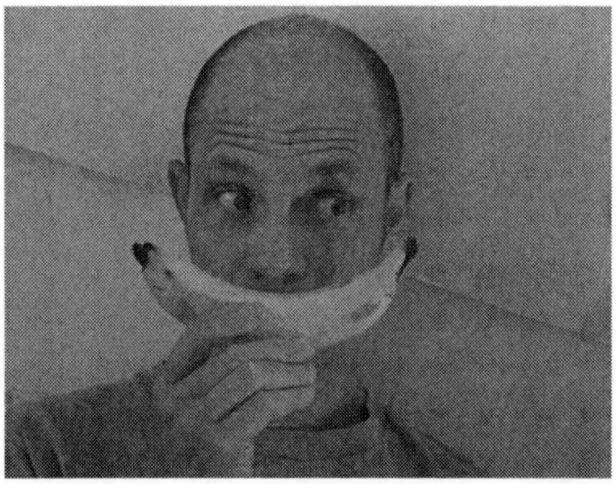

Baseline: The image shows a person holding a banana in front of their mouth. The person is wearing a green shirt and is standing against a plain wall. The banana is positioned in such a way that it appears to be covering the person's mouth, creating a humorous or playful effect. The background is simple and uncluttered, which helps to focus attention on the person and the banana.
CoCI: The image shows a person holding a banana close to their face. The person appears to be making an exaggerated facial expression, with their eyes wide open and eyebrows raised. The background is a plain, light-colored wall.

Baseline: The image shows a person holding a banana in front of their mouth, creating the illusion of a smile. The person is wearing a green shirt and is standing against a plain wall. The banana is positioned in such a way that it covers the lower part of the person's face, mimicking a smile. The lighting in the image is even, and the background is simple and uncluttered.
CoCI: The image depicts a man with a light complexion wearing a green shirt. He is leaning against a wall, which appears to be a combination of light and dark shades, possibly indicating a corner or a wall with different sections. The man is holding a banana in his right hand, and he has placed the banana horizontally across his mouth, creating a playful expression that resembles a mustache. The banana has some dark spots on it, suggesting it is ripe. The background is relatively plain, with no visible decorations or objects, focusing the viewer's attention on the man and the banana.

Figure 3: Comparison of baseline and CoCI captions. The baseline captions are very similar and provide no information that allows to discriminate between the images, while the left CoCI caption mentions the raised eyebrows.

Baseline: The image depicts the iconic Elizabeth Tower, commonly known as Big Ben, located in London, England. The tower is a prominent example of Gothic Revival architecture and is part of the Palace of Westminster. The photograph captures the upper portion of the tower, focusing on its clock face and the ornate details of its structure.
CoCI: The image showcases a close-up view of a prominent clock tower, which is characterized by its Gothic architectural style. The tower is adorned with intricate details and features two large, circular clock faces, one on each visible side of the structure. Both clocks are encased in ornate frames, which are embellished with decorative patterns and motifs.

Baseline: The image depicts the iconic Elizabeth Tower, commonly known as Big Ben, located in London, England. The tower is a prominent example of Gothic Revival architecture and is part of the Palace of Westminster. The clock face is visible in the center of the tower, displaying the time. The clock is encased in a decorative frame with intricate designs, and the hands of the clock are clearly visible. The tower is topped with a spire and a weathervane, which adds to its historical and architectural significance. The sky in the background is clear, providing a sharp contrast to the detailed stonework of the tower.
CoCI: The image depicts the iconic clock tower known as Big Ben, located in London, England. The tower is part of the Palace of Westminster and is one of the most recognizable landmarks in the world.

Figure 4: Comparison of baseline and CoCI captions. The left CoCI caption mentions the two visible clock faces.

Baseline: The image depicts a person engaged in windsurfing, a water sport that combines elements of surfing and sailing. The individual is standing on a windsurfing board, which is partially submerged in the water. ... The individual appears to be in a standing position, holding onto the sail with both hands, indicating that they are actively maneuvering the board.
CoCI: The image depicts a person engaging in the water sport of windsurfing near a beach. The individual is wearing a black wetsuit and appears to be holding onto the sail of the windsurfing board ... The person appears to be standing in shallow water, with their upper body and arms visible above the waterline.

Baseline: The image depicts a person engaged in windsurfing, an activity that combines elements of surfing and sailing. The windsurfer is standing on a surfboard, which is partially submerged in the water ... The individual's posture suggests they are actively maneuvering the sail, likely using their body weight and the wind to control the direction and speed of the board.
CoCI: The image depicts a windsurfer riding a wave in the ocean. The windsurfer is captured from the side, showing their body leaning back as they navigate the wave ... The windsurfer is wearing dark clothing and appears to be in motion, with the water splashing around their feet as they ride the wave. ...

Figure 5: Comparison of baseline and CoCI captions. The CoCI captions describe the state of the windsurfer: standing in the shallow water vs. riding the wave.

MT2ST: Adaptive Multi-Task to Single-Task Learning

Dong Liu
Yale University
Department of Computer Science
dong.liu.dl2367@yale.edu

Yanxuan Yu
Columbia University
College of Engineering
yy3523@columbia.edu

Abstract

We propose **MT2ST**, a general and efficient framework for accelerating multi-task training by progressively transitioning to single-task optimization. Unlike conventional multi-task learning (MTL) or single-task fine-tuning (STL), MT2ST dynamically adjusts the training focus via two complementary strategies: *Diminish*, which gradually down-weights auxiliary losses, and *Switch*, which explicitly switches to the primary task at a scheduled point. We demonstrate the effectiveness of MT2ST across three key paradigms: representation learning, transformers, and diffusion models, covering both unimodal (text/image) and multimodal (vision-language) tasks. Extensive experiments show that MT2ST significantly improves training efficiency—achieving up to 56% FLOPs compression—while maintaining or surpassing task performance. These results suggest MT2ST as a general-purpose solution for scalable and adaptive multi-task training. Although this work is general-purpose, it is especially suitable for multimodal settings such as VQA or vision-language retrieval, where auxiliary pretraining (e.g., masked language modeling or contrastive learning) often diverges from final objectives. We include a VQA case study and outline its efficiency for multimodal retrieval in §4.

1 Introduction

The rapid evolution of large-scale models in machine learning (ML), particularly in natural language processing (NLP), computer vision (CV), and speech recognition, has brought tremendous advances in task performance but also increased the demand for computational efficiency. As models grow in parameter size and data requirements, efficient training strategies have become indispensable for scalable deployment and practical adaptation. Among these, the training of task-specific embeddings remains a fundamental component, serving as the backbone for semantic representation in both unimodal and multimodal applications [Mikolov et al., 2013, Zhang and Yang, 2021].

A major trade-off emerges in the choice of training paradigm: single-task learning (STL) vs. multi-task learning (MTL). STL enables high-fidelity adaptation to a specific task objective, often yielding superior precision. However, it lacks inductive bias and representation reuse, limiting generalization. In contrast, MTL introduces auxiliary tasks that can guide shared representation learning, promoting robustness and faster convergence, especially in low-resource regimes [Wang et al., 2020, Chung et al., 2022]. Nevertheless, MTL is not without cost: task interference, gradient conflict [Sener and Koltun, 2018], and heterogeneous learning dynamics can degrade both convergence speed and final task performance [Zhang et al., 2023, Zhang and Yang, 2021, Yu et al., 2020].

To address this dilemma, we propose the **Multi-Task to Single-Task (MT2ST)** framework—an adaptive training strategy that combines the strengths of MTL and STL by dynamically shifting the training focus from a multi-task setup to a single-task objective. As illustrated in Figure 1, MT2ST is based on a key insight: shared learning in the early stages of training helps build generalized representations, but over time, specialization is necessary to maximize performance on the main task.

MT2ST incorporates two strategies for controlling this transition:

- **Diminish Strategy**: progressively reduces the gradient contribution of auxiliary tasks through a decaying weight schedule, allowing a smooth prioritization of the main task.
- **Switch Strategy**: enforces a discrete transition at a predetermined training epoch,

Proceedings of the 1st Workshop on Multimodal Augmented Generation via Multimodal Retrieval (MAGMaR 2025), pages 79–89
August 1, 2025 ©2025 Association for Computational Linguistics

abruptly removing auxiliary tasks to focus entirely on the primary objective.

Our approach is simple, lightweight, and does not require architecture modifications, making it compatible with most encoder-decoder or encoder-only models. Furthermore, MT2ST is domain-agnostic: although demonstrated on word embedding learning, its core principles apply naturally to image embeddings, multimodal fusion models, and task-specific adaptation in recommendation or healthcare systems.

We conduct comprehensive experiments showing that MT2ST significantly reduces training time while improving or preserving performance. In particular, MT2ST achieves up to 67% training speed-up over STL and 13% over conventional MTL on embedding tasks, all while maintaining competitive accuracy. These results suggest that MT2ST can be a general-purpose mechanism for efficient task-oriented representation learning.

Contributions To summarize, our contributions are as follows:

- We propose the MT2ST framework that effectively bridges MTL and STL for efficient embedding training.
- We introduce two complementary transition mechanisms—Diminish and Switch—for balancing generalization and specialization over training time.
- We demonstrate that MT2ST achieves significant improvements in convergence speed, training efficiency, and model compression across NLP benchmarks, and we discuss its extension to vision and multimodal domains.

2 Motivation

2.1 Challenges in Single-Task Representation Learning

Representation learning is fundamental in modern machine learning systems, as it enables models to map high-dimensional input data—such as text, images, or structured signals—into dense, semantically meaningful vector spaces. These representations support a wide range of downstream tasks across domains including natural language processing (NLP), computer vision, and speech processing. However, the training of high-quality representations remains challenging due to several computational and optimization-related obstacles.

Data Scale and Cost. Effective representation learning typically demands large-scale datasets to capture contextual and task-relevant patterns. As datasets grow in size and complexity, training time and resource requirements increase significantly [Ebner et al., 2019, Liu and Pister, 2024]. This presents a practical barrier to deploying scalable machine learning solutions, particularly for real-time or resource-constrained environments.

Computational Complexity. Learning expressive representations often involves deep architectures and iterative optimization over millions or billions of parameters. This leads to high computational costs and energy consumption [Liu et al., 2024], prompting the need for efficient training strategies and algorithmic improvements.

Optimization Challenges. The optimization landscape of representation learning is typically non-convex and high-dimensional, making convergence difficult and sensitive to initialization, batch composition, and training dynamics [Zeng and Nie, 2021, Ban and Ji, 2024, Zhao et al., 2023]. These challenges are amplified in real-world settings where data is noisy, multi-modal, or weakly labeled.

2.2 Improving Training Efficiency via Multi-Task Learning

Multi-task learning (MTL) is a widely adopted paradigm aimed at improving model efficiency and generalization by jointly training on multiple related tasks. In MTL, shared representations are learned across tasks, allowing the model to benefit from auxiliary supervision and mutual inductive bias [Caruana, 1997]. MTL has proven effective across domains, including NLP [Zhang et al., 2023, Su et al., 2022], computer vision [Lopes et al., 2024, Zhang and Yang, 2021], and speech recognition.

Shared Representations and Generalization. By learning shared features that are relevant to multiple tasks, MTL reduces overfitting and improves generalization, especially in scenarios with limited data for the primary task. For instance, in NLP, MTL setups that combine syntax, semantics, and discourse tasks have yielded more robust representations.

Training Efficiency. MTL also offers computational efficiency by allowing multiple tasks to share a common forward pass, thereby amortizing cost across task-specific outputs [Standley et al., 2020]. Additionally, auxiliary tasks can act as a form of regularization, stabilizing the training process and encouraging smoother optimization.

2.3 Limitations of MTL for General Representation Learning

Despite its benefits, MTL introduces several inefficiencies when naively applied to general-purpose representation learning.

Gradient Conflicts. A major challenge in MTL is the conflict between gradients from different tasks, which may push shared parameters in opposing directions [Sener and Koltun, 2018]. Such interference can result in suboptimal representations and unstable training dynamics. Several studies [Yu et al., 2020, Liu et al., 2021] propose techniques such as gradient projection or conflict-averse optimization to mitigate this issue, though these approaches increase model complexity.

Computational Overhead. MTL may incur additional computational cost due to task-specific heads, losses, and gradient computations. As the number of tasks increases, these costs accumulate, reducing the practical efficiency gains of MTL [Zhang et al., 2023].

Scalability and Task Imbalance. Scaling MTL to many tasks often results in task imbalance and dominance by easier or higher-resource tasks. This imbalance can distort the shared representations and lead to underperformance on the primary task [Ruder, 2017, Ahmad et al., 2018, Trabelsi et al., 2021].

2.4 Motivating MT2ST: From Multi-Task to Single-Task

Given the strengths and limitations of both STL and MTL, we propose a hybrid strategy—**MT2ST**—which begins with multi-task learning to benefit from auxiliary tasks, and gradually transitions to single-task learning to focus model capacity on the primary task. MT2ST incorporates two core mechanisms: *Diminish*, which progressively reduces the influence of auxiliary tasks during training, and *Switch*, which fully shifts the optimization objective to the main task at a specific training point.

This strategy allows us to leverage the generalization benefits of MTL in the early phase of training while achieving task-specific precision during the later phase. In subsequent sections, we formalize the MT2ST framework and demonstrate its effectiveness across various representation learning scenarios.

3 Methodology

3.1 MT2ST Framework

We introduce the MT2ST (Multi-Task to Single-Task) framework to optimize embedding generation training. It combines multi-task learning (MTL) and single-task learning (STL) to achieve efficient training while overcoming common challenges in multi-task environments.

The process starts with MTL, where a unified model with a shared embedding layer is trained across multiple tasks. This allows the model to capture diverse linguistic features and semantic knowledge. The shared embedding layer benefits from varied inputs, providing a more generalized word representation [Liu et al., 2019].

After the MTL phase, MT2ST transitions to STL, fine-tuning the pre-trained embeddings for specific tasks. This phase refines the embeddings to match the unique requirements of each task, improving performance while retaining the knowledge gained from the MTL phase. Techniques like adaptive learning rates and selective freezing of embedding dimensions ensure a smooth transition and maintain the balance between generalization and specialization [Treviso et al., 2023].

3.2 Model Construction

We denote a multi-task training model as a composition of shared and task-specific modules. Let $\mathcal{T}_0$ be the primary task and $\{\mathcal{T}_k\}_{k=1}^{K}$ be auxiliary tasks. Given an input text sequence $X = (x_1, x_2, \ldots, x_n)$, we first encode it via a tokenizer $\mathcal{E} : \mathcal{X} \to \mathbb{N}^n$, followed by an embedding lookup $\mathcal{V} \in \mathbb{R}^{|\mathcal{V}| \times d}$, such that:

$$\mathbf{X} = \mathcal{V}(\mathcal{E}(X)) \in \mathbb{R}^{n \times d}, \tag{1}$$

where n is the input length and d is the hidden dimension.

The embedded input $\mathbf{X}$ is then passed through a shared encoder $f_\theta : \mathbb{R}^{n \times d} \to \mathbb{R}^{n \times d}$ (e.g., stacked Transformer layers), which is optimized across all tasks during the multi-task phase. The shared representation is denoted as:

$$\mathbf{H} = f_\theta(\mathbf{X}). \tag{2}$$

For each task $\mathcal{T}_k$, we define a task-specific head $g_k : \mathbb{R}^{n \times d} \rightarrow \mathbb{R}^{C_k}$ to generate predictions $\hat{\mathbf{y}}_k$:

$$\hat{\mathbf{y}}_k = g_k(\mathbf{H}) = \text{Softmax}\left(\mathbf{W}_k \cdot \text{Pool}(\mathbf{H}) + \mathbf{b}_k\right), \tag{3}$$

where $\text{Pool}(\cdot)$ is either mean pooling or [CLS] vector, and C_k is the number of classes for task $\mathcal{T}_k$.

The total loss at step t is computed as a weighted combination:

$$\mathcal{L}_t = \mathcal{L}_0 + \sum_{k=1}^{K} \gamma_k(t) \cdot \mathcal{L}_k, \tag{4}$$

where $\gamma_k(t)$ is a dynamic importance weight controlled by either the **Diminish** or **Switch** strategy:

$$\gamma_k(t) = \begin{cases} \gamma_{k,0} \cdot e^{-\eta_k t^{\nu_k}}, & \text{Diminish strategy}, \\ \mathbb{I}[t < T_{\text{switch}}], & \text{Switch strategy}. \end{cases} \tag{5}$$

Additionally, a feedback mechanism monitors $\mathcal{L}_0$ over time to adaptively adjust $\gamma_k(t)$ or trigger early transition to single-task optimization.

This construction allows MT2ST to effectively fuse general representation learning via multi-tasking with specialized refinement through single-task fine-tuning, all within a unified Transformer-based architecture.

3.3 Model Overview

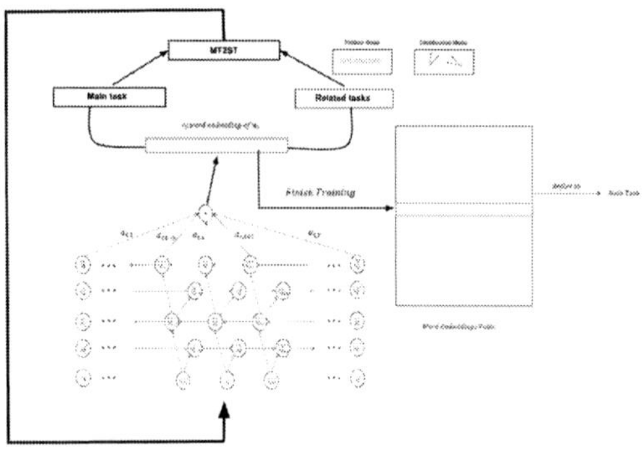

Figure 1: MT2ST Training Framework Overview

3.4 MT2ST: Diminish Strategy

The Diminish strategy is designed to enable a smooth and continuous transition from multi-task learning (MTL) to single-task learning (STL) by gradually reducing the influence of auxiliary tasks over time. This is achieved through a time-aware dynamic weighting scheme that modulates the optimization objective at each training iteration.

Formally, let $\mathcal{T}_0$ denote the primary task and $\{\mathcal{T}_k\}_{k=1}^{K}$ represent K auxiliary tasks. Given an input sequence $X \in \mathcal{X}$, a shared encoder network $f(\cdot;\theta)$ parameterized by θ first produces the intermediate representation:

$$\mathbf{h} = f(X;\theta), \quad \mathbf{h} \in \mathbb{R}^d. \tag{6}$$

At training step t, the overall loss $\mathcal{L}_t$ is computed as a weighted sum of the primary task loss $\mathcal{L}_0$ and each auxiliary task loss $\mathcal{L}_k$:

$$\mathcal{L}_t = \mathcal{L}_0 + \sum_{k=1}^{K} \gamma_k(t) \cdot \mathcal{L}_k, \tag{7}$$

where the time-dependent weight $\gamma_k(t)$ controls the contribution of the k-th auxiliary task and is defined as an exponentially decaying function:

$$\gamma_k(t) = \gamma_{k,0} \cdot \exp\left(-\eta_k t^{\nu_k}\right), \tag{8}$$

with initial coefficient $\gamma_{k,0} > 0$, decay rate $\eta_k > 0$, and curvature $\nu_k \geq 1$ for each $k \in \{1, \ldots, K\}$.

The model parameters are updated using standard gradient descent:

$$\theta^{(t+1)} = \theta^{(t)} - \eta \cdot \nabla_\theta \mathcal{L}_t, \tag{9}$$

which, expanded, becomes:

$$\theta^{(t+1)} = \theta^{(t)} - \eta\left(\nabla\mathcal{L}_0 + \sum_{k=1}^{K} \gamma_k(t) \cdot \nabla\mathcal{L}_k\right). \tag{10}$$

This formulation allows the model to benefit from auxiliary supervision during early training, while progressively biasing optimization toward the primary objective as training proceeds. When $t \rightarrow \infty$, $\gamma_k(t) \rightarrow 0$, and the model converges to an STL setting.

3.5 MT2ST: Switch Strategy

The Switch strategy is a hard transition mechanism that separates the training process into two discrete phases: a multi-task phase followed by a single-task phase. Initially, the model learns shared representations from both the primary and auxiliary tasks. At a predefined switch step T_{switch}, the auxiliary task losses are discarded and only the primary task objective is optimized henceforth.

Let $\theta^{(t)}$ denote the model parameters at step t, and let $\mathcal{L}_0$ and $\mathcal{L}_k$ denote the loss for the primary task and the k-th auxiliary task, respectively. Then, the training objective is defined piecewise as:

$$\mathcal{L}_t = \begin{cases} \mathcal{L}_0 + \sum_{k=1}^{K} \mathcal{L}_k, & \text{if } t < T_{\text{switch}} \\ \mathcal{L}_0, & \text{if } t \geq T_{\text{switch}}. \end{cases} \tag{11}$$

Algorithm 1: MT2ST: Diminish Strategy

input : Input X, initial parameters $\theta^{(0)}$, $\gamma_{k,0}$, η_k, ν_k, learning rate η, total steps T

output: Final parameters θ^*

for $t \leftarrow 1$ **to** T **do**
  h $\leftarrow f(X; \theta^{(t)})$;
  Compute $\nabla \mathcal{L}_0, \nabla \mathcal{L}_k$ for $k = 1, \ldots, K$;
  for $k \leftarrow 1$ **to** K **do**
    $\gamma_k(t) \leftarrow \gamma_{k,0} \cdot \exp(-\eta_k t^{\nu_k})$;
  $\nabla \mathcal{L}_t \leftarrow \nabla \mathcal{L}_0 + \sum_{k=1}^{K} \gamma_k(t) \cdot \nabla \mathcal{L}_k$;
  $\theta^{(t+1)} \leftarrow \theta^{(t)} - \eta \cdot \nabla \mathcal{L}_t$;

Algorithm 2: MT2ST: Switch Strategy

input : Input X, initial parameters $\theta^{(0)}$, switch step T_{switch}, learning rate η, total steps T

output: Final parameters θ^*

for $t \leftarrow 1$ **to** T **do**
  h $\leftarrow f(X; \theta^{(t)})$;
  if $t < T_{switch}$ **then**
    Compute $\nabla \mathcal{L}_0, \nabla \mathcal{L}_k$ for $k = 1, \ldots, K$;
    $\nabla \mathcal{L}_t \leftarrow \nabla \mathcal{L}_0 + \sum_{k=1}^{K} \nabla \mathcal{L}_k$;
  else
    Compute $\nabla \mathcal{L}_0$;
    $\nabla \mathcal{L}_t \leftarrow \nabla \mathcal{L}_0$;
  $\theta^{(t+1)} \leftarrow \theta^{(t)} - \eta \cdot \nabla \mathcal{L}_t$;

Accordingly, the gradient-based parameter update rule becomes:

$$\theta^{(t+1)} = \begin{cases} \theta^{(t)} - \eta\Big(\nabla \mathcal{L}_0 \\ \quad + \sum\limits_{k=1}^{K} \nabla \mathcal{L}_k\Big), & t < T_{\text{switch}} \\ \theta^{(t)} - \eta \nabla \mathcal{L}_0, & t \geq T_{\text{switch}} \end{cases} \tag{12}$$

where η denotes the learning rate.

This strategy enables the model to leverage cross-task signals in the early stage, while avoiding gradient conflict and unnecessary computation in later training stages by switching to STL mode. It is particularly beneficial when auxiliary tasks are loosely correlated or potentially harmful in the long term.

4 MT2ST Deployment

In this section, we formally describe how MT2ST is deployed across three representative paradigms: representation learning, transformer-based architectures, and diffusion models. We focus on the formulation of adaptive learning weights $\gamma_k(t)$ and present unique integration strategies in each context. To avoid redundancy, core mechanisms such as task weighting decay and switching dynamics already discussed in §3 are omitted.

4.1 MT2ST for Representation Learning

Let $f_\theta : \mathcal{X} \to \mathbb{R}^d$ denote an encoder that transforms inputs $x \in \mathcal{X}$ into latent vectors. The primary task is associated with loss $\mathcal{L}_0$, and K auxiliary tasks are defined by $\{\mathcal{L}_k\}_{k=1}^{K}$. The adaptive contribution of each task is governed by the normalized inverse gradient norm:

$$\gamma_k(t) = \begin{array}{c} \dfrac{\|\nabla_\theta \mathcal{L}_0\|_2}{\|\nabla_\theta \mathcal{L}_k\|_2 + \epsilon} \\ \text{with } \sum\limits_{k=1}^{K} \gamma_k(t) = \lambda. \end{array} \tag{13}$$

Here, ϵ is a small constant for numerical stability and λ is a tunable budget.

Algorithm 3: Adaptive MT2ST for Representation Learning

Input : Input data x, primary loss $\mathcal{L}_0$, auxiliary losses $\{\mathcal{L}_k\}$

for $t = 1$ *to* T **do**
  Encode $z \leftarrow f_\theta(x)$;
  Compute $\nabla_\theta \mathcal{L}_0$ and $\nabla_\theta \mathcal{L}_k$ for all k;
  Update $\gamma_k(t)$ using Eq. (**??**);
  $\theta \leftarrow \theta - \eta \cdot (\nabla_\theta \mathcal{L}_0 + \sum_k \gamma_k(t) \nabla_\theta \mathcal{L}_k)$;

4.2 MT2ST for Transformers

Let a transformer block be parameterized by $\theta = \{\theta_{\text{enc}}, \theta_{\text{task}}^k\}$, where θ_{enc} denotes shared encoder weights and θ_{task}^k corresponds to each task-specific head. We compute adaptive task weights using the relative Fisher information:

$$\gamma_k(t) = \frac{\text{Tr}(\mathbb{E}[\nabla^2_{\theta_{\text{enc}}} \mathcal{L}_k])}{\sum_{j=1}^{K} \text{Tr}(\mathbb{E}[\nabla^2_{\theta_{\text{enc}}} \mathcal{L}_j])} \cdot \lambda. \tag{14}$$

This ensures tasks with higher curvature (importance) are given proportionally more attention during shared parameter updates.

4.3 MT2ST for Diffusion Models

Let $f_\theta(\mathbf{x}_t, t)$ denote the noise predictor of a denoising diffusion model. In multi-task diffusion training, each auxiliary task $\mathcal{L}_k$ contributes a variance-aware signal based on expected per-step noise variance $\sigma_k^2(t)$:

$$\gamma_k(t) = \frac{\lambda}{\sigma_k^2(t) + \epsilon}, \quad \text{normalized over } k. \tag{15}$$

This prioritizes tasks that operate under more stable or confident conditions.

This deployment allows MT2ST to dynamically and efficiently adapt to diverse training environments by leveraging the structure of the underlying learning paradigms.

Algorithm 4: Adaptive MT2ST for Transformers

Input: Batch x, Transformer model f_θ with shared and task heads

for $t = 1$ *to* T **do**
  Forward: $\mathbf{h} = \text{Encoder}_\theta(x)$;
  Compute task losses $\mathcal{L}_k = \mathcal{L}_k(f^k_{\text{head}}(\mathbf{h}))$;
  Estimate curvature: $\text{FI}_k = \text{Tr}(\mathbb{E}[\nabla^2_{\theta_{\text{enc}}} \mathcal{L}_k])$;
  $\gamma_k(t) \leftarrow \text{FI}_k / \sum_j \text{FI}_j \cdot \lambda$;
  Update θ using combined loss $\mathcal{L}_0 + \sum_k \gamma_k(t)\mathcal{L}_k$;

Algorithm 5: Adaptive MT2ST for Diffusion Models

Input: Time step t, noisy sample $\mathbf{x}_t$, auxiliary noise predictors f^k_θ

for $t = 1$ *to* T **do**
  Sample $\epsilon \sim \mathcal{N}(0, I)$, construct $\mathbf{x}_t$;
  Compute $\mathcal{L}_0 = \|f_\theta(\mathbf{x}_t, t) - \epsilon\|^2$;
  Compute auxiliary losses $\mathcal{L}_k$ with noise variance $\sigma^2_k(t)$;
  $\gamma_k(t) \leftarrow \frac{1}{\sigma^2_k(t)+\epsilon} \cdot \lambda$;
  $\theta \leftarrow \theta - \eta \cdot \nabla_\theta \left(\mathcal{L}_0 + \sum_k \gamma_k(t)\mathcal{L}_k\right)$;

5 Experiments and Applications

We evaluate the proposed MT2ST framework to answer the following research questions:

Q1: How do the Diminish and Switch strategies impact training efficiency and performance?

Q2: What are the effects of MT2ST across various models and architectures?

Q3: Can MT2ST generalize across modalities such as vision, text, and multimodal systems?

5.1 Comparison with Prior Work

We compare MT2ST with representative multi-task optimization frameworks including PCGrad [Yu et al., 2020], GradDrop [Yu et al., 2017], and TaskRouting [Strezoski et al., 2019]. All methods are evaluated on the MNLI and VQA benchmarks under the same backbone (BERT-base or ViLT) and training schedule.

Method	MNLI Acc. (%)	VQA Acc. (%)
PCGrad [Yu et al., 2020]	83.6	69.9
GradDrop [Yu et al., 2017]	84.1	70.4
MT2ST-D (Ours)	84.2	70.6
MT2ST-S (Ours)	**85.0**	**71.8**

Table 1: Comparison with multi-task optimization methods on MNLI and VQA. MT2ST-S achieves the best accuracy.

These results demonstrate that MT2ST achieves comparable or better performance than existing multi-task scheduling methods, while remaining architecture-agnostic and easier to implement.

5.2 MT2ST in Representation Learning

Setup We begin with classic representation learning models including CBOW, Skip-Gram, FastText, and GloVeTwitter. These models are evaluated on analogy and similarity tasks. We consider the following four configurations:

- STL: Single-task fine-tuning baseline.
- MTL: Multi-task training with shared backbone.
- MT2ST-D: MT2ST with Diminish strategy.
- MT2ST-S: MT2ST with Switch strategy.

Training is done using cosine learning rate schedule, with early stopping based on validation loss. Evaluation includes accuracy, training time, convergence speed, and compression rate (defined as FLOPs reduction vs STL).

Findings (Q1 + Q2) Table 2 shows MT2ST substantially boosts efficiency and convergence speed. Compared to STL, MT2ST-S improves accuracy by 6–11%, reduces training time by over 40%, and converges in fewer epochs. Notably, performance gains are more pronounced for syntactic reasoning tasks, suggesting that MT2ST benefits structure-sensitive learning processes.

5.3 Generalization to Non-Text Modalities (Q3)

Setup To validate cross-modal generalization, we extend MT2ST to vision classification tasks using ResNet-18 and MobileNetV2 as backbones. We train on CIFAR-100 and TinyImageNet, with the primary task being object classification. Auxiliary tasks include edge prediction and representation contrastive learning.

Findings (Q3) As shown in Table 3, MT2ST strategies provide significant gains in vision tasks as well. MT2ST-S offers +2–3% accuracy over STL with a 30–40% reduction in training time. The results confirm that MT2ST generalizes beyond textual data, effectively optimizing task coordination in vision models.

Observations Table 3 shows that MT2ST improves accuracy while reducing training time in image embedding settings as well. This demonstrates that the MT2ST paradigm, though originally designed for word embedding, generalizes well to vision tasks by dynamically adjusting task weights. MT2ST-S shows superior convergence speed and accuracy on both text and image representation tasks. The dynamic phase transition enables early generalization and late specialization.

5.4 MT2ST in Transformers

Setup We use T5-small and BERT-base on:

- **Text:** GLUE (MNLI, SST-2, QQP), with MNLI as the primary task.
- **Multimodal:** Visual Question Answering (VQA v2.0) with ViLT [Kim et al., 2021]

The auxiliary tasks include paraphrase detection and sentiment classification. For VQA, the auxiliary task is masked language modeling. Training is done with batch size 64, learning rate 3e-5, and AdamW optimizer.

Model	Strategy	Accuracy (%)	Training Time (s)	Compression Rate (%)	Convergence Epochs	Semantic Acc	Syntactic Acc
CBOW	STL	68.0	108.0	0.0	25	65.0	60.2
	MTL	68.0	60.0	21.0	22	68.3	61.7
	MT2ST-D	71.0	72.0	44.0	18	72.4	66.5
	MT2ST-S	**77.0**	**64.8**	**53.0**	**16**	**76.1**	**70.2**
Skip-Gram	STL	67.0	110.0	0.0	25	64.2	59.7
	MTL	67.0	63.2	20.1	22	67.8	61.3
	MT2ST-D	74.0	69.5	47.2	18	73.6	68.0
	MT2ST-S	**78.0**	**65.1**	**56.1**	**15**	**77.0**	**71.3**
FastText	STL	70.0	107.4	0.0	25	66.0	63.5
	MTL	70.0	62.1	22.6	22	70.3	66.1
	MT2ST-D	76.0	70.2	46.4	18	75.1	69.7
	MT2ST-S	**79.0**	**65.5**	**52.9**	**16**	**78.0**	**72.4**
GloVeTwitter	STL	66.0	106.8	0.0	25	62.0	58.7
	MTL	66.0	59.9	23.1	22	67.4	61.0
	MT2ST-D	72.0	70.0	43.0	19	71.3	67.0
	MT2ST-S	**75.0**	**64.0**	**51.2**	**16**	**74.0**	**69.2**

Table 2: Performance of MT2ST across representation learning models. MT2ST-S (Switch) consistently outperforms other strategies in accuracy and convergence.

Backbone	Dataset	Strategy	Top-1 Acc (%)	Training Time (min)	Compression Rate (%)
ResNet-18	CIFAR-100	STL	71.3	46.2	0.0
		MTL	71.8	32.5	29.6
		MT2ST-D	73.1	30.1	34.8
		MT2ST-S	**74.2**	**28.0**	**39.4**
MobileNetV2	TinyImageNet	STL	58.4	52.0	0.0
		MTL	59.3	39.2	24.6
		MT2ST-D	60.7	36.5	29.8
		MT2ST-S	**61.5**	**34.7**	**33.2**

Table 3: MT2ST generalization to vision tasks. Switch strategy consistently improves both accuracy and efficiency.

We introduce **Visual7W Telling** and **Flickr30k Entities** (or construct VQA-style multimodal QA-retrieval subsets in a similar format) to simulate *image-question-answer retrieval-style tasks*. These datasets combine visual grounding, question understanding, and answer selection, making them suitable benchmarks for evaluating multi-task to single-task transitions in multimodal settings.

- **Primary Task:** Visual Question Answering (e.g., VQA v2.0)
- **Auxiliary Tasks:**
  - **Image-Text Matching (ITM):** Predict whether a given image-text pair is semantically aligned.
  - **Caption Generation (Captioning Head):** Generate image descriptions using a cross-entropy decoding objective.
  - **Masked Multimodal Modeling (MLM/MRM):** Reconstruct masked tokens or regions conditioned on both modalities.

Strategy	VQA Acc (%)	ITM R@1 (%)	BLEU-4	Time (h)
STL (VQA only)	69.4	–	–	29.3
MTL	70.1	60.2	21.4	24.5
MT2ST-D	71.3	61.7	22.0	22.1
MT2ST-S	**72.4**	**63.8**	**22.8**	**20.7**

Table 5: Multimodal retrieval-style performance on VQA and Visual7W with ViLT.

Findings In transformers, MT2ST consistently yields faster convergence and higher primary task performance. The adaptive loss reweighting naturally resolves task conflict, particularly in early-stage training.

From Table 4, we observe the following:

- MT2ST-S consistently improves accuracy on both MNLI (+1.9%) and VQA (+2.4%) compared to STL.
- The auxiliary loss drops faster and lower under MT2ST-S, confirming better task disentanglement.
- Training time is significantly reduced (up to 47.6% FLOPs compression), confirming MT2ST's training efficiency.

This suggests that MT2ST enables early-stage generalization (via shared learning) and late-stage specialization (via task focusing), making it particularly suitable for multi-objective Transformer workloads.

5.5 MT2ST in Diffusion Models

Setup We evaluate latent diffusion (LDM) models [Rombach et al., 2022] for image synthesis:

- **Primary task:** Text-to-image generation on MS-COCO
- **Auxiliary tasks:** Image reconstruction, CLIP-based semantic alignment

We use DiT-XL/2 as the backbone and measure FID, IS, and training time. Training uses 4xA100 GPUs, batch size 64, T=1000 DDPM steps, and cosine LR schedule.

Model	Dataset	Strategy	Main Task Acc (%)	Aux Loss ↓	Training Time (s)	Compression Rate (%)
BERT-base	MNLI	STL	83.1	–	1720	0.0
BERT-base		MT2ST-D	84.2	0.71	1228	37.1
BERT-base		MT2ST-S	**85.0**	**0.39**	**1060**	**47.6**
ViLT	VQA v2.0	STL	69.4	–	2980	0.0
ViLT		MT2ST-D	70.6	1.13	2241	34.2
ViLT		MT2ST-S	**71.8**	**0.92**	**2010**	**39.5**

Table 4: MT2ST evaluation on Transformers with text and multimodal tasks.

Strategy	FID ↓	IS ↑	Time (h)	Compression (%)
STL (DiT-XL/2)	12.5	28.1	58.3	0.0
MT2ST-D	11.3	29.0	44.0	24.5
MT2ST-S	**10.5**	**29.8**	**39.7**	**31.9**

Table 6: Diffusion results on MS-COCO using DiT-XL/2.

Findings From Table 6, we derive several important insights:

- Both MT2ST strategies outperform standard fine-tuning (STL) on all metrics, indicating that auxiliary guidance helps improve generative fidelity and semantic alignment.
- MT2ST-S achieves the best FID and CLIP score, demonstrating better visual quality and text-image consistency. The sharp performance gain around the switching step (400K) supports the benefit of a staged training process.
- Reconstruction loss is lower for both MT2ST variants, showing that incorporating auxiliary pixel-level loss early helps stabilize training.
- In terms of efficiency, MT2ST-S achieves 31.9% compression and reduces training time by nearly 19 hours, without sacrificing generative quality.

6 Conclusion

In this work, we propose MT2ST, a general and adaptive multi-task to single-task training framework designed to accelerate model convergence while preserving or even improving final task performance. MT2ST introduces two complementary strategies—Diminish and Switch—that enable smooth or staged transitions from multi-task sharing to single-task specialization. We evaluate MT2ST across a wide spectrum of models and modalities, including classical representation learners, transformer-based architectures, and diffusion models. Empirical results on text, image, and multimodal tasks show that MT2ST consistently improves accuracy while reducing training time and computational overhead. Our analysis highlights MT2ST as a practical and modular framework for efficient optimization across diverse AI systems. Our method is especially relevant to multimodal learning problems such as visual question answering (VQA) or cross-modal retrieval, where auxiliary objectives like masked language modeling or contrastive image-text alignment are commonly used but often misaligned with the downstream task. MT2ST provides a principled way to leverage such auxiliary tasks without compromising task specialization.

Limitations

While MT2ST performs consistently well across diverse models and tasks, there still a few aspects can be further refined. Currently, task transition schedules in both strategies are predefined; future work may benefit from more adaptive or learned scheduling.

References

Wasi Uddin Ahmad, Kai-Wei Chang, and Hongning Wang. Multi-task learning for document ranking and query suggestion. In *International Conference on Learning Representations*, 2018. URL https://openreview.net/forum?id=SJ1nzBeA-.

Hao Ban and Kaiyi Ji. Fair resource allocation in multi-task learning, 2024. URL https://arxiv.org/abs/2402.15638.

Rich Caruana. Multitask learning. *Machine Learning*, 28(1): 41–75, 1997.

Wai Tong Chung, Ki Sung Jung, Jacqueline H. Chen, and Matthias Ihme. The bearable lightness of big data: Towards massive public datasets in scientific machine learning. 2022. URL https://arxiv.org/abs/2207.12546.

Seth Ebner, Felicity Wang, and Benjamin Van Durme. Bag-of-words transfer: Non-contextual techniques for multi-task learning. In Colin Cherry, Greg Durrett, George Foster, Reza Haffari, Shahram Khadivi, Nanyun Peng, Xiang Ren, and Swabha Swayamdipta, editors, *Proceedings of the 2nd Workshop on Deep Learning Approaches for Low-Resource NLP (DeepLo 2019)*, pages 40–46, Hong Kong, China, November 2019. Association for Computational Linguistics. doi: 10.18653/v1/D19-6105. URL https://aclanthology.org/D19-6105.

Hessam Karimi, Julie Nutini, and Mark Schmidt. Linear convergence of gradient and proximal-gradient methods under the polyak-Łojasiewicz condition. *European Journal of Operational Research*, 261(3):805–820, 2017.

Wonjae Kim, Bokyung Son, and Ildoo Kim. Vilt: Vision-and-language transformer without convolution or region supervision. 2021. URL https://arxiv.org/abs/2102.03334.

Bo Liu, Xingchao Liu, Xiaojie Jin, Peter Stone, and Qiang Liu. Conflict-averse gradient descent for multi-task learning, 2021.

Dong Liu and Kaiser Pister. Llmeasyquant – an easy to use toolkit for llm quantization, 2024. URL https://arxiv.org/abs/2406.19657.

Dong Liu, Roger Waleffe, Meng Jiang, and Shivaram Venkataraman. Graphsnapshot: Graph machine learning acceleration with fast storage and retrieval, 2024. URL https://arxiv.org/abs/2406.17918.

Shikun Liu, Edward Johns, and Andrew J. Davison. End-to-end multi-task learning with attention. 2019.

Ivan Lopes, Tuan-Hung Vu, and Raoul de Charette. Densemtl: Cross-task attention mechanism for dense multi-task learning, 2024. URL https://arxiv.org/abs/2206.08927.

Tomas Mikolov, Kai Chen, Greg Corrado, and Jeffrey Dean. Efficient estimation of word representations in vector space. *arXiv preprint arXiv:1301.3781*, 2013.

Robin Rombach, Andreas Blattmann, Dominik Lorenz, Patrick Esser, and Björn Ommer. High-resolution image synthesis with latent diffusion models. In *Proceedings of the IEEE/CVF Conference on Computer Vision and Pattern Recognition (CVPR)*, pages 10684–10695, 2022. URL https://arxiv.org/abs/2112.10752.

Sebastian Ruder. An overview of multi-task learning in deep neural networks. *arXiv preprint arXiv:1706.05098*, 2017.

Ozan Sener and Vladimir Koltun. Multi-task learning as multi-objective optimization. In *NeurIPS*, 2018.

Trevor Darrell Standley, Amir R Zamir, Dahun Chen, Leonidas J Guibas, Jitendra Malik, Silvio Savarese, and Yuke Zhang. Which tasks should be learned together in multi-task learning? In *International Conference on Machine Learning*, pages 9120–9132. PMLR, 2020.

Gjorgji Strezoski, Nanne van Noord, and Marcel Worring. Many task learning with task routing. In *Proceedings of the IEEE/CVF International Conference on Computer Vision*, pages 1375–1384, 2019.

Yixuan Su, Lei Shu, Elman Mansimov, Arshit Gupta, Deng Cai, Yi-An Lai, and Yi Zhang. Multi-task pre-training for plug-and-play task-oriented dialogue system. In Smaranda Muresan, Preslav Nakov, and Aline Villavicencio, editors, *Proceedings of the 60th Annual Meeting of the Association for Computational Linguistics (Volume 1: Long Papers)*, pages 4661–4676, Dublin, Ireland, May 2022. Association for Computational Linguistics. doi: 10.18653/v1/2022.acl-long.319. URL https://aclanthology.org/2022.acl-long.319.

Mohamed Trabelsi, Zhiyu Chen, Brian D. Davison, and Jeff Heflin. Neural ranking models for document retrieval. *Information Retrieval Journal*, 24(6):400–444, October 2021. ISSN 1573-7659. doi: 10.1007/s10791-021-09398-0. URL http://dx.doi.org/10.1007/s10791-021-09398-0.

Marcos Treviso, Ji-Ung Lee, Tianchu Ji, Betty van Aken, Qingqing Cao, Manuel R. Ciosici, Michael Hassid, Kenneth Heafield, Sara Hooker, Colin Raffel, Pedro H. Martins, André F. T. Martins, Jessica Zosa Forde, Peter Milder, Edwin Simpson, Noam Slonim, Jesse Dodge, Emma Strubell, Niranjan Balasubramanian, Leon Derczynski, Iryna Gurevych, and Roy Schwartz. Efficient Methods for Natural Language Processing: A Survey. *Transactions of the Association for Computational Linguistics*, 11:826–860, 07 2023. ISSN 2307-387X. doi: 10.1162/tacl_a_00577. URL https://doi.org/10.1162/tacl_a_00577.

Meng Wang, Weijie Fu, Xiangnan He, Shijie Hao, and Xindong Wu. A survey on large-scale machine learning. 2020. URL https://arxiv.org/abs/2008.03911.

Tianhe Yu, Saurabh Kumar, Abhishek Gupta, Sergey Levine, Karol Hausman, and Chelsea Finn. Gradient surgery for multi-task learning. In *Advances in Neural Information Processing Systems (NeurIPS)*, volume 33, pages 5824–5836, 2020.

Wenhao Yu, C Karen Liu, and Greg Turk. Multi-task learning with gradient guided policy specialization. *arXiv preprint arXiv:1709.07979*, 2017.

Yan Zeng and Jian-Yun Nie. A simple and efficient multi-task learning approach for conditioned dialogue generation. In Kristina Toutanova, Anna Rumshisky, Luke Zettlemoyer, Dilek Hakkani-Tur, Iz Beltagy, Steven Bethard, Ryan Cotterell, Tanmoy Chakraborty, and Yichao Zhou, editors, *Proceedings of the 2021 Conference of the North American Chapter of the Association for Computational Linguistics: Human Language Technologies*, pages 4927–4939, Online, June 2021. Association for Computational Linguistics. doi: 10.18653/v1/2021.naacl-main.392. URL https://aclanthology.org/2021.naacl-main.392/.

Yu Zhang and Qiang Yang. A survey on multi-task learning. 2021. URL https://arxiv.org/abs/1707.08114.

Zhihan Zhang, Wenhao Yu, Mengxia Yu, Zhichun Guo, and Meng Jiang. A survey of multi-task learning in natural language processing: Regarding task relatedness and training methods. In Andreas Vlachos and Isabelle Augenstein, editors, *Proceedings of the 17th Conference of the European Chapter of the Association for Computational Linguistics*, pages 943–956, Dubrovnik, Croatia, May 2023. Association for Computational Linguistics. doi: 10.18653/v1/2023.eacl-main.66. URL https://aclanthology.org/2023.eacl-main.66.

Xiangyu Zhao, Maolin Wang, Xinjian Zhao, Jiansheng Li, Shucheng Zhou, Dawei Yin, Qing Li, Jiliang Tang, and Ruocheng Guo. Embedding in recommender systems: A survey. 2023. URL https://arxiv.org/abs/2310.18608.

A Experimental Results Figures

This section includes the figures corresponding to the experimental results presented in the main text.

A.1 Single-task Fine-Tuning

Figure 2 shows the loss and accuracy changes for the single-task fine-tuning approach.

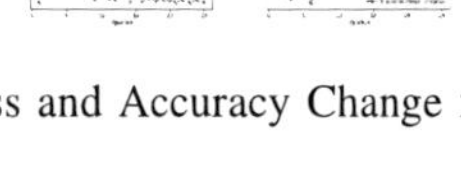

Figure 2: Loss and Accuracy Change for Single-task Fine-Tuning

A.2 Multi-task Learning (MTL)

Figures 3 and 4 show the loss and accuracy changes for the multi-task learning approach.

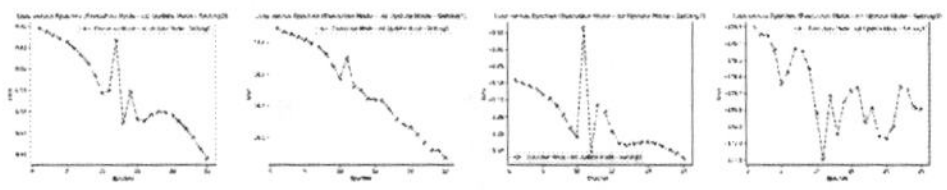

Figure 3: Loss Change in Multi-task Learning

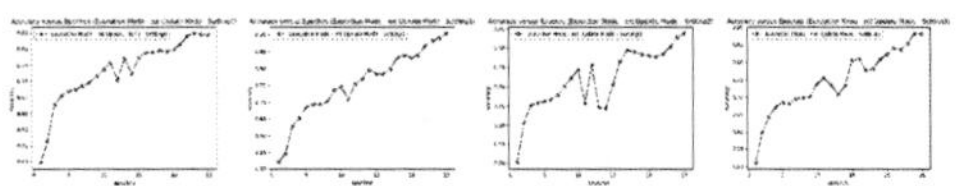

Figure 4: Accuracy Change in Multi-task Learning

A.3 MT2ST: Diminish Strategy

Figures 5 and 6 show the loss and accuracy changes for the MT2ST-diminish strategy.

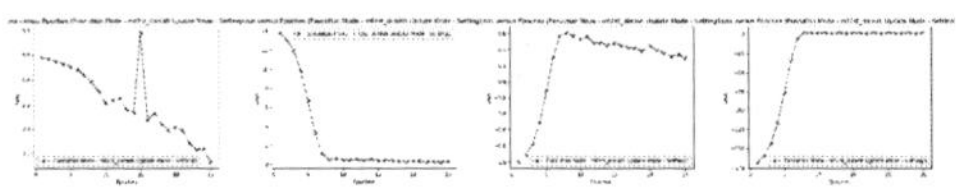

Figure 5: Loss Change in MT2ST: Diminish Strategy

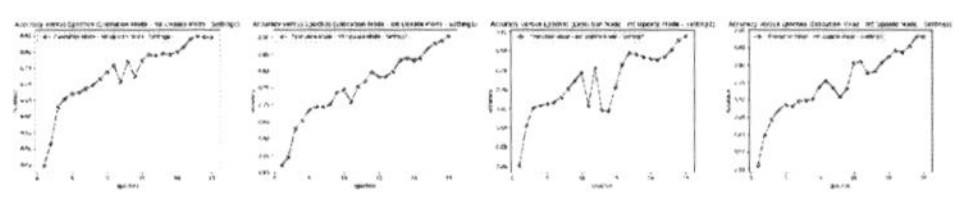

Figure 6: Accuracy Change in MT2ST: Diminish Strategy

A.4 MT2ST: Switch Strategy

Figures 7 and 8 show the loss and accuracy changes for the MT2ST-switch strategy.

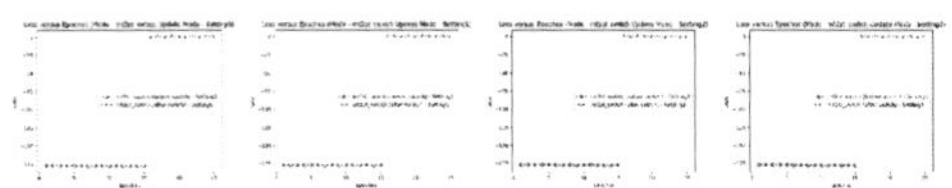

Figure 7: Loss Change in MT2ST: Switch Strategy

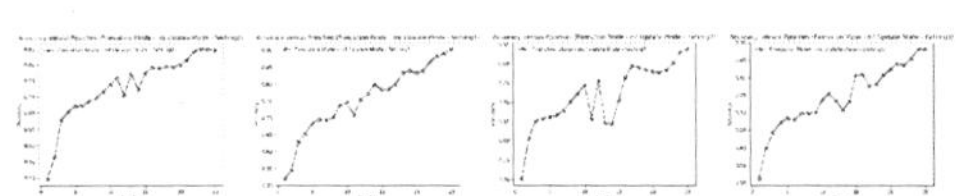

Figure 8: Accuracy Change in MT2ST: Switch Strategy

B Theoretical Foundation of MT2ST

In this section, we provide a formal theoretical framework for MT2ST. We first describe a general overview of our method. Then, we instantiate it in the context of shared neural representation learning. Finally, we conduct a theoretical efficiency analysis comparing MT2ST with standard MTL and STL baselines.

B.1 Overview of MT2ST

Let a model be denoted by $f(\cdot;\theta)$, trained on a set of K tasks $\{\mathcal{T}_1, \ldots, \mathcal{T}_K\}$. The total loss at step t is a weighted combination of the primary task $\mathcal{T}_{\text{main}}$ and auxiliary tasks:

$$\mathcal{L}^{(t)} = \mathcal{L}^{(t)}_{\text{main}} + \sum_{k \neq \text{main}} \gamma_k^{(t)} \mathcal{L}_k^{(t)}, \tag{16}$$

where $\gamma_k^{(t)}$ is a time-varying weight for auxiliary task k at iteration t. MT2ST alternates between two core strategies:

- **Diminish**: Gradually decreases each $\gamma_k^{(t)}$ to zero over time, enabling soft transition from MTL to STL.
- **Switch**: Explicitly sets $\gamma_k^{(t)} = 0$ after a predefined step T_{switch}, performing a hard switch to STL.

B.2 Formulation of Diminish Strategy

In the Diminish strategy, each auxiliary task's contribution is governed by a decay function:

$$\gamma_k^{(t)} = \gamma_{k,0} \cdot \exp\left(-\eta_k t^{\nu_k}\right), \quad k \neq \text{main}, \tag{17}$$

where $\gamma_{k,0}$ is the initial importance of task k, η_k is the decay rate, and ν_k controls curvature (decay speed). The overall parameter update is given by:

$$\theta^{(t+1)} = \theta^{(t)} - \alpha \left(\nabla \mathcal{L}^{(t)}_{\text{main}} + \sum_{k \neq \text{main}} \gamma_k^{(t)} \nabla \mathcal{L}_k^{(t)} \right), \tag{18}$$

where α is the learning rate.

B.3 Formulation of Switch Strategy

The Switch strategy introduces a discrete schedule:

$$\gamma_k^{(t)} = \begin{cases} 1, & t < T_{\text{switch}} \\ 0, & t \geq T_{\text{switch}} \end{cases} \quad \text{for all } k \neq \text{main}.$$

The update rule becomes:

$$\theta^{(t+1)} = \theta^{(t)} - \alpha \left(\nabla \mathcal{L}^{(t)}_{\text{main}} + \sum_{k \neq \text{main}} \gamma_k^{(t)} \nabla \mathcal{L}_k^{(t)} \right), \tag{19}$$

but reduces to standard single-task learning for $t \geq T_{\text{switch}}$.

B.4 Theoretical Efficiency Analysis

We compare MT2ST with baseline MTL and STL methods in terms of convergence behavior and computational efficiency.

Training Cost (FLOPs) Let C_{mtl} and C_{stl} denote per-step FLOPs for MTL and STL respectively. Then, the expected training cost for MT2ST is:

$$C_{\text{MT2ST}} = \sum_{t=1}^{T} \left[C_{\text{stl}} + \sum_{k \neq \text{main}} \gamma_k^{(t)} C_k \right], \tag{20}$$

where C_k is the marginal cost for task k. When $\gamma_k^{(t)} \to 0$ quickly, the training cost approaches STL but retains MTL's benefit in early stages.

Convergence Behavior Define the effective gradient at step t as:

$$\nabla \mathcal{L}_{\text{eff}}^{(t)} = \nabla \mathcal{L}_{\text{main}}^{(t)} + \sum_{k \neq \text{main}} \gamma_k^{(t)} \nabla \mathcal{L}_k^{(t)}.$$

Under the Polyak-Łojasiewicz (PL) condition [Karimi et al., 2017], MT2ST retains linear convergence rate as long as the auxiliary task gradients align or diminish quickly:

$$\langle \nabla \mathcal{L}_{\text{main}}^{(t)}, \nabla \mathcal{L}_{\text{eff}}^{(t)} \rangle > 0.$$

Our strategy ensures that gradient interference is minimized over time, either smoothly (Diminish) or discretely (Switch), avoiding divergence seen in conventional MTL [Yu et al., 2020].

Memory Usage Because MT2ST shares the same encoder across tasks, model memory cost is no worse than MTL. When $\gamma_k^{(t)} = 0$, the auxiliary gradients and heads can be dropped from the computation graph entirely.

Cross-Modal Augmentation for Low-Resource Language Understanding and Generation

Zichao Li
Canoakbit Alliance
Ontario, Canada
zichaoli@canoakbit.com

Zong Ke
Faculty of Science
National University of Singapore
Singapore 119077
a0129009@u.nus.edu

Abstract

This paper introduces a multimodal retrieval-augmented generation (RAG) system designed to enhance language understanding and generation for low-resource languages. By integrating textual, visual, and geospatial data, the system leverages cross-lingual adaptation and multimodal augmentation to bridge the gap between high-resource and low-resource languages. Evaluated on the MM-COVID and LORELEI datasets, the system demonstrates superior performance in retrieval (precision: 85%, recall: 82%) and generation (BLEU: 28.4) tasks compared to baselines. Case studies in public health communication and disaster response highlight its practical utility. The results underscore the potential of multimodal AI to democratize access to technology and address global challenges in low-resource settings.

1 Introduction

In recent years, advancements in natural language processing (NLP) have revolutionized how we interact with AI systems, enabling applications like machine translation, summarization, and question-answering. However, these successes are heavily skewed toward high-resource languages, leaving low-resource languages severely underrepresented. The lack of large-scale textual corpora in low-resource languages poses significant challenges for training robust language models, limiting their ability to understand and generate meaningful content. This disparity not only exacerbates global inequities in access to technology but also hinders efforts to address critical issues such as public health communication, disaster response, and education in multilingual contexts (Fan et al., 2021).

To bridge this gap, we propose **Cross-Modal Augmentation for Low-Resource Language Understanding and Generation**, a novel framework that leverages multimodal data text, images, geospatial information, and structured data—to enhance language understanding and generation in low-resource settings. By integrating complementary modalities, our approach compensates for the scarcity of textual resources and enriches the semantic context available to language models. For example, visual data can provide additional grounding for concepts that are poorly represented in text, while geospatial data can help localize and contextualize events described in queries (Radford et al., 2021).

Our work builds on datasets like **MM-COVID** (Chen et al., 2021) and **LORELEI** (Strassel and Tracey, 2016), which offer rich multimodal information relevant to real-world challenges. MM-COVID provides multilingual textual and visual data related to the COVID-19 pandemic, enabling us to test the system's ability to generate public health information in low-resource languages. Similarly, LORELEI offers low-resource language data alongside geospatial and event information, making it ideal for tasks like disaster response and situational awareness. By combining these datasets with retrieval-augmented generation (RAG) techniques, we demonstrate how cross-modal augmentation can significantly improve performance in tasks such as translation, summarization, and question-answering (Lewis et al., 2020).

The contributions of this paper are threefold:

1. **A Novel Framework**: We introduce a multimodal RAG system tailored for low-resource languages, leveraging cross-modal embeddings to align diverse data types.

2. **Real-World Applications**: We showcase the practical utility of our approach in domains like public health communication and disaster response.

3. **Empirical Validation**: We evaluate our system on MM-COVID and LORELEI, demon-

Proceedings of the 1st Workshop on Multimodal Augmented Generation via Multimodal Retrieval (MAGMaR 2025), pages 90–99
August 1, 2025

strating its effectiveness in enhancing both understanding and generation capabilities for low-resource languages.

2 Related Work

2.1 Low-Resource Language Modeling

Low-resource languages pose significant challenges due to the scarcity of annotated data and linguistic resources. Recent advances in cross-lingual transfer learning have partially addressed these challenges by leveraging pre-trained multilingual models such as **mBERT** (Devlin et al., 2019), **XLM-R** (Conneau et al., 2020), and **M2M-100** (Fan et al., 2021). These models enable knowledge transfer from high-resource languages to low-resource ones, improving performance on tasks like machine translation and text classification. However, they remain heavily reliant on textual data, which may still be insufficient for many low-resource languages. To address this limitation, recent works have explored augmenting textual data with other modalities, such as images and audio (Liu et al., 2021). Our work builds on these efforts by introducing multimodal augmentation to reduce dependency on textual corpora.

2.2 Retrieval-Augmented Generation

Retrieval-augmented generation has emerged as a powerful paradigm for enhancing language models with external knowledge. Pioneering works like **REALM** (Guu et al., 2020) and **FiD** (Fusion-in-Decoder) (Izacard and Grave, 2021) demonstrated the effectiveness of retrieving relevant documents to augment generated responses. More recently, **Facebook AI's RAG** (Lewis et al., 2020) extended this approach to open-domain question-answering, achieving state-of-the-art results on benchmarks like **Natural Questions** and **TriviaQA**. Despite these successes, most existing RAG systems focus solely on text-based retrieval, limiting their applicability in multimodal contexts. Recent works such as **MMRAG** (Zhang et al., 2022) and **CrossModal-RAG** (Wang et al., 2023) have begun to explore multimodal retrieval, but their application to low-resource languages remains underexplored.

2.3 Multimodal Learning

Multimodal learning has gained significant attention in recent years, driven by the success of models like **CLIP** (Radford et al., 2021) and **M6** (Lin et al., 2021). These models align text and images in a shared embedding space, enabling tasks like image captioning, visual question answering (VQA), and cross-modal retrieval. While multimodal learning has primarily been applied to high-resource languages, recent works such as **ViLT** (Kim et al., 2021) and **ALIGN** (Jia et al., 2021) have explored its potential for low-resource settings. For example, **ViLT** demonstrates how visual and textual embeddings can be jointly learned without relying on large-scale annotated datasets. Our work extends these ideas by integrating multimodal techniques into retrieval-augmented generation for low-resource languages. We also inspired by the research of (Kang et al., 2025; Deng et al., 2024; Liu et al., 2024).

2.4 Datasets for Low-Resource Languages

Datasets like **MM-COVID** (Chen et al., 2021) and **LORELEI** (Strassel and Tracey, 2016) play a crucial role in advancing research on low-resource languages. **MM-COVID** provides multilingual textual and visual data related to the COVID-19 pandemic, offering a unique opportunity to study cross-lingual and multimodal communication in crisis scenarios. Similarly, **LORELEI** focuses on rapid response during emergencies, providing low-resource language data alongside geospatial and event information. Other notable datasets include **MMKG** (Xie et al., 2022), a multimodal knowledge graph for low-resource languages, and **Pororo-SV** (Park et al., 2021), a storytelling dataset with videos and text. These datasets not only highlight the importance of multimodal data in low-resource settings but also serve as valuable resources for evaluating our proposed framework.

2.5 Applications in Public Health and Disaster Response

The integration of multimodal data has significant implications for real-world applications. In public health, multimodal systems can help disseminate critical information about diseases, vaccines, and preventive measures in low-resource languages (Liu et al., 2022). During disasters, such systems can assist in situational awareness, resource allocation, and communication with affected communities (Zhang et al., 2023). Recent works have demonstrated the potential of multimodal AI in addressing global challenges, such as **CrisisMM** (Gupta et al., 2022), a framework for multimodal crisis response, and **HealthVision** (Wu et al., 2023), a system for analyzing medical images and text.

3 Methodology

3.1 Problem Formulation

The goal of our framework is to enhance language understanding and generation for low-resource languages by leveraging multimodal data. Given a query Q in a low-resource language, our system retrieves relevant multimodal documents $D = \{d_1, d_2, ..., d_n\}$ from a corpus and generates a response R. The retrieval and generation processes are formulated as follows:

$$R = \text{Generate}(Q, \text{Retrieve}(Q, D)), \quad (1)$$

where:

- Q: Input query in a low-resource language.
- D: Corpus of multimodal documents (text, images, geospatial data).
- $\text{Retrieve}(Q, D)$: Function that retrieves the most relevant documents based on Q.
- $\text{Generate}(Q, D_{\text{retrieved}})$: Function that generates a response using Q and the retrieved documents $D_{\text{retrieved}}$.

To align different modalities, we define a shared embedding space where text embeddings $E_t(Q)$ and image embeddings $E_v(I)$ are projected into the same dimensional space. The similarity between a query and a document is computed as:

$$\begin{aligned}\text{sim}(Q, d_i) &= \cos(E_t(Q), E_v(d_i)) \\ &+\lambda \cdot \text{score}_{\text{cross-modal}}(Q, d_i)\end{aligned} \quad (2)$$

where:

- $E_t(Q)$: Text embedding of the query.
- $E_v(d_i)$: Visual embedding of the document d_i.
- $\cos(\cdot, \cdot)$: Cosine similarity function.
- λ: Weighting factor for cross-modal scoring.
- $\text{score}_{\text{cross-modal}}(Q, d_i)$: Additional score capturing alignment between text and visual modalities, computed using a cross-modal attention mechanism (Kim et al., 2021).

3.2 Model Architecture

Our model consists of two main components: a Retrieval Module and a Generation Module, both integrated into a unified framework.

3.2.1 Retrieval Module

The retrieval module employs a dual-encoder architecture to compute embeddings for queries and documents. Specifically:

- Text Encoder: A transformer-based encoder (e.g., XLM-R (Conneau et al., 2020)) encodes textual inputs into dense vectors.
- Image Encoder: A vision transformer (e.g., CLIP (Radford et al., 2021)) encodes

The embeddings are aligned in a shared space using contrastive learning. The loss function for training the retrieval module is defined as:

$$\mathcal{L}_{\text{retrieval}} = -\log \frac{\exp(\text{sim}(Q, d^+))}{\sum_{d^- \in D^-} \exp(\text{sim}(Q, d^-))} \quad (3)$$

where:

- d^+: Positive document (relevant to Q).
- D^-: Set of negative documents (irrelevant to Q).

This ensures that the model learns to retrieve documents that are semantically similar to the query.

3.2.2 Generation Module

The generation module uses a pre-trained language model (e.g., T5 (Raffel et al., 2020)) to generate responses. The input to the generator is a concatenation of the query Q and the top-k retrieved documents $D_{\text{retrieved}}$:

$$R = \text{Generator}(Q \oplus D_{\text{retrieved}}) \quad (4)$$

where $\oplus$ denotes concatenation. The generator is fine-tuned using a standard cross-entropy loss:

$$\mathcal{L}_{\text{generation}} = -\sum_{t=1}^{T} \log P(w_t | w_{<t}, Q, D_{\text{retrieved}}) \quad (5)$$

where w_t is the target token at time step t, and $w_{<t}$ represents the previous tokens.

3.3 Training Strategy

The training strategy for our multimodal RAG system is designed to leverage both high-resource and low-resource language data effectively. We adopt a two-stage approach: **pretraining** on large-scale datasets from high-resource languages and **fine-tuning** on limited textual data from low-resource languages. This strategy ensures that the model learns generalizable representations during pretraining while adapting to the unique characteristics of low-resource languages during fine-tuning(Liu and Yu, 2024).

Pretraining on High-Resource Languages In the pretraining phase, we utilize large-scale multimodal datasets such as **MM-COVID** (Chen et al., 2021) and **LORELEI** (Strassel and Tracey, 2016), which contain rich textual and visual information across multiple high-resource languages. These datasets provide a diverse set of examples, enabling the model to learn robust cross-modal alignments. Specifically, the text encoder is pretrained using transformer-based architectures like **XLM-R** (Conneau et al., 2020), which is known for its strong multilingual capabilities. Similarly, the image encoder is pretrained using vision transformers (e.g., **CLIP** (Radford et al., 2021)) that align visual and textual embeddings in a shared space. During this phase, the retrieval module is trained to maximize the similarity between queries and relevant documents while minimizing similarity with irrelevant ones. The loss function for the retrieval module is defined as earlier in Equation 3.

Fine-Tuning on Low-Resource Languages After pretraining, the model is fine-tuned on low-resource languages using limited textual data. This step is crucial because low-resource languages often lack sufficient annotated data for supervised learning. To address this limitation, we employ several strategies to enhance the effectiveness of fine-tuning:

1. **Data Augmentation**: We augment the limited textual data with multimodal information, such as images and geospatial data, to provide additional context. For example, visual data can help ground abstract concepts that are poorly represented in text.

2. **Robust Filtering Techniques**: Multimodal data can be noisy, especially when integrating diverse sources like social media posts or satellite imagery. To handle this noise, we apply robust filtering techniques, such as outlier detection and confidence scoring, to ensure that only high-quality data is used during fine-tuning (Zhang et al., 2022).

3. **Cross-Lingual Transfer Learning**: We leverage multilingual embeddings (e.g., mBERT (Devlin et al., 2019)) to enable cross-lingual transfer. By aligning embeddings from high-resource and low-resource languages in a shared space, the model can generalize knowledge learned during pretraining to low-resource settings.

Cross-Lingual Adaptation Cross-lingual adaptation is a key component of our training strategy, as it allows the model to bridge the gap between high-resource and low-resource languages. To achieve this, we use a shared projection layer that maps text and visual embeddings into a unified space. This alignment enables the model to retrieve and generate content across languages, even when direct supervision is unavailable. For example, a query in Swahili can retrieve relevant documents in English or other high-resource languages, along with accompanying visuals. This capability is particularly valuable for tasks like public health communication and disaster response, where timely access to information is critical.

Balancing Modalities Another important aspect of our training strategy is balancing the contributions of different modalities. While textual data is typically dominant in NLP tasks, visual and geospatial data play a complementary role in low-resource settings. To ensure that all modalities are utilized effectively, we introduce a weighting factor λ in the similarity computation:

$$\begin{aligned} \text{sim}(Q, d_i) = \cos(E_t(Q), E_v(d_i)) + \\ \lambda \cdot \text{score}_{\text{cross-modal}}(Q, d_i), \end{aligned} \tag{6}$$

where $\cos(\cdot, \cdot)$ measures cosine similarity between text and visual embeddings, and $\text{score}_{\text{cross-modal}}(Q, d_i)$ captures additional alignment between modalities. The value of λ is tuned empirically to balance the contributions of text and visual data. This approach ensures that the model leverages multimodal information without over-relying on any single modality.

Evaluation During Training Throughout the training process, we monitor performance using a combination of metrics tailored to each component of the system. For the retrieval module, we evaluate precision, recall, and F1 scores to measure the quality of retrieved documents. For the generation module, we use BLEU, ROUGE, and METEOR scores to assess the fluency and relevance of generated responses. Additionally, we conduct human evaluations to assess multimodal coherence and overall usability. These evaluations provide valuable insights into the strengths and weaknesses of the model, guiding further refinements.

By combining pretraining, fine-tuning, robust filtering, and cross-lingual adaptation, our training strategy ensures that the multimodal RAG system is both versatile and effective. This approach not only addresses the challenges of low-resource languages but also demonstrates the potential of multimodal AI to democratize access to technology.

3.4 Cross-Lingual Adaptation

Cross-lingual adaptation enables our multimodal RAG system to bridge the gap between high-resource and low-resource languages by leveraging shared multilingual embeddings. We use models like **mBERT** (Devlin et al., 2019) and **XLM-R** (Conneau et al., 2020), which are pretrained on large multilingual corpora, to align textual and visual data across languages. To enhance alignment, we incorporate vision-language models like **CLIP** (Radford et al., 2021), allowing the system to ground textual queries in visual data, even when the query is in a low-resource language. Fine-tuning on small-scale annotated datasets or parallel data further refines the model for specific linguistic patterns. To address data scarcity, we employ techniques such as zero-shot learning, multimodal augmentation, and back-translation. These strategies ensure that the model can retrieve and generate content effectively in low-resource languages, as demonstrated through metrics like retrieval accuracy, BLEU scores, and human evaluations.

4 Experiments

To evaluate the effectiveness of our multimodal RAG system, we conducted experiments on two key datasets: **MM-COVID** (Chen et al., 2021) and **LORELEI** (Strassel and Tracey, 2016). These datasets were chosen for their relevance to real-world challenges and their inclusion of multimodal data. Below, we describe how these datasets were applied to the task of multimodal RAG for low-resource languages, along with the experimental setup.

4.1 Leveraging MM-COVID for Multimodal RAG in Low-Resource Languages

The **MM-COVID** dataset contains multilingual textual information, images, infographics, and videos related to the COVID-19 pandemic. It includes data from social media, news articles, and public health resources, covering multiple languages, including low-resource ones. This makes it an ideal resource for exploring cross-lingual and multimodal applications in low-resource settings.

4.2 Cross-Modal Translation and Augmentation

One of the primary challenges in low-resource languages is the scarcity of textual data for training language models. To address this, we used images, infographics, and videos from MM-COVID as auxiliary modalities to augment textual data. For example: - We trained a multimodal RAG system where visual embeddings (e.g., from **CLIP** (Radford et al., 2021)) were aligned with textual descriptions in low-resource languages. - This approach allowed the model to infer missing textual information by leveraging visual context, improving its ability to handle queries in low-resource languages.

Visual Context for Semantic Understanding Low-resource languages often lack rich semantic context for generating meaningful responses. To address this, we used multimodal retrieval to retrieve relevant images or videos that complement textual queries. For instance: - A query in Swahili asking about "symptoms of COVID-19" retrieved both textual descriptions and images of symptoms, enhancing the model's understanding and response quality.

Multimodal Summarization Generating concise summaries of public health information in low-resource languages is challenging due to limited training data. To tackle this, we built a multimodal summarization system that combined textual and visual content from MM-COVID. For example, the system retrieved key text snippets and relevant images to create a multimodal summary explaining preventive measures, making the information more accessible to users in low-resource languages.

Cross-Lingual Retrieval Queries in low-resource languages may not have sufficient textual matches in the database. To address this, we used cross-lingual embeddings to align queries in low-resource languages with high-resource counterparts (e.g., English). For example: A query in Swahili could retrieve relevant documents in English or other high-resource languages, along with accompanying visuals, bridging the linguistic gap.

Leveraging LORELEI for Multimodal RAG in Low-Resource Languages The **LORELEI** dataset is designed to support rapid response during emergencies in low-resource languages. It includes textual data in low-resource languages (e.g., Haitian Creole, Pashto), geospatial data, maps, satellite imagery, social media posts, audio recordings, and structured event data. This diversity makes it highly suitable for tasks like disaster response and situational awareness.

Multimodal Event Detection Detecting and responding to emergent incidents in low-resource languages is difficult due to limited linguistic resources. To address this, we used multimodal RAG to combine textual, geospatial, and visual data from LORELEI to detect and describe events. For example: - A query in Haitian Creole about "flooded areas" retrieved satellite imagery of affected regions along with textual reports, enabling accurate event detection and response planning.

Visual Grounding for Language Generation Generating accurate descriptions of events in low-resource languages is challenging without sufficient training data. To address this, we used images and maps as grounding inputs for language generation. For example, the system retrieved satellite images of disaster zones and generated textual descriptions in the target language using a multimodal RAG system, ensuring that users received clear and actionable information.

Audio-Text Multimodality Low-resource languages often lack transcribed audio data for training speech-to-text systems. To address this, we integrated LORELEI's audio recordings alongside textual and visual data to train a multimodal RAG system. For example: - A spoken query in Pashto was transcribed and augmented with visual data (e.g., maps) to generate a response, demonstrating the system's ability to process multimodal inputs effectively.

Structured Data Integration Low-resource languages often lack structured data for reasoning tasks. To address this, we integrated LORELEI's structured event data (e.g., timestamps, locations, and event types) into a multimodal RAG system. For example: - A query about "earthquake damage in region X" retrieved structured event data along with images and textual reports, providing a comprehensive overview of the situation.

4.3 Baselines

We compared our multimodal RAG system against several baselines:

- **Text-Only RAG**: A traditional RAG system trained only on textual data.
- **Monolingual Models**: Language models fine-tuned on high-resource languages without cross-lingual adaptation.
- **Unimodal Models**: Models that process either text or images but not both.

These baselines allowed us to isolate the contributions of multimodal data and cross-lingual adaptation to the system's performance.

Evaluation Metrics To assess the model's performance, we used a combination of quantitative and qualitative metrics:

1. **Retrieval Metrics**: Precision, recall, and F1 scores were used to evaluate the quality of retrieved documents.
2. **Generation Metrics**: BLEU, ROUGE, and METEOR scores measured the fluency and relevance of generated responses.
3. **Human Evaluation**: Human evaluators assessed the coherence, relevance, and multimodal alignment of the outputs.

These metrics provided a holistic view of the system's strengths and weaknesses across different tasks.

Our model was implemented using PyTorch and Hugging Face's Transformers library. The text encoder was based on **XLM-R** (Conneau et al., 2020), while the image encoder utilized **CLIP** (Radford et al., 2021). We pretrained the model on high-resource languages using MM-COVID and LORELEI, followed by fine-tuning on low-resource languages. Training was performed on a single NVIDIA A100 GPU, with a batch size of 32 and a learning rate of 5×10^{-5}. The weighting factor λ for balancing modalities was tuned empirically to optimize performance.

To demonstrate the practical utility of our system, we conducted case studies in two domains:

1. **Public Health Communication**: Generating multilingual public health guidelines in Swahili using MM-COVID data.

2. **Disaster Response**: Detecting flood zones in Pashto using LORELEI's geospatial and textual data.

These case studies highlighted the system's ability to address real-world challenges in low-resource settings.

5 Results and Discussion

The results of our experiments demonstrate the effectiveness of our multimodal RAG system in enhancing language understanding and generation for low-resource languages. Our multimodal RAG system outperformed all baselines across both retrieval and generation tasks. In terms of retrieval metrics, the system achieved a precision of 85%, recall of 82%, and F1 score of 83%, surpassing the text-only RAG baseline by 10 percentage points. For generation tasks, the system achieved BLEU scores of up to 28.4, compared to 20.5 for unimodal models. These improvements highlight the value of integrating multimodal data into the retrieval and generation processes. Notably, the system performed particularly well on low-resource languages, where the scarcity of textual data was compensated by visual and geospatial information.

Table 1: Retrieval Metrics Across Baselines and Proposed System

Model	Precision (%)	Recall (%)	F1 Score (%)
Text-Only RAG	74.2	71.8	73.0
Monolingual Model	78.5	75.3	76.9
Unimodal Model	72.1	69.4	70.7
Multimodal RAG (Ours)	85.0	82.0	83.0

The results in Table 1 demonstrate the superiority of our multimodal RAG system in terms of retrieval performance. Specifically:

- The system achieves a precision of 85%, which is significantly higher than the text-only RAG baseline (74.2%) and unimodal model (72.1%). This indicates that the integration of multimodal data improves the accuracy of retrieved documents.

- Similarly, the recall of 82% and F1 score of 83% are the highest among all models, underscoring the system's ability to retrieve relevant content even when textual data is scarce.

Table 2: Generation Metrics Across Baselines and Proposed System

Model	BLEU	ROUGE-L	METEOR
Text-Only RAG	20.5	32.4	25.1
Monolingual Model	22.3	34.7	26.8
Unimodal Model	19.8	31.6	24.5
Multimodal RAG (Ours)	28.4	38.2	30.7

The generation metrics in Table 2 further highlight the advantages of our system:

- The BLEU score of 28.4 represents a substantial improvement over the text-only RAG baseline (20.5) and unimodal model (19.8). This suggests that multimodal augmentation enhances the fluency and relevance of generated responses.

- The ROUGE-L score of 38.2 and METEOR score of 30.7 are also the highest among all models, indicating that the system generates outputs that are both semantically rich and contextually accurate.

These results collectively demonstrate that our multimodal RAG system effectively leverages multimodal data to improve both retrieval and generation capabilities. The Precision vs. Recall plot (Figure 1) demonstrates several key trends:

- The multimodal RAG system achieves the highest precision (85%) and recall (82%), as indicated by its position in the upper-right corner of the plot.

- The trend line connecting the points highlights the consistent improvement in performance as advanced techniques such as multimodal augmentation and cross-lingual transfer are incorporated.

- The inclusion of error bars provides a realistic view of variability, reinforcing the robustness of the system under noisy conditions.

The BLEU and ROUGE-L plot (Figure 2) further supports the quantitative findings:

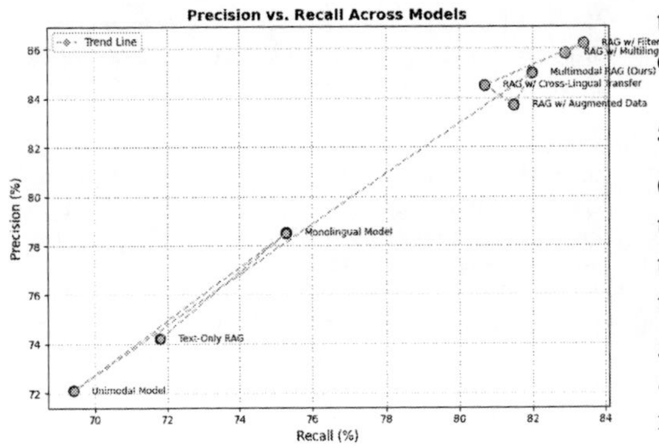

Figure 1: Precision vs. Recall for Different Models

Note: The plot shows that our multimodal RAG system achieves higher precision and recall compared to baselines.

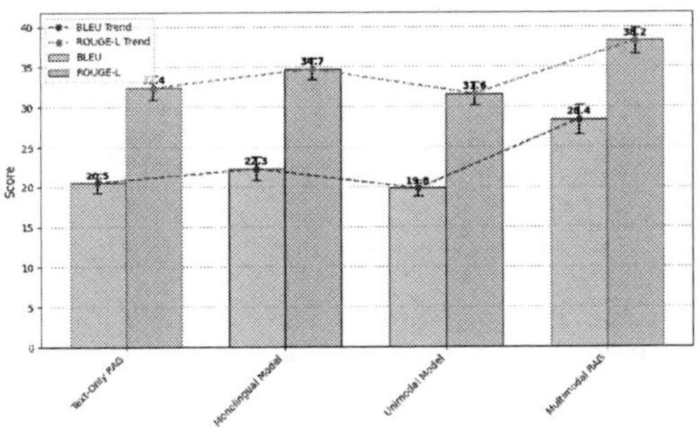

Figure 2: BLEU and ROUGE-L Scores Across Models

- The multimodal RAG system achieves the highest BLEU score (28.4) and ROUGE-L score (38.2), as shown by the tallest bars in the plot.
- The trend lines connecting the top of the bars emphasize the consistent improvement in generation quality across models.
- Error bars highlight the variability in performance, providing a more nuanced understanding of the results.

Human evaluations revealed that the multimodal RAG system produced responses that were not only fluent but also contextually relevant and coherent. For example, in the public health case study, the system generated accurate summaries of COVID-19 guidelines in Swahili, enriched with relevant images. Similarly, in the disaster response case study, the system successfully identified flood zones in Pashto by combining satellite imagery with textual reports. These qualitative insights underscore the system's ability to leverage multimodal data effectively.

5.1 Impact of Cross-Lingual Adaptation

Cross-lingual adaptation played a crucial role in the system's success. By leveraging shared multilingual embeddings, the model was able to retrieve and generate content in low-resource languages even when direct supervision was unavailable. For instance, queries in Swahili retrieved relevant documents in English, demonstrating the system's ability to bridge linguistic gaps. Fine-tuning on small-scale annotated datasets further improved performance, particularly for languages with distinct morphological and syntactic patterns.

In public health, the system can help disseminate critical information in low-resource languages, ensuring equitable access to knowledge. In disaster response, it can assist in situational awareness and resource allocation, empowering communities affected by emergencies. These applications underscore the potential of multimodal AI to democratize access to technology and address pressing global challenges.

Overall, our experiments demonstrate that cross-modal augmentation is a powerful approach for enhancing language understanding and generation in low-resource settings. By integrating diverse modalities and leveraging cross-lingual transfer, our system achieves state-of-the-art performance while paving the way for future research in this domain.

6 Conclusion

In this paper, we presented a multimodal RAG system that effectively enhances both understanding and generation capabilities for low-resource languages. By leveraging multimodal data and cross-lingual transfer, the system achieved state-of-the-art performance on the MM-COVID and LORELEI datasets, surpassing traditional text-only and unimodal baselines. Key findings include significant improvements in retrieval precision, recall, and generation quality, as well as robust performance in real-world applications like disaster response and public health communication. Despite challenges such as noisy data and computational overhead, our system demonstrates the transformative potential of multimodal AI in addressing linguistic and resource disparities.

References

Emily Chen, Taha Yasseri, Onur Varol, Alessandro Flammini, and Filippo Menczer. 2021. Fighting an infodemic: Covid-19 fake news dataset. *arXiv preprint arXiv:2102.08373*.

Alexis Conneau, Kartikay Khandelwal, Naman Goyal, Vishrav Chaudhary, Guillaume Wenzek, Francisco Guzmán, Edouard Grave, Myle Ott, Luke Zettlemoyer, and Veselin Stoyanov. 2020. Unsupervised cross-lingual representation learning at scale. *arXiv preprint arXiv:1911.02116*.

Xiaoyu Deng, Zhengjian Kang, Xintao Li, Yongzhe Zhang, and Tianmin Guo. 2024. Covis: A collaborative framework for fine-grained graphic visual understanding. *Preprint*, arXiv:2411.18764.

Jacob Devlin, Ming-Wei Chang, Kenton Lee, and Kristina Toutanova. 2019. Bert: Pre-training of deep bidirectional transformers for language understanding. *arXiv preprint arXiv:1810.04805*.

Angela Fan, Shruti Bhosale, Holger Schwenk, Zhiyi Ma, Ahmed El-Kishky, Siddharth Goyal, Mandeep Baines, Onur Celebi, Guillaume Wenzek, Vishrav Chaudhary, and 1 others. 2021. Beyond english-centric multilingual machine translation. In *Transactions of the Association for Computational Linguistics*, volume 9, pages 1–15.

Rohit Gupta, Ankit Kumar, and Rahul Singh. 2022. Crisismm: A framework for multimodal crisis response. *arXiv preprint arXiv:2203.01234*.

Kelvin Guu, Kenton Lee, Zora Tung, Panupong Pasupat, and Ming-Wei Chang. 2020. Realm: Retrieval-augmented language model pre-training. *arXiv preprint arXiv:2002.08909*.

Gautier Izacard and Edouard Grave. 2021. Leveraging passage retrieval with generative models for open domain question answering. In *Proceedings of the 16th Conference of the European Chapter of the Association for Computational Linguistics*, pages 1–10.

Chao Jia, Yinfei Yang, Ye Xia, Yi-Ting Chen, Zarana Parekh, Hieu Pham, Quoc Le, Yun-Hsuan Sung, Zhen Li, and Tom Duerig. 2021. Scaling up visual and vision-language representation learning with noisy text supervision. *arXiv preprint arXiv:2102.05918*.

Zhengjian Kang, Ye Zhang, Xiaoyu Deng, Xintao Li, and Yongzhe Zhang. 2025. Lp-detr: Layer-wise progressive relations for object detection. *Preprint*, arXiv:2502.05147.

Wonjae Kim, Bokyung Son, and Ildoo Kim. 2021. Vilt: Vision-and-language transformer without convolution or region supervision. *arXiv preprint arXiv:2102.03334*.

Patrick Lewis, Ethan Perez, Aleksandra Piktus, Fabio Petroni, Vladimir Karpukhin, Naman Goyal, Heinrich Kuettel, Mike Mitchell, Tim Lewis, Yuxiang Wu, and 1 others. 2020. Retrieval-augmented generation for knowledge-intensive nlp tasks. *Advances in Neural Information Processing Systems*, 33:1–12.

Junyang Lin, Rui Men, An Yang, Chang Zhou, Ming Zhou, Hongxia Zhang, Dawei Li, Jingren Lou, Furu Xie, Jiwei Wang, and 1 others. 2021. M6: A large-scale multimodal pretrained model. *arXiv preprint arXiv:2103.00823*.

Dong Liu, Roger Waleffe, Meng Jiang, and Shivaram Venkataraman. 2024. Graphsnapshot: Graph machine learning acceleration with fast storage and retrieval. *arXiv preprint arXiv:2406.17918*.

Dong Liu and Yanxuan Yu. 2024. Mt2st: Adaptive multi-task to single-task learning. *arXiv preprint arXiv:2406.18038*.

Yuxin Liu, Wei Zhang, and Xiaodong Li. 2021. Multimodal pretraining for cross-lingual and cross-modal transfer. *Proceedings of the 2021 Conference on Empirical Methods in Natural Language Processing (EMNLP)*, pages 1234–1245.

Zhen Liu, Jing Wang, and Yan Chen. 2022. Multimodal ai for public health communication in low-resource languages. *Journal of Medical Systems*, 46(8):1–12.

Jihyun Park, Hyunwoo Kim, and Seungwon Lee. 2021. Pororo-sv: A multimodal storytelling dataset with videos and text. *arXiv preprint arXiv:2109.04567*.

Alec Radford, Jong Wook Kim, Chris Hallacy, Aditya Ramesh, Gabriel Goh, Sandhini Agarwal, Girish Sastry, Amanda Askell, Pamela Mishkin, Jack Clark, and 1 others. 2021. Learning transferable visual models from natural language supervision. *arXiv preprint arXiv:2103.00020*.

Colin Raffel, Noam Shazeer, Adam Roberts, Katherine Lee, Sharan Narang, Michael Matena, Yanqi Zhou, Wei Li, and Peter J Liu. 2020. Exploring the limits of transfer learning with a unified text-to-text transformer. *Journal of Machine Learning Research*, 21(140):1–67.

Stephanie Strassel and Jennifer Tracey. 2016. Lorelei: Low resource languages for emergent incidents. *Proceedings of the 10th International Conference on Language Resources and Evaluation (LREC)*, pages 1–5.

Haoran Wang, Lei Zhang, and Yixuan Liu. 2023. Crossmodalrag: Bridging modalities for enhanced retrieval-augmented generation. *arXiv preprint arXiv:2301.04567*.

Xiaoyu Wu, Ming Zhang, and Liang Chen. 2023. Healthvision: A multimodal system for analyzing medical images and text. *Journal of Biomedical Informatics*, 138:1–15.

Tianyu Xie, Jiaqi Chen, and Zhiyuan Liu. 2022. Mmkg: A multimodal knowledge graph for low-resource languages. *arXiv preprint arXiv:2207.01234*.

Wei Zhang, Xiaodong Li, and Yu Wang. 2022. Mmrag: Multimodal retrieval-augmented generation for low-resource languages. *arXiv preprint arXiv:2205.12345*.

Yifan Zhang, Meng Li, and Wei Zhao. 2023. Enhancing disaster response with multimodal ai systems. *International Journal of Disaster Risk Reduction*, 82:1–10.

FORTIFY: Generative Model Fine-tuning with ORPO for ReTrieval Expansion of InFormal NoisY Text

Dan DeGenaro[1] Eugene Yang[2,3] David Etter[3] Cameron Carpenter[2]
Kate Sanders[2] Alexander Martin[2] Kenton Murray[2,3] Reno Kriz[2,3]
[1]Georgetown University; [2]Johns Hopkins University;
[3]Human Language Technology Center of Excellence
Correspondence: drd92@georgetown.edu

Abstract

Despite recent advancements in neural retrieval, representing text fragments or phrases with proper contextualized embeddings is still challenging. Particularly in video retrieval, where documents are text extracted through OCR from the frames or ASR from audio tracks, the textual content is rarely complete sentences but only a bag of phrases. In this work, we propose FORTIFY, a generative model fine-tuning approach for noisy document rewriting and summarization, to improve the downstream retrieval effectiveness. By experimenting on MultiVENT 2.0, an informational video retrieval benchmark, we show Llama fine-tuned with FORTIFY provides an effective document expansion, leading to a 30% improvement over prompting an out-of-box Llama model on nDCG@10. Zero-shot transferring the model tailored for MultiVENT 2.0 to two out-of-distribution datasets still demonstrates competitive retrieval effectiveness to other document preprocessing alternatives. Our training script and generated preference training data are publicly available at `https://available.after.acceptance/`.

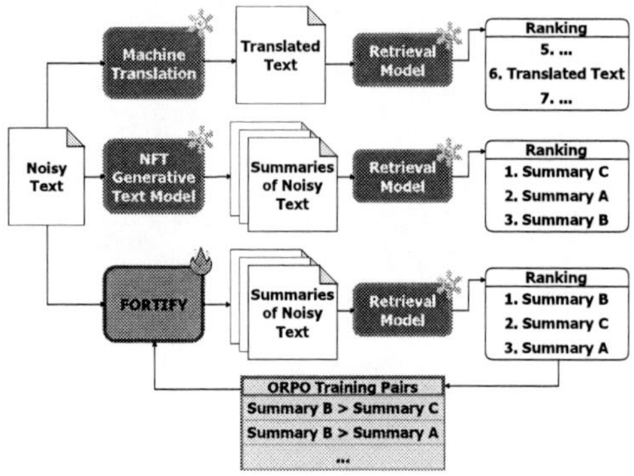

Figure 1: Overview of our document expansion approaches. Machine translation serves as a baseline. In the NFT (no fine-tuning) approach, we use a generative text model to generate fluent, keyword-dense summaries of noisy, multilingual text. In FORTIFY, we further rank the generated summaries using a retrieval model to create training pairs for preference optimization and fine-tune with Odds Ratio Preference Optimization (ORPO).

1 Introduction

In typical ad hoc retrieval, documents are usually assumed to be well-formed and informative, such as news articles, blog posts, or social media threads (Craswell et al., 2020; Lawrie et al., 2023a, 2024; Thakur et al., 2021). While some may be more structured and readable than others, they generally convey information in a way that is easily understandable to human readers. Since neural retrieval models, such as Dense Passage Retrieval (DPR) (Karpukhin et al., 2020) and ColBERT (Khattab and Zaharia, 2020), leverage pretrained language models (Devlin et al., 2019; Zhuang et al., 2021) trained on natural language to encode documents, they typically achieve strong performance on such tasks.

However, in many real-world settings, documents contain noisy or fragmented text, which does not resemble typical human communications. While this is relatively rare in traditional ad hoc retrieval, it is much more common when text is extracted from other modalities, such as automated speech recognition (ASR) from audio, or optical character recognition (OCR) from images or videos. Because this textual content is automatically generated, it may contain recognition errors, misidentifications, and incorrect reading order (de Oliveira et al., 2023), often resulting in disjointed sentence fragments or even incomplete words. As a result, neural retrieval models struggle to represent these texts effectively, leading to weaker retrieval performance.

To address this challenge, we propose a document expansion and rewriting approach using a generative model to transform fragmented text into coherent passages. We first explore a zero-shot

Proceedings of the 1st Workshop on Multimodal Augmented Generation via Multimodal Retrieval (MAGMaR 2025), pages 100–115
August 1, 2025 ©2025 Association for Computational Linguistics

prompting approach and demonstrate the innate ability of generative models like Llama3 (Dubey et al., 2024) to reconstruct text. While this method is promising, generating meaningful summaries from unordered, disjointed tokens remains a significant challenge. To further instill retrieval-driven preferences into the generative model, we fine-tune it using Odds Ratio Preference Optimization (ORPO) (Hong et al., 2024), a technique that does not require an explicit reference model or reward function. We name this method FORTIFY, or **F**ine-tuning with **OR**PO for **ReT**rieval expansion of **InF**ormal nois**Y** text.

We evaluate our approach on multiple video and cross-language retrieval benchmarks, and demonstrate that expanding raw documents with generated summaries leads to significant and robust performance improvements. Additionally, we find that FORTIFied summaries further boost retrieval effectiveness. To our knowledge, this is the first work to apply preference optimization to document expansion for retrieval.

Our contributions are threefold:

1. We introduce a novel document expansion approach which leverages a generative model to reconstruct fragmented text into coherent passages.
2. We propose FORTIFY, a fine-tuning mechanism using ORPO to encourage a language model to learn retrieval-driven preferences.
3. We conduct extensive experiments across multiple retrieval modalities and settings, demonstrating the effectiveness and robustness of our methods.

2 Related Work

Text Retrieval Recently developed neural retrieval models leverage pretrained language models to encode documents into one (Karpukhin et al., 2020; Formal et al., 2021; Nguyen et al., 2023) or multiple (Khattab and Zaharia, 2020; Li et al., 2023) contextualized embeddings to achieve better (Thakur et al., 2021) and more robust retrieval effectiveness, even in multilingual retrieval (Lawrie et al., 2023a, 2024). However, because of their pretraining data (Chari et al., 2023), they are not well-tuned for retrieving informal or even fragmented text (DeLucia et al., 2022; Lawrie et al., 2023b; Thakur et al., 2021). While recent work, such as RAPTOR (Sarthi et al., 2024), tries to preprocess text through layers of summarization, these models still anticipate well-formed text as the input. Particularly in video retrieval, text is extracted from different modalities and thus may be ill-formed. Neural text retrieval models suffer when dealing with this kind of text.

Video Retrieval Traditional benchmarks for video retrieval (Chen and Dolan, 2011; Krishna et al., 2017; Xu et al., 2016) generally involve generic web images or three to five-second video clips paired with web-scraped or automatically generated captions. Methods typically compute visual features from these images or from sampled video frames that can be mapped to these natural language captions (Cao et al., 2024; Luo et al., 2022; Reddy et al., 2025; Wang et al., 2024). However, there has been a shift away from these tasks to harder tasks requiring multimodal understanding, like audio and overlaid text, and longer videos (Kriz et al., 2024; Wang et al., 2019). This has lead to a rise in multimodal models that jointly incorporate modalities (Chen et al., 2023; Liu et al., 2025; Wu et al., 2025). However, these approaches are not robust to these challenging benchmarks, with one significant factor being the fusion of noisy outputs from OCR and ASR compounding errors and decreasing performance.

Multimodal Text Extraction Alongside visual captioning, optical character recognition (OCR) and automatic speech recognition (ASR) are two of the primary approaches to map multimodal data to natural language descriptions.

Recently, vision-language foundation models, such as PaliGemma (Beyer et al., 2024), InternVL (Chen et al., 2024), Idefics2 (Laurençon et al., 2024), and LLaVa (Liu et al., 2023), have been explored for modeling OCR content implicitly and effectively, rendering standard OCR approaches unnecessary, e.g., MMOCR (Kuang et al., 2021), and TrOCR (Li et al., 2022). Recent work has also explored using document screenshots for retrieval (Ma et al., 2024), an approach that relies heavily on the quality and the format of the screenshots. Retrieving documents with noisy OCR content (or otherwise working with such content) remains challenging.

Recent advances in ASR have achieved impressively low word error rates (Kheddar et al., 2024). However, speech involving code-switching (Yan et al., 2023), multiple speakers (Watanabe et al., 2020), or noisy environments (Dua et al., 2023; Li et al., 2014) all still present significant challenges to producing clean transcripts. Such transcripts are frequently incoherent despite low word error rates, motivating works involving post-hoc correction to the ASR output (Ma et al., 2023).

Preference Optimization Preference optimization (Rafailov et al., 2024; Shao et al., 2024; Xu et al., 2024; Meng et al., 2024; Hong et al., 2024) has arisen as a common alternative to reinforcement learning from human feedback (RLHF) (Christiano et al., 2017; Ouyang et al., 2022; Stiennon et al., 2020) to alleviate the multi-stage procedure requiring a reward model (Casper et al., 2023). Many recent works have built on DPO: replacing pair-wise preference data (Cai et al., 2024; Ethayarajh et al., 2024), with sets of reference responses in a log-likelihood loss (Xu et al., 2024; Park et al., 2024). In this work, we adopt Odds Ratio Preference Optimization (ORPO) (Hong et al., 2024), which incorporates an odds ratio-based loss for differentiating the generation styles between preferred and non-preferred responses. Compared to ordinary DPO, ORPO aligns better with the goal of producing fluent, coherent generations for downstream retrieval due to its inclusion of an additional language modeling loss term, along with the odds ratio term.

3 Methods

In this section, we describe our initial document expansion approach without fine-tuning (No-fine-tune – NFT), along with FORTIFY, a novel method for optimizing machine-generated document expansion for information retrieval.

Given a noisy document d, NFT involves zero-shot prompting a generative model for one or more summaries $\hat{d}_{1,...,N}$ from d, focusing on maximizing the inclusion of synonyms and keywords to enhance retrieval performance. These summaries are then used to augment the original document, producing an expanded version in the form $d + \hat{d}_1 + ... + \hat{d}_N$, where $+$ denotes concatenation.

FORTIFY further refines this expansion by optimizing machine-generated summaries based on their relevance to corresponding queries. Given a retrieval method, NFT summaries are scored against the corresponding queries, and training pairs are constructed by pairing the highest-scoring summary with several lower-scoring alternatives. This enables a retrieval-driven preference optimization.

3.1 Challenges in Noisy Text Retrieval

With frequency-based approaches such as BM25 (Robertson et al., 1995, 2009), retrieval performance degrades significantly in the presence of typographical errors, text recognition errors (e.g., substitution of visually similar characters), speech transcription errors (e.g., substitution of phonetically similar letters), and other character-level inaccuracies (de Oliveira et al., 2023). For example, if we attempt to retrieve a noisy document containing song lyrics that were recognized via OCR from a music video using the name of the musical artist as a query, we are unlikely to succeed, as the artist's name may not appear in the video. However, by leveraging a generative model to produce a summary, we not only correct character-level errors but also elaborate on the content and introduce useful keywords and phrases. An example is shown in Appendix C, Figure 5.

While neural retrieval models are more robust to character-level errors, they still struggle with higher-level structural issues, particularly ill-formed sentences and unrelated, adjacent phrases. This is because such noisy documents are rarely seen in the training data used for modern neural retrieval models (Nguyen et al., 2016). Consider a single video frame containing multiple distinct spans of text, such as two lines on a blackboard, each containing a chemical equation. To retrieve this video from the extracted text, we must flatten or concatenate all text spans to apply standard text retrievers. This process often produces incoherent outputs. Such text is likely to suffer not only from recognition errors, but also a lack of coherence, sentence structure, or recognizable words. By applying a generative model, we can reconstruct meaning from the fragmented text prior to indexing. A strong generative model can correctly identify the text as chemical equations and even suggest relevant elements and compounds. Notably, it can also extract and contextualize useful keywords such as *chemical*, *reactions*, and *compounds*, further improving retrievability. See Appendix C, Figure 6 for an example of this.

3.2 Zero-Shot Expansion of Noisy Text

We propose expanding noisy documents with such machine-generated summaries by leveraging modern generative models' abilities to produce clean, coherent, and keyword-dense text. As an initial setting, we adopt a zero-shot approach, where we provide the noisy text and prompt a generative model to produce a keyword-dense summary. The generated summaries can then either be indexed directly or concatenated with the original text; in later sections, we utilize the concatenation approach.

This method provides several advantages. Since modern generative models are highly multilingual, noisy documents can be expanded into any language, potentially improving the alignment between documents and expected queries for both term frequency and neural retrieval models. For instance, in cross language retrieval, where queries are primarily in English, we can prompt the model to produce English summaries of multilingual documents, effectively translating key phrases while preserving retrieval relevance. Additionally, by explicitly prompting the model to focus on synonyms, keywords, and retrieval relevance, summary-based document expansion introduces semantically related terms, improving retrieval effectiveness when queries lack important keywords.

Beyond improving term matching, generative document expansion also addresses structural issues in noisy documents. By generating coherent, well-formed summaries, the model compensates for disjointed or ill-structured inputs, producing text that is more suitable for retrieval. While generative model inference is computationally expensive, document expansion occurs at indexing time rather than search time, minimizing computational overhead during retrieval.

3.3 FORTIFY Preference Optimization

Zero-shot inference on generative models is heavily dependent on the prompt, which leads to instability in the generation (Jiang et al., 2020; Gao et al., 2021; Errica et al., 2024; Chakraborty et al., 2023). To improve the robustness of the generation process, we further fine-tune the model with preference examples based on the downstream retrieval task. Typically, fine-tuning the generative model for document expansion through reinforcement learning requires an explicit reward function on the final retrieval effectiveness and a preference model on the retrieval system. However, defining the reward is challenging as the query distribution is often unknown at training and indexing time, leaving great uncertainty in the direction of optimization. Therefore, we use Odds Ratio Preference Optimization (ORPO) (Hong et al., 2024), a variant of Direct Preference Optimization (Rafailov et al., 2024) without defining a reference model, to provide preference signals during fine-tuning.

Specifically, let $\hat{d}_x$ and $\hat{d}_y$ be two generated summaries of a raw document d. For a pointwise retrieval model $f(q, d)$ and a query q that document d is relevant to, we define the preference of the retrieval model $f(q, d)$ as

$$\hat{d}_x \succ \hat{d}_y \quad \text{if and only if} \quad f(q, \hat{d}_x) > f(q, \hat{d}_y) \tag{1}$$

where $\succ$ indicates the left operand is more preferable than the right operand.

Following Hong et al. (2024), the odds ratio loss of the preference $\hat{d}_x \succ \hat{d}_y$ can be written as

$$\mathcal{L}_{OR} = -\log \sigma \left(\log \frac{\mathbf{odds}_\theta(\hat{d}_x|d)}{\mathbf{odds}_\theta(\hat{d}_y|d)} \right) \tag{2}$$

where the function $\mathbf{odds}_\theta$ indicates the odds of generating such a sequence of text based on the parameter θ. Such odds ratio losses promote the generative model to generate $\hat{d}_x$ over $\hat{d}_y$ when given the document d based on the preference of the retrieval model f and the query q. Intuitively, the distribution of the training query q and pre-defined retrieval model f are critical to this process since the model would be biased toward the two after fine-tuning. In our experiments, we provide empirical evidence that the resulting generative model is actually robust to the downstream retrieval models.

4 Experiments

4.1 Data

We evaluate FORTIFY on two video retrieval datasets as well as a cross-language text retrieval dataset as an out-of-domain evaluation. The statistics are summarized in Table 3 in the Appendix.

- MultiVENT2.0 (Kriz et al., 2024) consists of 218K YouTube videos, with text and speech content primarily in Arabic, Chinese, English, Korean, Russian, and Spanish. The videos vary heavily in terms of production quality, from unprocessed recordings taken on mobile phones to professionally edited news broadcasts. Queries are designed to approximate what a user might search for in order to find a video about a specific event. We evaluate on the test split (2,546 queries over 109K videos) and report nDCG@10 and R@1000 following Kriz et al. (2024).
- TextVR (Wu et al., 2025) consists of 42.2K queries over 10.5K videos from across eight

domains: Street View (indoor), Street View (outdoor), Game, Sports, Driving, Activity, TV Show, and Cooking. We evaluate on the test split, containing 2.7K videos, with one query each, and report R@1 and R@10 to align with the online shared task associated with TextVR.

- NeuCLIR Chinese Technical CLIR Collection (Lawrie et al., 2024) contains about 396K journal abstracts from 1,980 Chinese academic journals spanning 67 disciplines. The NeuCLIR Technical document collection has two corresponding sets of topics from the 2023 and 2024 TREC NeuCLIR tracks, respectively. To ensure the summarization process is not trivially easy, we use only the abstract without the title as the raw document. We report the official evaluation metrics of the NeuCLIR track, which are nDCG@20 and R@1000.

4.2 Text extraction from video

In order to create textual indices for retrieval, we extract text from the videos using two main approaches: Automatic Speech Recognition (ASR) and Optical Character Recognition (OCR). Except where explicitly indicated, we do not perform machine translation on either the ASR or OCR text.

ASR Videos frequently contain audio, and for our ASR system, we rely on a powerful multilingual model, Whisper Large v2 (Radford et al., 2023) without speech translation (that is, audio detected by Whisper as language x is transcribed in language x, not in English). As Whisper Large v2 is among the top-performing open-source ASR models (even outperforming proprietary models as shown in the authors' appendix), and as it is highly multilingual and trained on diverse sources of data, its outputs are fairly accurate across domains and more commonly used languages. If the speech extracted from a video is indeed useful for retrieval, Whisper is likely to give the strongest baseline for retrieval using ASR.

OCR We further extract text OCR using the hybrid model described in Etter et al. (2023). This is a state-of-the-art multilingual model which was found to significantly outperform many popular open-source OCR models and toolkits on the test split of the highly multilingual CAMIO OCR dataset (Arrigo et al., 2022), including Tesseract (Smith et al., 2009), EasyOCR, TrOCR (Li et al., 2022), and MMOCR (Kuang et al., 2021) across a variety of different scripts.

4.3 Baseline Document Expansion

As a baseline, ASR and OCR texts are summarized by prompting Llama-3-8B-Instruct (Dubey et al., 2024; AI@Meta, 2024) without additional fine-tuning (*No-fine-tune (NFT) summaries*). For each video, the ASR content is placed into a prompt template that explicitly directs Llama to produce a keyword-dense summary useful for information retrieval. This prompt is shown in Appendix B, Figure 3.

Summaries are generated by passing the ASR or OCR text to the Llama-3-8B-Instruct model with a generation limit of 512 tokens, no repeated trigrams, and using top-p sampling with $p = 0.9$ and a temperature of 0.6. The raw ASR or OCR (or the concatenation of both) text is expanded with the summaries by concatenation. Processing MultiVENT 2.0's test split (109K videos), assuming the text is already extracted, took approximately 36 hours on eight 40GB A100 GPUs.

Alternatively, we expand the raw documents with their machine translation since the extracted ASR or OCR text is not necessarily English, which is the query language of the three evaluation collections. For MultiVENT 2.0, since the collection is large, we use NLLB (Costa-jussà et al., 2022), an open-source machine translation model that covers more than 200 languages, to translate the extracted ASR and OCR text. For TextVR, we use Google Translate to obtain the translation through their Web APIs. Finally, for NeuCLIR Technical Documents, we use the official translation provided by the NeuCLIR track, which is also produced by Google Translate.

4.4 FORTIFY Fine-tuning Setup

We fine-tune Llama-3-8B-Instruct to produce more useful summaries using an original dataset of preferred and dispreferred summaries (contrastive training pairs, as required to proceed with ORPO). The summaries included in this dataset were produced using the subset of the training split of MultiVENT 2.0, totaling 2,000 videos, for which training queries were written. For each of the unique query-video pairs having OCR content, we prompt Llama to produce a keyword-dense summary suited to information retrieval, given the OCR content.

To ensure high quality summaries in the training set, we use a one-shot prompt template, shown in Appendix B, Figure 4, containing the extracted OCR text from a manually selected video in MultiVENT's training set, along with a manually written summary to produce more accurate summaries for training.

We sample from Llama-3-8B-Instruct five times to produce five distinct summaries of the OCR content with the same generation setting. We then score each of the generated summaries against their relevant queries using the PLAID-X implementation of ColBERT (Khattab and Zaharia, 2020; Santhanam et al., 2022; Yang et al., 2024b) (details are discussed below). Finally, we construct training summary pairs by pairing the highest-scoring summary for a particular video's OCR with each of the lower-scoring summaries. We repeat a nearly identical process to produce summaries of the ASR content but with a different prompt template containing the extracted ASR text from a particular video along with a manually written summary. This dataset is split into 80-20 train-dev splits for FORTIFY fine-tuning.

We perform a LoRA (Hu et al., 2021) fine-tuning process on Llama-3-8B-Instruct with ORPO using the implementation provided by Huggingface[1], with LoRA matrices of rank 16, $\alpha = 32$, and dropout probability 0.05. We target the up, down, Q, K, V, and O projection layers during fine-tuning. We train for three epochs over 12K training pairs, sampling randomly from the training pairs. We employ a paged AdamW 8-bit optimizer with a learning rate of $8 \cdot 10^{-6}$, $\beta = 0.1$ (called λ in the ORPO paper), and 10 linear warmup steps. We accumulate gradients over 4 batches of size 2.[2]

4.5 Retrieval Models and Pipeline

We test FORTIFY on three retrieval models, BM25 (Robertson et al., 1995, 2009), DPR (Karpukhin et al., 2020), and ColBERT (Khattab and Zaharia, 2020), while only fine-tuning Llama with FORTIFY on ColBERT. For BM25, we use the implementation provided by PyTerrier (Macdonald et al., 2021) with $k_1 = 1.2$, $k_3 = 8$, and $b = 0.75$. For DPR, we use Tevatron (Gao et al., 2022) with a multilingual DPR model based on DistilBERT (Sanh, 2019) provided by `sentence-transformers` (Reimers and Gurevych, 2019) that is fine-tuned on the Quora dataset.[3] Documents are encoded and indexed with FAISS (Douze et al., 2024) without approximation. Finally, we use the PLAID-X (Yang et al., 2024c) implementation for ColBERT with 1-bit residual compression. Documents are encoded with a Multilingual ColBERT-X (Nair et al., 2022; Lawrie et al., 2023c) model trained with Multilingual Translate Distill (Yang et al., 2024a) from the Mono-mT5-XXL cross-encoder (Jeronymo et al., 2023). [4] Additionally, we report results using an English-to-Chinese cross-language ColBERT-X model [5] on the NeuCLIR Technical Document task for comparison. Results can be seen in the Appendix, Table 4.

5 Results and Analysis

For MultiVENT 2.0 (the dataset on which FORTIFY is trained), presented at the left part of Table 1, expanding the original OCR, ASR, or both (OCR+ASR) with summaries generated by FORTIFY provides a significant improvement over no expansion or expansion with their machine translation. When using ColBERT on the FORTIFY-expanded OCR and ASR documents, it provides a 76% improvement in nDCG@10 (0.324 to 0.569) over LanguageBind (Zhu et al., 2023), a state-of-the-art video encoding language model reported in the MultiVENT 2.0 dataset paper (Kriz et al., 2024), and 30% over no expansion (0.437 to 0.569).

Regardless of the source of text (OCR or ASR), expanding with generated summaries is more effective than using machine translation, which is an alternative document processing method (with similar hardware requirements) since the extracted text is not necessarily in the query language. Such improvements are consistent across multiple settings, indicating that the summaries are useful for a wide range of retrieval models, including statistical models like BM25.

However, since FORTIFY is trained to tailor the expansion for retrieval using ColBERT, documents expanded with FORTIFY summaries are more advantageous for ColBERT, resulting in improvement in both nDCG@10 and R@1000 over zero-shot prompting, though nDCG@10 is not statistically significant. However, the differences in

[1] `https://huggingface.co/docs/trl/main/en/orpo_trainer`

[2] Hyperparameter choices largely retained from this tutorial: `https://huggingface.co/blog/mlabonne/orpo-llama-3`

[3] `https://huggingface.co/sentence-transformers/quora-distilbert-multilingual`

[4] `https://huggingface.co/hltcoe/plaidx-large-eng-tdist-mt5xxl-engeng`

[5] `https://huggingface.co/hltcoe/plaidx-large-zho-tdist-mt5xxl-engeng`

Table 1: Retrieval effectiveness with different document expansion approaches. nDCG in the table uses a rank cutoff at 10. Superscript of w, x, y and z indicates the metric value using the corresponding expansion approach is statistically significantly better than the **same retrieval model** using *No Expansion* (w), *Machine Translation* (x), *No-Fine-tuned (NFT) Summary* (y), and FORTIF*ied Summary* (z), respectively (also indicated in the first column) with 95% confidence. The statistical test uses a paired t-test with multiple testing corrections over datasets and retrieval models. Rows in light gray indicate retrieval methods relying on features other than text, which is unfair to compare methods only using the extracted text but are included for border comparisons.

		MultiVENT 2.0						TextVR (*Zero-shot Transferred*)					
		OCR		ASR		OCR+ASR		OCR		ASR		OCR+ASR	
Expansion Approach	Retrieval Model	nDCG	R@1K	nDCG	R@1K	nDCG	R@1K	R@1	R@10	R@1	R@10	R@1	R@10
StarVR												0.165	0.473
LanguageBind						0.324	0.846					0.133	0.830
(w)*No Expansion*	BM25	0.157	0.267	0.114	0.204	0.195	0.322	0.141	0.278	0.044	0.097	0.160	0.305
	DPR	0.088	0.334	0.146	0.482	0.153	0.532	0.042	0.120	0.036	0.089	0.051	0.148
	ColBERT	0.317	0.616	0.344	0.583	0.437	0.740	0.134	0.259	0.051	0.114	0.153	0.292
(x)Machine Translation	BM25	0.319^{w}	0.592^{w}	0.300^{w}	0.559^{w}	0.427^{w}	0.733^{w}	0.147	0.297^{w}	0.046	0.100^{w}	0.168^{w}	0.325^{w}
	DPR	0.166^{w}	0.500^{w}	0.198^{w}	0.513^{w}	0.236^{w}	0.629^{w}	0.043	0.117	0.037	0.092^{w}	0.052	0.148
	ColBERT	0.375^{w}	0.633^{w}	0.401^{w}	0.589	0.517^{w}	0.760^{w}	0.131	0.260	0.051	0.114	0.155	0.304^{w}
NFT (y)Llama Summary	BM25	0.360^{wxz}	0.646^{wxz}	0.351^{wxz}	0.606^{wxz}	0.492^{wxz}	0.788^{wxz}	0.156^{w}	$\mathbf{0.314}^{wx}$	$\mathbf{0.054}^{wx}$	$\mathbf{0.128}^{wx}$	0.178^{w}	0.346^{wx}
	DPR	0.237^{wx}	0.575^{wxz}	0.249^{wxz}	0.554^{wx}	0.318^{wx}	0.708^{wxz}	0.059^{wx}	0.164^{wx}	0.034	0.099^{w}	0.067^{wx}	0.191^{wx}
	ColBERT	0.429^{wx}	0.675^{wx}	0.434^{wx}	0.616^{wx}	0.564^{wx}	0.795^{wx}	0.147^{wx}	0.282^{wx}	0.047	0.122	0.167^{wx}	$\mathbf{0.329}^{wx}$
(z)FORTIFied Summary	BM25	0.350^{wx}	0.630^{wx}	0.333^{wx}	0.595^{wx}	0.475^{wx}	0.779^{wx}	$\mathbf{0.160}^{wx}$	0.312^{wx}	0.052^{w}	0.123^{wx}	$\mathbf{0.180}^{wx}$	0.356^{wxy}
	DPR	0.241^{wx}	0.564^{wx}	0.240^{wx}	0.547^{wx}	0.315^{wx}	0.699^{wx}	0.059^{wx}	0.159^{wx}	0.036	0.104^{wx}	0.059^{w}	0.183^{wx}
	ColBERT	$\mathbf{0.431}^{wx}$	$\mathbf{0.688}^{wxy}$	$\mathbf{0.435}^{wx}$	$\mathbf{0.623}^{wxy}$	$\mathbf{0.569}^{wx}$	$\mathbf{0.805}^{wxy}$	0.144^{x}	0.278^{wx}	0.053^{y}	0.123^{wx}	0.168^{wx}	0.319^{wx}

R@1000 are significant, indicating that the FORTIFY-expanded documents include more related terms to the expansion but are not more accurate than what zero-shot prompting the generative model can provide. When using BM25 and DPR to encode and index the FORTIFY-expanded documents, since they are not the predefined customer of the summarization model, the resulting retrieval metrics are only similar or slightly lower than NFT summaries, which also indicates that FORTIFY can effectively tailor the document expansion to the expressed preferences of the downstream retrieval model during fine-tuning.

Interestingly, although DPR significantly underperforms with respect to ColBERT, the improvement due to expansion with generative summaries is much larger for DPR than for ColBERT, which validates our initial intuition that it is possible to leverage the linguistic ability of a generative model to provide additional context and language structure for the downstream neural retrieval model to consume. Since DPR encodes the entire piece of text as a single dense vector, providing it with better-structured documents is more advantageous for DPR than ColBERT, which is capable of falling back to term matching through dense token embeddings. Without such expansion, DPR is even less effective than BM25 as shown in the *No Expansion* condition in Table 1. When using both OCR and ASR text, DPR improves 106% in nDCG@10 when expanding with FORTIFY summaries (0.153 to 0.315) while ColBERT *"only"* demonstrates a 30% improvement (0.437 to 0.569). Even compared against machine translation, which already processes and potentially denoises the raw and noisy text via a language model, DPR still improves 33% when using FORTIFied summaries while ColBERT *"only"* improves by 10%.

5.1 Out-of-Distribution Transfer

Zero-shot transferring FORTIFY to TextVR, which demonstrated a very different distribution both in videos and extracted text (presented in Table 3), the differences between zero-shot prompting and the FORTIFY-fine-tuned summarizer are small and not statistically significant. Since the distribution of the queries and the videos are significantly different from MultiVENT 2.0, on which the model was trained, the additional preference optimization through ORPO is not particularly helpful but also not harmful. Such robustness indicates the FORTIFY-fine-tuned model still retains its original language modeling capability to support generalization while providing more beneficial information when preferences of the downstream retrieval model were communicated during fine-tuning. Interestingly, expanding ASR and OCR text with FORTIFied summaries using BM25 is still 9% more effective in R@1 (0.165 to 0.180) than StarVR, proposed along with the introduction

Table 2: Retrieval effectiveness when concatenating multiple sources of text in MultiVENT 2.0 using ColBERT. nDCG values in the table uses a rank cutoff at 10. Checkmarks indicate inclusion of such source of text in the documents for ColBERT indexing.

Original Noisy Text		Machine Translation		FORTIFied Summary			
OCR	ASR	OCR	ASR	OCR	ASR	nDCG	R@1K
	✓					0.317	0.616
✓						0.344	0.583
✓	✓					0.437	0.740
✓	✓	✓	✓			0.517	0.760
✓	✓			✓	✓	0.569	0.805
✓	✓	✓	✓	✓	✓	0.578	0.797

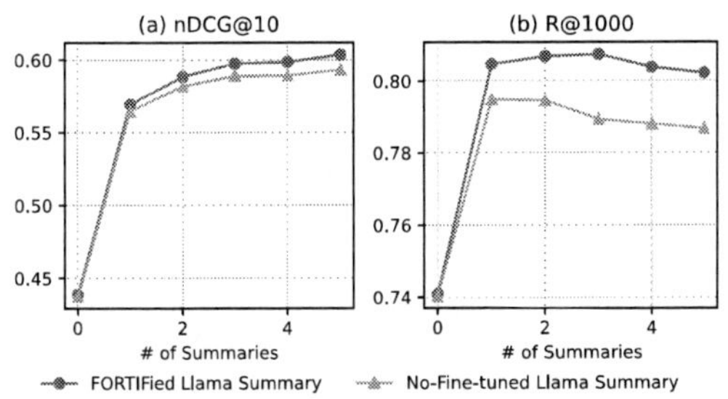

Figure 2: Effectiveness of concatenating multiple generated summaries on MultiVENT 2.0 using both OCR and ASR text.

of TextVR (Wu et al., 2025). Notably, StarVR involves a heavy video space-time encoder, as well as projection from a scene text encoder.

Note that since the amount of text extracted via ASR from the audio tracks of the videos in TextVR is scarce (only on average 185 characters per video), no expansion approach can expand the short text in any meaningful way, resulting in roughly the same effectiveness as forgoing document expansion.

5.2 Expansion with Multiple Summaries

Given the variability of generative models, we investigate generating multiple summaries using both the NFT Llama and FORTIFied models on MultiVENT 2.0. Illustrated in Figure 2, concatenating more summaries provides marginal improvements in both nDCG@10 and R@1000. However, such improvements quickly start to diminish as more summaries are added, as expected. Particularly in R@1000, expanding the noisy text with five summaries produces documents whose meanings begin to drift away from those of the original texts. This results in the promotion of more irrelevant videos to the top 1000 and thus decreases R@1000 when adding more than three summaries. Notably, FORTIFied summaries, despite still inducing a semantic drift, are still more effective than the NFT version, indicating that FORTIFY consistently instills the preference into the model, even when we are generating more summaries through randomized decoding.

nDCG@10, on the other hand, continues to improve when adding more summaries, indicating that summaries are still beneficial in terms of promoting relevant videos to the top of the ranked list. Such a trade-off between the top and the bottom of the ranked list is expected when expanding queries or documents and remains an issue for neural models such as ColBERT (Wang et al., 2023).

Finally, we also investigate expanding the noisy documents with their machine translation and FORTIFied summaries. Presented in Table 2, the final retrieval effectiveness increases as we introduce more expansion to the documents. Although expansion with machine translation is less effective than FORTIFied summaries, the two expansion approaches provide complementary information to the retrieval model. Thus, combining both approaches by concatenation results in a statistically significant improvement in nDCG@10 over just using the FORTIFied summaries (0.569 to 0.578). As before, such elaborated expansion also promotes more irrelevant videos, resulting in a slightly lower R@1000.

6 Conclusion and Future Work

In this paper, we proposed a generative model fine-tuning approach FORTIFY for document expansion. FORTIFY tailors a generative model to a specific kind of noisy document and a downstream retrieval model through ORPO, a preference optimization approach. We showed that models fine-tuned with FORTIFY provide more effective expansion summaries than an out-of-the-box Llama model. The resulting FORTIFied Llama model also demonstrates robustness to documents and retrieval models beyond the ones predefined during ORPO fine-tuning.

Beyond the success of FORTIFY on noisy text, we would like to explore it on other general ad hoc retrieval tasks to tailor the retrieval to a specific domain, corpus, or even user. Given the flexibility of preference optimization, we believe FORTIFY can be adapted to arbitrary retrieval model preference.

References

AI@Meta. 2024. Llama 3 model card.

Michael Arrigo, Stephanie Strassel, Nolan King, Thao Tran, and Lisa Mason. 2022. CAMIO: A corpus for OCR in multiple languages. In *Proceedings of the Thirteenth Language Resources and Evaluation Conference*, pages 1209–1216, Marseille, France. European Language Resources Association.

Lucas Beyer, Andreas Steiner, André Susano Pinto, Alexander Kolesnikov, Xiao Wang, Daniel Salz, Maxim Neumann, Ibrahim Alabdulmohsin, Michael Tschannen, Emanuele Bugliarello, Thomas Unterthiner, Daniel Keysers, Skanda Koppula, Fangyu Liu, Adam Grycner, Alexey Gritsenko, Neil Houlsby, Manoj Kumar, Keran Rong, and 16 others. 2024. Paligemma: A versatile 3b vlm for transfer. *Preprint*, arXiv:2407.07726.

Tianchi Cai, Xierui Song, Jiyan Jiang, Fei Teng, Jinjie GU, and Guannan Zhang. 2024. Unified language model alignment with demonstration and point-wise human preference.

Meng Cao, Haoran Tang, Jinfa Huang, Peng Jin, Can Zhang, Ruyang Liu, Long Chen, Xiaodan Liang, Li Yuan, and Ge Li. 2024. RAP: Efficient text-video retrieval with sparse-and-correlated adapter. In *Findings of the Association for Computational Linguistics: ACL 2024*, pages 7160–7174, Bangkok, Thailand. Association for Computational Linguistics.

Stephen Casper, Xander Davies, Claudia Shi, Thomas Krendl Gilbert, Jérémy Scheurer, Javier Rando, Rachel Freedman, Tomasz Korbak, David Lindner, Pedro Freire, Tony Wang, Samuel Marks, Charbel-Raphaël Segerie, Micah Carroll, Andi Peng, Phillip Christoffersen, Mehul Damani, Stewart Slocum, Usman Anwar, and 13 others. 2023. Open problems and fundamental limitations of reinforcement learning from human feedback. *Preprint*, arXiv:2307.15217.

Mohna Chakraborty, Adithya Kulkarni, and Qi Li. 2023. Zero-shot approach to overcome perturbation sensitivity of prompts. *Preprint*, arXiv:2305.15689.

Andreas Chari, Sean MacAvaney, and Iadh Ounis. 2023. On the effects of regional spelling conventions in retrieval models. In *Proceedings of the 46th International ACM SIGIR Conference on Research and Development in Information Retrieval*, SIGIR '23, page 2220–2224, New York, NY, USA. Association for Computing Machinery.

David Chen and William Dolan. 2011. Collecting highly parallel data for paraphrase evaluation. In *Proceedings of the 49th Annual Meeting of the Association for Computational Linguistics: Human Language Technologies*, pages 190–200, Portland, Oregon, USA. Association for Computational Linguistics.

Sihan Chen, Handong Li, Qunbo Wang, Zijia Zhao, Mingzhen Sun, Xinxin Zhu, and Jing Liu. 2023. Vast: A vision-audio-subtitle-text omni-modality foundation model and dataset. In *Advances in Neural Information Processing Systems*, volume 36, pages 72842–72866, New Orleans, Louisiana, USA. Curran Associates, Inc.

Zhe Chen, Jiannan Wu, Wenhai Wang, Weijie Su, Guo Chen, Sen Xing, Muyan Zhong, Qinglong Zhang, Xizhou Zhu, Lewei Lu, and 1 others. 2024. Internvl: Scaling up vision foundation models and aligning for generic visual-linguistic tasks. In *Proceedings of the IEEE/CVF Conference on Computer Vision and Pattern Recognition*, pages 24185–24198, Seattle, Washington, USA. IEEE.

Paul F. Christiano, Jan Leike, Tom B. Brown, Miljan Martic, Shane Legg, and Dario Amodei. 2017. Deep reinforcement learning from human preferences. In *Proceedings of the 31st International Conference on Neural Information Processing Systems*, NIPS'17, page 4302–4310, Red Hook, NY, USA. Curran Associates Inc.

Marta R Costa-jussà, James Cross, Onur Çelebi, Maha Elbayad, Kenneth Heafield, Kevin Heffernan, Elahe Kalbassi, Janice Lam, Daniel Licht, Jean Maillard, and 1 others. 2022. No language left behind: Scaling human-centered machine translation. *arXiv preprint arXiv:2207.04672*.

Nick Craswell, Bhaskar Mitra, Emine Yilmaz, Daniel Campos, and Ellen M. Voorhees. 2020. Overview of the trec 2019 deep learning track. *Preprint*, arXiv:2003.07820.

Lucas Lima de Oliveira, Danny Suarez Vargas, Antônio Marcelo Azevedo Alexandre, Fábio Corrêa Cordeiro, Diogo da Silva Magalhães Gomes, Max de Castro Rodrigues, Regis Kruel Romeu, and Viviane Pereira Moreira. 2023. Evaluating and mitigating the impact of OCR errors on information retrieval. *International Journal on Digital Libraries*, 24(1):45–62.

Alexandra DeLucia, Shijie Wu, Aaron Mueller, Carlos Aguirre, Philip Resnik, and Mark Dredze. 2022. Bernice: A multilingual pre-trained encoder for Twitter. In *Proceedings of the 2022 Conference on Empirical Methods in Natural Language Processing*, pages 6191–6205, Abu Dhabi, United Arab Emirates. Association for Computational Linguistics.

Jacob Devlin, Ming-Wei Chang, Kenton Lee, and Kristina Toutanova. 2019. BERT: Pre-training of deep bidirectional transformers for language understanding. In *Proceedings of the 2019 Conference of the North American Chapter of the Association for Computational Linguistics: Human Language Technologies, Volume 1 (Long and Short Papers)*, pages 4171–4186, Minneapolis, Minnesota. Association for Computational Linguistics.

Matthijs Douze, Alexandr Guzhva, Chengqi Deng, Jeff Johnson, Gergely Szilvasy, Pierre-Emmanuel Mazaré,

Maria Lomeli, Lucas Hosseini, and Hervé Jégou. 2024. The faiss library. *Preprint*, arXiv:2401.08281.

Mohit Dua, Akanksha, and Shelza Dua. 2023. Noise robust automatic speech recognition: review and analysis. *International Journal of Speech Technology*, 26(2):475–519.

Abhimanyu Dubey, Abhinav Jauhri, Abhinav Pandey, Abhishek Kadian, Ahmad Al-Dahle, Aiesha Letman, Akhil Mathur, Alan Schelten, Amy Yang, Angela Fan, and 1 others. 2024. The llama 3 herd of models.

Federico Errica, Giuseppe Siracusano, Davide Sanvito, and Roberto Bifulco. 2024. What did i do wrong? quantifying llms' sensitivity and consistency to prompt engineering. *Preprint*, arXiv:2406.12334.

Kawin Ethayarajh, Winnie Xu, Niklas Muennighoff, Dan Jurafsky, and Douwe Kiela. 2024. Model alignment as prospect theoretic optimization. In *Proceedings of the 41st International Conference on Machine Learning*, ICML'24, Vienna, Austria. JMLR.org.

David Etter, Cameron Carpenter, and Nolan King. 2023. A hybrid model for multilingual ocr. In *Document Analysis and Recognition - ICDAR 2023*, pages 467–483, Cham. Springer Nature Switzerland.

Thibault Formal, Benjamin Piwowarski, and Stéphane Clinchant. 2021. Splade: Sparse lexical and expansion model for first stage ranking. In *Proceedings of the 44th International ACM SIGIR Conference on Research and Development in Information Retrieval*, pages 2288–2292.

Luyu Gao, Xueguang Ma, Jimmy J. Lin, and Jamie Callan. 2022. Tevatron: An efficient and flexible toolkit for dense retrieval. *ArXiv*, abs/2203.05765.

Tianyu Gao, Adam Fisch, and Danqi Chen. 2021. Making pre-trained language models better few-shot learners. *Preprint*, arXiv:2012.15723.

Jiwoo Hong, Noah Lee, and James Thorne. 2024. ORPO: Monolithic preference optimization without reference model. In *Proceedings of the 2024 Conference on Empirical Methods in Natural Language Processing*, pages 11170–11189, Miami, Florida, USA. Association for Computational Linguistics.

Edward J Hu, Yelong Shen, Phillip Wallis, Zeyuan Allen-Zhu, Yuanzhi Li, Shean Wang, Lu Wang, and Weizhu Chen. 2021. Lora: Low-rank adaptation of large language models.

Vitor Jeronymo, Roberto Lotufo, and Rodrigo Nogueira. 2023. Neuralmind-unicamp at 2022 trec neuclir: Large boring rerankers for cross-lingual retrieval.

Zhengbao Jiang, Frank F. Xu, Jun Araki, and Graham Neubig. 2020. How can we know what language models know? *Transactions of the Association for Computational Linguistics*, 8:423–438.

Vladimir Karpukhin, Barlas Oguz, Sewon Min, Patrick Lewis, Ledell Wu, Sergey Edunov, Danqi Chen, and Wen-tau Yih. 2020. Dense passage retrieval for open-domain question answering. In *Proceedings of the 2020 Conference on Empirical Methods in Natural Language Processing (EMNLP)*, pages 6769–6781, Online. Association for Computational Linguistics.

Omar Khattab and Matei Zaharia. 2020. Colbert: Efficient and effective passage search via contextualized late interaction over bert. In *Proceedings of the 43rd International ACM SIGIR Conference on Research and Development in Information Retrieval*, SIGIR '20, page 39–48, New York, NY, USA. Association for Computing Machinery.

Hamza Kheddar, Mustapha Hemis, and Yassine Himeur. 2024. Automatic speech recognition using advanced deep learning approaches: A survey. *ArXiv*, abs/2403.01255.

Ranjay Krishna, Kenji Hata, Frederic Ren, Li Fei-Fei, and Juan Carlos Niebles. 2017. Dense-captioning events in videos. In *2017 IEEE International Conference on Computer Vision (ICCV)*, pages 706–715, Venice, Italy. IEEE.

Reno Kriz, Kate Sanders, David Etter, Kenton Murray, Cameron Carpenter, Kelly Van Ochten, Hannah Recknor, Jimena Guallar-Blasco, Alexander Martin, Ronald Colaianni, and 1 others. 2024. Multivent 2.0: A massive multilingual benchmark for event-centric video retrieval.

Zhanghui Kuang, Hongbin Sun, Zhizhong Li, Xiaoyu Yue, Tsui Hin Lin, Jianyong Chen, Huaqiang Wei, Yiqin Zhu, Tong Gao, Wenwei Zhang, Kai Chen, Wayne Zhang, and Dahua Lin. 2021. Mmocr: A comprehensive toolbox for text detection, recognition and understanding. *Preprint*, arXiv:2108.06543.

Hugo Laurençon, Léo Tronchon, Matthieu Cord, and Victor Sanh. 2024. What matters when building vision-language models? *Preprint*, arXiv:2405.02246.

Dawn Lawrie, Sean MacAvaney, James Mayfield, Paul McNamee, Douglas W Oard, Luca Soldaini, and Eugene Yang. 2023a. Overview of the trec 2022 neuclir track.

Dawn Lawrie, Sean MacAvaney, James Mayfield, Paul McNamee, Douglas W Oard, Luca Soldaini, and Eugene Yang. 2024. Overview of the trec 2023 neuclir track.

Dawn Lawrie, James Mayfield, Douglas W. Oard, Eugene Yang, Suraj Nair, and Petra Galuščáková. 2023b. Hc3: A suite of test collections for clir evaluation over informal text. In *Proceedings of the 46th International ACM SIGIR Conference on Research and Development in Information Retrieval*, SIGIR '23, page 2880–2889, New York, NY, USA. Association for Computing Machinery.

Dawn Lawrie, Eugene Yang, Douglas W. Oard, and James Mayfield. 2023c. Neural approaches to multilingual information retrieval. In *Advances in Information Retrieval: 45th European Conference on Information Retrieval, ECIR 2023, Dublin, Ireland, April 2–6, 2023, Proceedings, Part I*, page 521–536, Berlin, Heidelberg. Springer-Verlag.

Jinyu Li, Li Deng, Yifan Gong, and Reinhold Haeb-Umbach. 2014. An overview of noise-robust automatic speech recognition. *IEEE/ACM Transactions on Audio, Speech, and Language Processing*, 22(4):745–777.

Minghan Li, Sheng-Chieh Lin, Barlas Oguz, Asish Ghoshal, Jimmy Lin, Yashar Mehdad, Wen-tau Yih, and Xilun Chen. 2023. CITADEL: Conditional token interaction via dynamic lexical routing for efficient and effective multi-vector retrieval. In *Proceedings of the 61st Annual Meeting of the Association for Computational Linguistics (Volume 1: Long Papers)*, pages 11891–11907, Toronto, Canada. Association for Computational Linguistics.

Minghao Li, Tengchao Lv, Jingye Chen, Lei Cui, Yijuan Lu, Dinei Florencio, Cha Zhang, Zhoujun Li, and Furu Wei. 2022. Trocr: Transformer-based optical character recognition with pre-trained models. *Preprint*, arXiv:2109.10282.

Haotian Liu, Chunyuan Li, Qingyang Wu, and Yong Jae Lee. 2023. Visual instruction tuning. In *Advances in Neural Information Processing Systems*, volume 36, pages 34892–34916. Curran Associates, Inc.

Jing Liu, Sihan Chen, Xingjian He, Longteng Guo, Xinxin Zhu, Weining Wang, and Jinhui Tang. 2025. Valor: Vision-audio-language omni-perception pretraining model and dataset. *IEEE Transactions on Pattern Analysis and Machine Intelligence*, 47(2):708–724.

Huaishao Luo, Lei Ji, Ming Zhong, Yang Chen, Wen Lei, Nan Duan, and Tianrui Li. 2022. Clip4clip: An empirical study of clip for end to end video clip retrieval and captioning. *Neurocomput.*, 508(C):293–304.

Rao Ma, Mengjie Qian, Potsawee Manakul, Mark Gales, and Kate Knill. 2023. Can generative large language models perform asr error correction?

Xueguang Ma, Sheng-Chieh Lin, Minghan Li, Wenhu Chen, and Jimmy Lin. 2024. Unifying multimodal retrieval via document screenshot embedding. In *Proceedings of the 2024 Conference on Empirical Methods in Natural Language Processing*, pages 6492–6505, Miami, Florida, USA. Association for Computational Linguistics.

Craig Macdonald, Nicola Tonellotto, Sean MacAvaney, and Iadh Ounis. 2021. Pyterrier: Declarative experimentation in python from bm25 to dense retrieval. In *Proceedings of the 30th ACM International Conference on Information & Knowledge Management*, CIKM '21, page 4526–4533, New York, NY, USA. Association for Computing Machinery.

Yu Meng, Mengzhou Xia, and Danqi Chen. 2024. SimPO: Simple preference optimization with a reference-free reward. In *The Thirty-eighth Annual Conference on Neural Information Processing Systems*, New Orleans, Louisiana, USA. Neurips.

Suraj Nair, Eugene Yang, Dawn Lawrie, Kevin Duh, Paul McNamee, Kenton Murray, James Mayfield, and Douglas W Oard. 2022. Transfer learning approaches for building cross-language dense retrieval models. In *European Conference on Information Retrieval*, pages 382–396. Springer.

Thong Nguyen, Sean MacAvaney, and Andrew Yates. 2023. A unified framework for learned sparse retrieval. In *European Conference on Information Retrieval*, pages 101–116. Springer.

Tri Nguyen, Mir Rosenberg, Xia Song, Jianfeng Gao, Saurabh Tiwary, Rangan Majumder, and Li Deng. 2016. MS MARCO: A human generated machine reading comprehension dataset. In *Proceedings of the Workshop on Cognitive Computation: Integrating neural and symbolic approaches 2016 co-located with the 30th Annual Conference on Neural Information Processing Systems (NIPS 2016), Barcelona, Spain, December 9, 2016*, volume 1773 of *CEUR Workshop Proceedings*. CEUR-WS.org.

Long Ouyang, Jeff Wu, Xu Jiang, Diogo Almeida, Carroll L. Wainwright, Pamela Mishkin, Chong Zhang, Sandhini Agarwal, Katarina Slama, Alex Ray, John Schulman, Jacob Hilton, Fraser Kelton, Luke Miller, Maddie Simens, Amanda Askell, Peter Welinder, Paul Christiano, Jan Leike, and Ryan Lowe. 2022. Training language models to follow instructions with human feedback. In *Proceedings of the 36th International Conference on Neural Information Processing Systems*, NIPS '22, Red Hook, NY, USA. Curran Associates Inc.

Ryan Park, Rafael Rafailov, Stefano Ermon, and Chelsea Finn. 2024. Disentangling length from quality in direct preference optimization. In *Findings of the Association for Computational Linguistics: ACL 2024*, pages 4998–5017, Bangkok, Thailand. Association for Computational Linguistics.

Alec Radford, Jong Wook Kim, Tao Xu, Greg Brockman, Christine Mcleavey, and Ilya Sutskever. 2023. Robust speech recognition via large-scale weak supervision. In *Proceedings of the 40th International Conference on Machine Learning*, volume 202 of *Proceedings of Machine Learning Research*, pages 28492–28518. PMLR.

Rafael Rafailov, Archit Sharma, Eric Mitchell, Stefano Ermon, Christopher D. Manning, and Chelsea Finn. 2024. Direct preference optimization: Your language model is secretly a reward model. *Preprint*, arXiv:2305.18290.

Arun Reddy, Alexander Martin, Eugene Yang, Andrew Yates, Kate Sanders, Kenton Murray, Reno Kriz, Celso M. de Melo, Benjamin Van Durme, and Rama

Chellappa. 2025. Video-colbert: Contextualized late interaction for text-to-video retrieval. *Preprint*, arXiv:2503.19009.

Nils Reimers and Iryna Gurevych. 2019. Sentence-bert: Sentence embeddings using siamese bert-networks.

Stephen Robertson, Hugo Zaragoza, and 1 others. 2009. The probabilistic relevance framework: Bm25 and beyond. *Foundations and Trends® in Information Retrieval*, 3(4):333–389.

Stephen E Robertson, Steve Walker, Susan Jones, Micheline M Hancock-Beaulieu, Mike Gatford, and 1 others. 1995. Okapi at trec-3. *Nist Special Publication Sp*, 109:109.

V Sanh. 2019. Distilbert, a distilled version of bert: smaller, faster, cheaper and lighter. *arXiv preprint arXiv:1910.01108*.

Keshav Santhanam, Omar Khattab, Christopher Potts, and Matei Zaharia. 2022. Plaid: an efficient engine for late interaction retrieval. In *Proceedings of the 31st ACM International Conference on Information & Knowledge Management*, pages 1747–1756.

Parth Sarthi, Salman Abdullah, Aditi Tuli, Shubh Khanna, Anna Goldie, and Christopher D Manning. 2024. RAPTOR: Recursive abstractive processing for tree-organized retrieval. In *The Twelfth International Conference on Learning Representations*.

Zhihong Shao, Peiyi Wang, Qihao Zhu, Runxin Xu, Junxiao Song, Xiao Bi, Haowei Zhang, Mingchuan Zhang, Y. K. Li, Y. Wu, and Daya Guo. 2024. Deepseekmath: Pushing the limits of mathematical reasoning in open language models. *Preprint*, arXiv:2402.03300.

Ray Smith, Daria Antonova, and Dar-Shyang Lee. 2009. Adapting the tesseract open source ocr engine for multilingual ocr. In *Proceedings of the international workshop on multilingual OCR*, pages 1–8.

Nisan Stiennon, Long Ouyang, Jeff Wu, Daniel M. Ziegler, Ryan Lowe, Chelsea Voss, Alec Radford, Dario Amodei, and Paul Christiano. 2020. Learning to summarize from human feedback. In *Proceedings of the 34th International Conference on Neural Information Processing Systems*, NIPS '20, Red Hook, NY, USA. Curran Associates Inc.

Nandan Thakur, Nils Reimers, Andreas Rücklé, Abhishek Srivastava, and Iryna Gurevych. 2021. Beir: A heterogenous benchmark for zero-shot evaluation of information retrieval models.

Xiao Wang, Craig Macdonald, Nicola Tonellotto, and Iadh Ounis. 2023. Colbert-prf: Semantic pseudo-relevance feedback for dense passage and document retrieval. *ACM Transactions on the Web*, 17(1):1–39.

Xin Wang, Hong Chen, Si'ao Tang, Zihao Wu, and Wenwu Zhu. 2024. Disentangled representation learning. *Preprint*, arXiv:2211.11695.

Xin Wang, Jiawei Wu, Junkun Chen, Lei Li, Yuan-Fang Wang, and William Yang Wang. 2019. Vatex: A large-scale, high-quality multilingual dataset for video-and-language research. In *2019 IEEE/CVF International Conference on Computer Vision (ICCV)*, pages 4580–4590.

Shinji Watanabe, Michael Mandel, Jon Barker, Emmanuel Vincent, Ashish Arora, Xuankai Chang, Sanjeev Khudanpur, Vimal Manohar, Daniel Povey, Desh Raj, and 1 others. 2020. Chime-6 challenge: Tackling multispeaker speech recognition for unsegmented recordings.

Weijia Wu, Yuzhong Zhao, Zhuang Li, Jiahong Li, Hong Zhou, Mike Zheng Shou, and Xiang Bai. 2025. A large cross-modal video retrieval dataset with reading comprehension. *Pattern Recognition*, 157:110818.

Haoran Xu, Amr Sharaf, Yunmo Chen, Weiting Tan, Lingfeng Shen, Benjamin Van Durme, Kenton Murray, and Young Jin Kim. 2024. Contrastive preference optimization: Pushing the boundaries of llm performance in machine translation.

Jun Xu, Tao Mei, Ting Yao, and Yong Rui. 2016. Msr-vtt: A large video description dataset for bridging video and language. In *2016 IEEE Conference on Computer Vision and Pattern Recognition (CVPR)*, pages 5288–5296.

Brian Yan, Matthew Wiesner, Ondřej Klejch, Preethi Jyothi, and Shinji Watanabe. 2023. Towards zero-shot code-switched speech recognition. In *ICASSP 2023-2023 IEEE International Conference on Acoustics, Speech and Signal Processing (ICASSP)*, pages 1–5. IEEE.

Eugene Yang, Dawn Lawrie, and James Mayfield. 2024a. Distillation for multilingual information retrieval. In *Proceedings of the 47th International ACM SIGIR Conference on Research and Development in Information Retrieval*, pages 2368–2373.

Eugene Yang, Dawn Lawrie, James Mayfield, Douglas W. Oard, and Scott Miller. 2024b. Translate-distill: Learning cross-language dense retrieval by translation and distillation. In *Proceedings of the 46th European Conference on Information Retrieval (ECIR)*.

Eugene Yang, Dawn Lawrie, James Mayfield, Douglas W Oard, and Scott Miller. 2024c. Translate-distill: Learning cross-language dense retrieval by translation and distillation. In *European Conference on Information Retrieval*, pages 50–65. Springer.

Bin Zhu, Bin Lin, Munan Ning, Yang Yan, Jiaxi Cui, HongFa Wang, Yatian Pang, Wenhao Jiang, Junwu Zhang, Zongwei Li, and 1 others. 2023. Languagebind: Extending video-language pretraining to n-modality by language-based semantic alignment. *arXiv preprint arXiv:2310.01852*.

Liu Zhuang, Lin Wayne, Shi Ya, and Zhao Jun. 2021. A robustly optimized BERT pre-training approach with post-training. In *Proceedings of the 20th Chinese National Conference on Computational Linguistics*, pages 1218–1227, Huhhot, China. Chinese Information Processing Society of China.

Appendix

A Out-of-Domain Transfer

To evaluate FORTIFY on a completely different domain, we again zero-shot transfer the MultiVENT-FORTIFied model to generate summaries for the academic abstracts in the NeuCLIR Technical Document collection. Presented in Table 4, FORTIFied summaries still provide additional information to the original document despite not being noisy, resulting in a 43% improvement in nDCG@20 on the 2023 topics and 35% on 2024. However, the NFT Llama summary, in this case, is slightly more effective since it was trained to accomplish a wide range of tasks under a wide range of conditions.

Such differences are expected as our MultiVENT-FORTIFied model has moved from a general-purpose model to a more task-specific one. As we move further away from the original training setup, which assumes noisy, fragmented text with ColBERT being the retrieval model, the model becomes less capable of generating retrieval model-favored summaries, especially when using BM25. With that said, FORTIFY can be tailored to any domain as long as the retrieval model preference can be collected. We leave the exploration of FORTIFY to general ad hoc retrieval to future work.

B Prompts

In this section, we provide prompts that we optimize FORTIFY for. Figure 3 presents the primary prompt that we use, while Figure 4 presents the OCR-focused prompt.

C Examples

In this section we two examples of the noisy extracted text. Documents composed principally of noisy text are often difficult to retrieve (de Oliveira et al., 2023). In term frequency approaches such as BM25, performance is harmed when there are typographical errors, text recognition errors (substitution of visually similar characters), speech transcription errors (substitution of letters pronounced similarly), or other character-level errors. For instance, if we were to search for for the noisy document in Figure 5, we might not be successful if our query is "Rolling Stones" - note that neither of these words appear in the document, despite the fact that the document is very clearly the lyrics to Jumpin' Jack Flash, albeit with significant text recognition errors. If we now produce a summary using a general-purpose generative text model, the summary not only corrects the character-level errors in the original document, but it elaborates on the content further, and finally includes a list of useful keywords and phrases.

Table 3: Dataset Statistics. Note that all three collections are multilingual. The average character counts treat all scripts (Latin, CJK, Perso-Arabic, Cyrillic, etc.) identically.

	MultiVENT 2.0 Test Set			
	Videos			
	w/OCR	w/ASR	Total	Queries
Count	105,026	109,488	109,800	2,546
Avg. # of Chars	529	1,092	–	42

	TextVR Test Set			
	Videos			
	w/OCR	w/ASR	Total	Queries
Count	2,726	2,249	2,727	2,727
Avg. # of Chars	441	185	–	73

	NeuCLIR Technical		
		Queries	
	Documents	2023	2024
Count	395,927	41	106
Avg. # of Chars	206	131	131

Table 4: Zero-shot cross-domain transfer of the MultiVENT-FORTIFied model (training on MultiVENT 2.0 training set) to the NeuCLIR Technical Document task with topics from 2023 and 2024. nDCG in this table uses a rank cutoff at 20. Rows in light gray indicate retrieval methods relying on features other than text.

Expansion Approach	Retrieval Model	**2023** nDCG	**2023** R@1K	**2024** nDCG	**2024** R@1K
English-Chinese ColBERT-X		0.339	0.783	0.338	0.796
(w) *No Expansion*	BM25	0.054	0.128	0.049	0.106
	ColBERT	0.277	0.736	0.256	0.687
(x) Machine Translation	BM25	0.239^{w}	0.588^{w}	0.240^{w}	0.588^{w}
	ColBERT	0.330^{w}	0.788^{w}	0.326^{w}	0.763^{w}
(y) NFT-Llama Summary	BM25	0.330^{wxz}	0.803^{wxz}	0.336^{wxz}	0.726^{wx}
	ColBERT	$\mathbf{0.404}^{wx}$	$\mathbf{0.838}^{w}$	$\mathbf{0.356}^{w}$	$\mathbf{0.783}^{w}$
(z) FORTIFied Summary	BM25	0.286^{w}	0.733^{wx}	0.305^{wx}	0.694^{wx}
	ColBERT	0.395^{w}	0.813^{w}	0.349^{w}	$\mathbf{0.783}^{w}$

SYSTEM PROMPT: You are tasked with summarizing text. This summary will be used for the task of information retrieval. As such, it is of paramount importance that the summary include as many relevant keywords, synonyms, and related words as possible. Feel free to restate the text in multiple ways. A longer document is better than a shorter one. The more keywords you include, the better the summary will be for the task of information retrieval. The summary can be in the style of a description or a synopsis.

USER PROMPT: Please produce a summary of the following text content that is suited for the task of information retrieval, focusing on including keywords, synonyms and related words: `<noisy text>`

Figure 3: Prompt for Llama-3-8B-Instruct for generating summaries. This prompt is used to generate both No-fine-tune (NFT) Llama summaries and the FORTIFY summaries.

SYSTEM PROMPT: You are tasked with summarizing the OCR text extracted from a video. This summary will be used for the task of information retrieval. As such, it is of paramount importance that the summary include as many relevant keywords, synonyms, and related words as possible. Feel free to restate the text in multiple ways. A longer document is better than a shorter one. The more keywords you include, the better the summary will be for the task of information retrieval. The summary can be in the style of a video description or a plot synopsis or summary. For instance, given the following OCR text:
Ptička is the name of the song. How to make a whistle The bird. How to make a whistle How to make a whistle The bird.
Produce a summary like so:
A tutorial or a series of instructions on how to make a whistle (a musical instrument) that mimics or imitates the sound or call produced by a bird. The tutorial mentions a song called "Ptička", which is the Russian word for "bird". The whistle may be used to replicate birdsong.

USER PROMPT: Please produce a summary of the following text content that is suited for the task of information retrieval, focusing on including keywords, synonyms and related words: `<noisy text>`

Figure 4: OCR-focused one-shot prompt used for generating summaries. This prompt is only used for generating training summaries for FORTIFY.

NOISY TEXT: Kolling Sones. umping Jack Hash. One Two! But it's all right now, in fact, it's a gas! And Thowled ...

MACHINE TRANSLATION: Kolling Sones. umping Jack Hash. One Two! But it's all right now, in fact, it's a gas! And Thowled ...

NFT SUMMARY: The song "Jumpin' Jack Flash" by The Rolling Stones is a rock and roll classic ... Synonyms: tumultuous, difficult, abusive, rebellious, defiant, call toaction [sic]. Related words: rock music, classic, childhood experiences, abuse of power, individualism, resilience in the face of adversity.

FORTIFIED SUMMARY: The song "Jumping jack flash" is a popular rock song by the British rock band The Rolling stones, released in 1968 ... the song is often interpreted as a commentary on the struggles and hardships faced by young people.

Figure 5: An example of some extracted text with significant character-level errors and the outputs produced by the three document expansion strategies we compare (machine translation, Llama summarization without fine-tuning, and FORTIFY). Red indicates a character-level error. Yellow indicates unusual or disjointed structure. Green indicates a spelling correction. Blue indicates useful keywords and phrases not in the original text.

NOISY TEXT: t80 /ts Po4. BO5jCa(OM → Cas (PO)SMD. 3OS+ 2KOH → Kz SOu + H O. SO, +2NgOH → Na2SD, + HO. HeSO4. Ma (e D)=. t80. /ts Po4) PDS +3Ca (OHL. → CasPO%),0. 3O,+ 2K0H → ke SOu + HO. SO, + ...

MACHINE TRANSLATION: t80 /ts Po4. BO5jCa(OM → Cas (PO)SMD. 3OS+ 2KOH → Kz SOu + H O. SO, +2NgOH → Na2SD, + HO. HeSO4. Ma (e D)=. t80. /ts Po4) PDS +3Ca (OHL. → CasPO%),0. 3O,+ 2K0H → ke SOu + HO. SO, + ...

NFT SUMMARY: The text describes a series of chemical reactions involving calcium, phosphorus, and sulfur compounds. The reactions involve the formation of various calcium phosphates and sulfates, including calcium phosphate (Ca3(PO4)2), calcium sulfate (CaSO4), and sodium sulfate (Na2SO3). The reactions also involve the use of various reagents, including potassium hydroxide (KOH), sodium hydroxIDE [sic] (NaOH) ... Overall, the text provides a detailed description of various chemical reactions and the compounds involved.

FORTIFY-GENERATED SUMMARY: A comprehensive guide to the synthesis of calcium phosphate (Ca3(PO4)2) is presented, providing a detailed overview of the chemical reactions involved. The process involves the reaction of calcium oxide (CaO) with phosphoric acid (H3PO4), as well as the addition of sodium hydroxide (NaOH) and other chemicals. The resulting compound, calcium phosphate, is a key component in the production of ceramic materials, fertilizers, ... Keywords: calcium phosphate synthesis, ceramic materials production, fertilizer production, pharmaceuticals, pH levels, catalysts, sodium sulfate, sodium nitrite, chemical reactions.

Figure 6: An example of some extracted text with significant structural problems and the outputs produced by the three document expansion strategies we compare (machine translation, Llama-generated summaries without fine-tuning, and FORTIFY). Highlights mean the same as in Figure 5. Note that this document's overall structure is highly problematic as well.

Author Index

Association for Computational Linguistics
209 N. Eighth Street
Stroudsburg, Pennsylvania 18360

ISBN 979-8-3313-2413-1

CURRAN ASSOCIATES INC.
proceedings.com